Altered Destinies

Other Books by Gene I. Maeroff

Scholarship Assessed (1997), with Charles E. Glassick and
    Mary Taylor Huber
Team Building for School Change (1993)
Sources of Inspiration (1992), Editor
The School Smart Parent (1989)
The Empowerment of Teachers (1988)
School and College (1983)
Don't Blame the Kids (1981)
The Guide to Suburban Public Schools (1975), with Leonard Buder

Altered Destinies

Making Life Better for Schoolchildren in Need

Gene I. Maeroff

St. Martin's Griffin
New York

ISBN 0-312-17543-4 (cloth)
ISBN 0-312-22080-4 (paper)

Library of Congress Cataloging-in-Publication Data

Maeroff, Gene I.
    Altered destinies : making life better for schoolchildren in need
 / by Gene I. Maeroff.
       p.   cm.
    Includes bibliographical references and index.
    ISBN 0-312-17543-4
    1. Socially handicapped children—Education—United States.
    2. Educational equalization—United States. 3. Infrastructure
    (Economics)—United States.   I. Title.
    LC4091.M255   1998
    371.826'942'0973—dc21   97-38747
                                                        CIP

Design by Acme Art, Inc.
First edition: February, 1998
First Griffin paperback: May 1999
10 9 8 7 6 5 4 3 2 1

for Joyce

Contents

PART IV. A SENSE OF KNOWING

Preface

The genesis of this book was a meeting that the Charles Stewart Mott Foundation sponsored in Flint, Michigan, in March 1995, to inquire into the state of the community school concept, which Mott had played a major role in advancing some 60 years earlier. Representatives of a number of the programs described on these pages attended that two-day gathering. What I heard at that meeting and what I learned on inquiring further into the various programs persuaded me that there was a story to be told.

While the idea of the reconceived community school figures prominently in the chapters that follow, the fundamental focus is on students, not on schools. I decided early in my exploration that what was most important was not the delivery system itself but what it achieved for the children, especially for children who economic and social needs place at severe disadvantage. The community school in its latest configuration assumes importance in terms of what it offers these students that more traditional schools do not.

The American democracy will not be fully realized so long as millions of young people emerge from schools, both as dropouts and as high schools graduates, utterly unprepared to participate in any meaningful way in the life of this country. I believe that most middle-class Americans do not have the slightest idea of the severity of the situation. For the good of everyone, schools must contribute to helping the neediest students attain outcomes that approximate those that routinely accrue to advantaged children. This can happen only if schools and other agencies and institutions of society strive to provide the kind of support apparatus—social capital, if you will—that builds the networks and norms and engenders the trust that promote academic success.

The notion that students in the United States should be held to higher academic standards is simple and compelling. But it is not sufficient to endorse higher standards and thereby assume that the problems of the past will be obliterated. Higher standards mark a beginning, but they will come to naught unless, as in building the great cathedrals of the Middle Ages, mighty buttresses are put in place. Every aspect of a needy student's life needs reinforcement in order for him or her to concentrate on the work of the classroom. Children who suffer the ravages of poverty can best contend with the demands of school by having benefit of special measures that enable them to give education the attention that it needs and deserves. A sense of connectedness, a sense of well-being, a sense of academic initiative, a sense of knowing— all of these must figure in the effort to raise achievement levels.

While this book continually evokes images of children living in poverty and the dire circumstances that befall them, readers must bear in mind that schools and colleges are full of students who have overcome economic disadvantages. Generalizations, in other words, have exceptions. Failure is not preordained and the indomitableness of some demonstrates the capacity of others.

The absence of financial wherewithal is, regrettably, a dominating factor in the lives of at least one of every five American children. Any author who is sympathetic strives to write of these youngsters and their condition without patronizing them or their families. In referring to their poverty and identifying them as poor, the aim is purely descriptive, and in no way meant to be pejorative. Such phrases as "economically disadvantaged" or "lacking in financial resources," would avoid use of the adjective "poor," but would simply mask reality in verbose euphemism. Thus, references in this book to "children in need" or "poor children," for instance, are in no way intended to deny anyone's dignity. Rather, the aim is to remind readers of conditions that interfere with the ability of students to realize their God-given potential.

I do not pretend that these pages contain a panacea. What is offered here, however, is the outline of an approach that can be adapted for use anywhere. In identifying promising ventures, I have tried to provide a format by which schools can start to make a difference in the lives of students whose education has been victimized by poverty. From the various separate ways of attacking the problem emerge certain commonalities that hold promise in the education of economically disadvantaged students.

I was able to devote time to this book and to travel to numerous locales in more than ten states as a result of the financial support that I received for this work from the Charles Stewart Mott Foundation. There was no quid pro quo involved and I was totally unimpeded in my investigations and in reaching the conclusions that I settled upon. The quotes throughout this book, unless otherwise cited, were generally the result of personal interviews and observations during those many field visits. The organizational approach of the book and the ideas are totally mine. I am indebted to Donna Rhodes, who was a program officer with Mott when my work began and has more recently been an independent consultant, based in Maryland. Also, I am grateful to the Institute for Educational Leadership in Washington, D.C. for serving as the sponsoring agency for my study. Michael Usdan, its president, provided a sounding board and reviewed my work in progress.

When I began this book, I was a senior fellow at the Carnegie Foundation for the Advancement of Teaching, at that time located in Princeton, New Jersey. As in writing previous books and reports, I was able to make use of the resources of that organization, especially the information center and its director, Hinda Greenberg, as well as the assistance of her colleague Torrin Dilley. Before the manuscript was completed, I had relocated to Teachers College, Columbia University, where I also relied on the library. Finally, I am indebted to Michael Flamini, a senior editor at St. Martin's Press, for recognizing what this book had to offer.

I will not even try to thank by name the many people around the country who provided help and hospitality during my many field visits. Suffice to say, this book definitely could not have been written without their aid. I had the good fortune to receive assistance both from representatives of the various programs described on the pages that follow and from teachers, principals, and others who worked in the elementary and secondary schools in which these programs carried out their projects.

—Gene I. Maeroff
Teachers College, Columbia University
New York City
September 1997

Altered Destinies

Introduction: Social Capital for Schoolchildren in Need

Of all the riches denied to disadvantaged children, perhaps the most important have to do with the absence of a network of support that would allow them to thrive in school. The lack of this network and of the norms and values that underpin it place their education at risk from the day they first walk into classrooms across the United States. Often the backing they need is missing not only at home but also in the neighborhoods in which they dwell. It is not simply that their mothers had inadequate prenatal care or that picture books and toys were not part of their infancy or that they heard little of the kind of substantial conversation that promotes solid language development. More than that, their minds and hearts were not filled with the hopes, dreams, and aspirations from which to fashion academic success. They know neither what they are missing nor where to turn to get it, an affliction apt to continue throughout their schooling.

"The single most frustrating factor for urban teachers is the relentless intrusion of social problems into the classroom," said Kenneth Hitchner, a high school guidance counselor, writing an opinion piece in *The New York Times*. Explaining why students at a suburban high school had higher test scores than those in urban districts, he said of the suburban families: "They buy books and piano lessons and soccer programs; they take their children to musicals and baseball games and museums; they have paid a considerable amount for their own education, which they pass along to their children."[1]

Such experiences form the foundation stones on which schools help children construct an education. The mental associations that they make with what they learn away from the classroom provide the connectors to the knowledge that unfolds on the pages of their books and on the monitors of their computers. The networks of which they become a part, even as small children, lead them to get what they need for enriching their personal development and their education. Certainly all youngsters, however deprived, have experiences. But, for some, their experiences are anything but enriching. While an individual hardworking youngster may prevail over almost any adversity, major assistance is needed if substantial numbers of impoverished students are to achieve scholastic success. Families and communities require help if they are to structure relationships that provide their children with values and opportunities in harmony with productive learning.[2]

James S. Coleman, the sociologist of education, described the elements provided to a child's education by a strong family as *social capital*. Coleman found in his studies that variations among family backgrounds made more difference in achievement than did differences among schools. "A child approaches the tasks set by the school with a set of attitudes mainly brought from the home," he said. "The child's performance, whether in handwriting, in multiplication tables, or in learning advanced algebra, depends not only on the opportunities and demands the school provides for doing well but also upon the desire, the goals, the attitudes, and the effort with which the child addresses these opportunities. The school has some effect on these latter qualities, but they are qualities that the child largely brings from home."[3]

And so it is that a growing number of schools and other organizations and agencies throughout the United States seek to compensate for what students do not receive in the environments in which they are raised. It is fashionable today to say that every child can learn. Of course every child can learn. Just as certainly, however, fate has conspired against some youngsters, and it hardly can be asserted that they enjoy the same benefits as students from more advantaged backgrounds. Some students have been placed at a disadvantage; it is as if they have been asked to run a race with their shoelaces tied together.

A psychologist with the Neighborhood Academic Initiative, which worked with secondary students in Los Angeles said: "Our students lack something because of their environments. What comes naturally with more money is the time that parents have to talk to kids more about education and its value. These kids are surrounded by the environment of the inner city." During the week that the psychologist made that statement the class had discussed what a person must do when he or she visits someone in jail. The students got into a conversation in class in which they compared the security for visitors at different prisons. Every student in the group had visited someone who was incarcerated. Furthermore, 30 to 50 (from an entire program group of fewer than 200) had lost someone close to them to gang violence. The program counseled students in groups to help them learn to cope with losses of this kind.

The effort—the struggle—to build social capital for poor children represents one of the most important endeavors in the country today. The national dimensions of the struggle could be seen in a New York City public school housed in a former church in Brooklyn's Williamsburg section, in a public school situated in a strip mall in St. Paul, Minnesota, and on the campus of the University of Southern California, where public school students from south-central Los Angeles spent part of their day. It could be seen in a public school in Newark, around the corner from an open market in drugs, and in a public school in South Tucson, where determined Arizonans hounded out of existence a nearby bar that was a rendezvous for prostitutes. It could be seen in one of the poorest counties in Appalachia, where success meant helping kids learn enough to leave, and in a school two blocks from a chic, gentrified neighborhood in Miami Beach, where the children of immigrants could barely imagine the American dream. In these places and many others, dedicated people were attempting to bolster families and neighborhoods, to build a sense of community among students, and to engage them in the kind of schooling that would secure for them a future bright with promise.

"Social capital is a product of the process," concluded a report by Rainbow Research on the school in Brooklyn's Williamsburg section, El Puente Academy for Peace and Justice. "They set out to develop the skills of their young people and of their parents; to develop values in their young people that encourage them to 'give back' to the community; to address police brutality; to clean up their environment, and to build relationships with others that are not part of El Puente."[4] This approach is in keeping with what Robert D. Putnam seemed to have in mind when he wrote that social capital refers to "features of social organization, such as networks, norms, and trust that facilitate coordination and cooperation for mutual benefit." Social capital, continued Putnam, who has written frequently on civic and community life, makes possible "the achievement of certain ends that would not be attainable in its absence."[5]

Barbara Schneider, a professor at the University of Chicago and a former colleague of James Coleman, pointed out that social capital "can be defined by its function, not its structure." It is a set of ties between and among people through which norms and trust are created that facilitate action.[6] The family itself becomes a conduit for social capital for members of certain enterprising immigrant groups that pool labor power and financial resources. Even with limited employment opportunities in the United States, these new Americans find upward mobility by relying on a network of support for their fledgling businesses provided by fellow immigrant family members.[7]

Social capital also assists long-established Americans who know how to use the system to achieve their goals. Recently, for instance, when the sons and daughters of certain well-connected families had trouble getting admitted to the University of California, contacts apparently were made to obtain acceptances that would not otherwise have been available.[8] For the advantaged it is not simply a matter of going to college—that is a given—but of going to the *right* college. Two professors, Philip J. Cook, who taught public policy at Duke University, and Robert H. Frank, who taught economics at Cornell University, maintained that "an increasingly small number of colleges and universities have become the gatekeepers for society's top-paying jobs."[9] The social capital put at the disposal of the children of the affluent makes it more likely they will be the ones who gain admission to those colleges and universities and get those jobs.

Then so be it if winning admission to a college of choice means spending thousands of dollars to pay the fees of private consultants who hold a student's hand each step of the way through the application process. This is the network—sustained by wealth, savvy, and connections—that directs a youngster toward the activities that will look best on a high school transcript, helps him or her select a college, cultivates the interest of the admissions office, and even writes the application essay. Compare these advantages with the plight of two young women in Appalachia in a recent graduating class at West Virginia's Clay High School. They both took Advanced Placement English but could not afford to pay for the national examination at the end of the course. The school got someone else to pay their fees, and both attained the top possible score of 5. No connections, but lots of brains.

The new struggle on behalf of schoolchildren in need distinguishes itself from the compensatory education of earlier times in that it confronts disadvantage on a wider and more comprehensive front. The federal government's original foray into the schools, the Elementary and Secondary Education Act of 1965, created the Title I program that has for more than three decades provided poor children with tutoring in reading and mathematics, particularly in elementary schools. What is different in most of the programs described on the following pages is their preoccupation with as much of the student's whole being as possible—social, emotional, physical, and psychological as well as intellectual—and the extension of this concern through secondary school. Therefore, comprehensive health services, links between school and home, connections by the school to the community, enriching cultural experiences, coaching for college admissions tests, and visits to college campuses figure in the various programs.

Those who desire improvements in classroom learning must realize and acknowledge that school reform, especially when it focuses on disadvantaged students, cannot easily succeed if it ignores the circumstances of their out-of-school lives. They spend most of their time beyond the schoolhouse walls, and, even inside the school, their learning bears the indelible stamp of outside influences. Improving educational outcomes for students in need requires more than attending to academic content and standards. The conditions in the neighborhoods that so much affect their ability to prosper as students also must be considered. When President Clinton in 1997 called for raising standards by instituting tests that would end social promotion,[10] he did not mention the other part of the problem of low achievement: Students with less advantaged backgrounds will not pass those tests unless the nation gives special attention to the obstacles in their paths, in and out of the classroom. After an examination of 44 programs designed to improve school-linked services for children, researchers concluded that the problems the programs faced had a mix of cultural, economic, political, and health causes. Solutions, said the researchers, must come from the community—from public and private agencies, local and state health and human services departments, business, and religious institutions—coordinated with the school's own services.[11] The problems are bigger than the school and cannot be solved by the school alone.

The underlying support system needs shoring up so that students will have a sturdy foundation on which to stand. Reformers must see the school as part of an ecosystem, the parts of which deeply affect each other. Capacity building for student learning has to consider the entire ecosystem, not only the portion visible within the classroom. The goal is to enlarge the capacity of the youngster's environment to provide the support needed to succeed in school. "[W]e must learn that the realm of educational policy extends beyond matters tradition-ally associated only with teachers, classroom, school-community relations, or school administrators," wrote sociology professor William L. Yancey and graduate student Salvatore J. Saporito of Temple University. They said that policies concerning unemployment, the location of manufacturing centers, family income, access to medical service, racial/ethnic discrimination, and intergroup conflict are also, in effect, educational policies.[12]

THE FOUR SENSES

The programs detailed in this book for building social capital for schoolchildren in need represent, collectively, an attempt to confront and deal with the many factors that obstruct the students' academic achievement. In sum, the programs, called enhancements, add up to a broad approach toward constructing the various pieces of the support structure without which few students can succeed. The programs share similar objectives in four main ways. Therefore, this book has four parts—entitled "a sense of connectedness," "a sense of well-being," "a sense of academic initiative," and "a sense of knowing"—each consisting of four chapters that examine these characteristics.

Together, these four characteristics can provide schoolchildren in need with a semblance of the kind of social capital available to other children by virtue of family socioeconomic status. Few of the programs provide all four characteristics in their entirety, and right now the best that can be hoped for is that students will gather bits and pieces of what they need. In fact, as they currently exist, some of the enhancement programs point in the right direction without delivering fully on their promise. What is most important, though, is the idea that a composite could be assembled, putting all the elements in place by enlarging on the approaches of the various programs. When youngsters gain connectedness to the people and institutions whose guidance and help will enable them to advance themselves, their social capital increases. At the same time, they can prosper as students only if they have emotional and physical underpinnings that keep them from being overwhelmed by their environments. They also need academic initiative to motivate and sustain their scholastic efforts. Finally, a sense of knowing allows them to accrue the academic and social learning that lets them select the route of their destiny in a society that otherwise would limit them to the Hobson's choice of no options at all.

A Sense of Connectedness

Students who are isolated and alienated lack the ties that can enable them to improve their lot in the world. Feelings of belonging set the stage for accepting the school's social and educational norms. The series of connections that a good program of enhancement puts in place helps young people navigate through otherwise treacherous waters. Connectedness leads to regular school attendance and engagement in the curriculum. It folds children into a web of support in which their academic efforts will be rewarded by people who help make sure that they complete high school and go to college.

Taken to another level, connectedness links the school to the community and the community to the school. A community that feels at one with a school lends its support to the school's goals. Schools and their neighborhoods tend toward interdependency. The ills of one inevitably affect the other. Schools and communities can aid in each other's revitalization. When a community is healthy, its children return from school each day, for instance, to settings in which they are safe and live in decent housing. A community that has a good school is a place where people want to make their homes.

Schools are strengthened when their communities take seriously the matter of supporting education and children. When those in poor neighborhoods turn to activism on behalf of their schools, they usually seek nothing more than the benefits that come to affluent youngsters almost as a matter of birthright. The work of enhancement programs to connect schools to parents also represents an effort to replicate bonds that are taken for granted among the affluent. Adults who are alienated from the schools their children attend, as many poor people are, less readily reinforce the goals of schooling.

A Sense of Well-Being

How prosaic it sounds to say that students who are unhealthy cannot prosper in school. It is so simple a proposition that it seems self-evident. Yet a sense of well-being is a luxury for poor children. When a school functions as a community center for students and their families, it provides them with amenities that a host of organizations and agencies make available in affluent communities.

Good health is fundamental to a student's well-being, yet many needy students lack the health care they require. Schools in some locales are entering collaborations with health care providers to ensure that students get necessary treatment. This care has to include services to minister to students' emotional and psychological well-being. The deprivations of poverty often create a psychic barrier to scholastic achievement. Imbued with healthy attitudes, children accept responsibility for self-control. A sense of well-being depends on feeling safe in school and when traveling to and from school. Part of a sense of well-being has to do with caring—the caring that others show for students and the caring that students show for others. Achieving such attitudes is difficult for youngsters whose homes and neighborhoods are places of social dysfunction. The stresses of poverty exact a mighty toll, even on children. Students must overcome these distractions if they are to attend diligently to schoolwork. Otherwise, they will be overwhelmed by larger concerns and schoolwork will have little significance.

A Sense of Academic Initiative

Academic achievement is underpinned by a work ethic that regards schoolwork with utmost seriousness. Such behavior can be learned. Many of the enhancements strive to instill in students attitudes supportive of scholastic success. Students have to learn how to organize themselves in the pursuit of learning. They are not born, for example, knowing how to take notes. Role models and mentors figure prominently in these efforts to change academic outcomes. How can students recognize the advantages of higher education if they know no one who has attended college? A student can be aided enormously by a single person who is willing to show the way, someone to whom to turn when adversity seems overwhelming.

Before anything else, however, students need motivation. This is a precursor to learning. Rewards ranging right up to the largest—free college tuition—figure in enhancement programs. The enhancement programs try to deal with the aspirations and perseverance of students who sometimes must contend with classmates who ridicule them for wanting to achieve in school. An important part of a sense of academic initiative has to do with expectations—what others expect of the student and what the student expects of him- or herself. Finally, engagement in learning and academic initiative go together. Sometimes this means tying schooling to the outside world so that it seems more authentic than so much of what occurs in the classroom. Engagement leads to learning.

A Sense of Knowing

Ultimately, education revolves around what someone knows and can do with that knowledge, a sense of knowing. This fourth characteristic closes the circle and gives the enhancements their full academic dimension. Connectedness, well-being, and academic initiative support a sense of knowing. Programs often take steps to extend the school day in order to make more time for knowing. Students who have been placed at a disadvantage by poverty need to devote more time to learning.

All knowledge that will advance the fortunes of schoolchildren in need is not academic, however. Invariably, enhancement programs strive to help students gain social competence. The programs place a high premium on enrichment—trips to museums, concerts, ball games, and other unfamiliar places are occasions for learning behavior that may not have been previously taught. Social knowledge is essential to gaining access to the mainstream. Isolation and poverty operate together to restrict opportunities for youngsters of need. Students whose home life is bereft of intellectual stimulation face formidable odds. It is never too late, though, to try to involve parents in reinforcing their children's education. The high academic expectations that increasingly accompany plans for educational improvement will be realized more readily if the home appreciates and values what is at stake. For the enhancement programs, this may mean trying to reach students through their parents.

For inner-city kids, the problem is not one of poverty alone. Impoverishment frequently causes and is caused by a lack of neighborliness and an absence of community. "The problems are not just school problems," said Ron Lewis, a vice president of Communities in Schools. "They are community problems." A hallmark of this sort of poverty is the fear bred by drugs, crime, and violence. This is the inescapable reality with which some youngsters live every day and night.

Picture the scene: A class in a Newark elementary school in which students were supposed to give current events reports based on the news of the day. One child tells of watching someone who was killed next door being carried out of the house in a body bag. Another tells of a police officer killed on the corner and how her older brother watched him draw his last breath. These are current events. "I have a constant awareness of the real struggle that they face—just to get up every morning thinking, 'There might be a bullet out there for me today because I'm in the wrong place at the wrong time,'" Frances

Lucerna, the principal of Brooklyn's El Puente Academy, said. Children in the United States have the highest rates of death by firearms in the industrialized world. The homicide rate among American children under the age of 15 is five times greater than in 25 other industrialized countries combined.[13]

The relevant social indicators affecting children who live in poverty have been cited so many times that the public has grown inured to them. *Kids Count Data Book,* an annual publication of the Annie E. Casey Foundation, provides the grim statistics. The portion of children living in poverty rose from 17 to 21 percent from 1975 to 1993,[14] and arrests of juveniles for violent crimes increased from 341 to 527 per 100,000 during the same period.[15] Abuse, poverty, drugs, death, failure in school—the syndrome is all too familiar. In a far-reaching study of teachers, Susan Moore Johnson , a Harvard professor, was told again and again by teachers "of impoverished students lacking adequate food, housing, or medical care," students who the teachers said they wished "might begin school equipped with a modicum of self-discipline."[16] Marian Wright Edelman, head of the Children's Defense Fund, organized Stand for Children, a demonstration that drew tens of thousands to Washington in 1996 to call for bettering the lives of America's children.

The figures just cited take on human proportions in a sixth-grade class in Newark that was part of a Communities in Schools program, where 9 of the 18 students lived in homes with neither biological parent. Many fathers never bothered seeing the children they begot, and mothers were absent because of addiction, AIDS, or chronic illness. Yet disregarding such evidence, the nation's governors and business leaders gathered with the president of the United States at a so-called Education Summit in 1996, declaring themselves in favor of tough, rigorous standards for the country's elementary and secondary schools. How did these leaders think that millions of downtrodden children could meet such standards? Why did they think that such children, living under a state of siege, would even care to do so? The truth is that all too many children have little interest in school and see no reason for persevering in their studies. No one has persuaded them that what schools ask of them has any connection to the rest of their lives.

Building Community

Efforts to create social capital for poor children involve the building of community—within the school and beyond its walls. The most ambitious of the enhancement programs recognize that revitalized neighborhoods can nurture and support students, becoming sources of services, guidance, employment, recreation, and cultural stimulation. The by-now hackneyed expression that it takes a village to raise a child says it all. And if the adage has grown stale, it is only because the advantaged part of the population takes its blessings for granted. People in Greenwich and Scarsdale, in Newton and Winnetka, in Bethesda and Beverly Hills never lack for a place to turn to fill their needs. Their "villages" are fully intact.

An exhaustive 1996 report by the federal government culled the research and concluded that student outcomes, even after controlling for family background, were negatively affected by living in poor neighborhoods. It stated: "While living in affluent neighborhoods increases IQ at age 5 for both poor and non-poor children, living in poor neighborhoods raises the odds of a child developing behavior problems, becoming pregnant as a teenager, and dropping out of school."[17] At their worst, these are neighborhoods in which the residue of civic life is as fragile as ashes in a windstorm. Even jobs have disappeared, a point made with abundant poignancy by Harvard University's William Julius Wilson.[18]

"The deterioration of the community prevents them from having social capital," El Puente's Frances Lucerna said of students who live in communities that are figuratively and literally on the wrong side of the tracks. She continued: "There is a deterioration of a sense of family. My background is in working with kids in day care, and I saw the lack of family structure there. This is not a situation unique to Williamsburg." Where once an urban neighborhood and the community in which it was embedded could support and sustain its children, now such sustenance is absent. Even many churches are shells of their former selves, attracting few congregants and teetering on the brink of insolvency. Schools in cities frequently stand as islands amid oceans of despair, repositories of potential benefits that students can find in few other places in their immediate surroundings. Yet rather than construct bridges to the surrounding community, schools may allow themselves to remain "cut off both geographically and culturally from their students' families and communities,"[19] according to the deliberations of a conference devoted to finding ways to end the isolation.

The best way, the ideal way, to equip young people with social capital would be to reinvigorate their entire surroundings, an idea perhaps not as Pollyannish as it may sound. A team from Harvard University's Graduate School of Business, working in conjunction with scholars from the Rutgers University business school at Newark, said that even that troubled city had resources for revitalizing itself, although those resources went largely unheralded. The professors cited Newark's strategic location near an international airport and a world-class port; the untapped local market demand of a poor but underserved population with an annual family income of $2 billion; the city's economic integration with regional clusters of manufacturers and other businesses; and the human resources available in a population, although undereducated, largely industrious and eager to work.[20]

To take this argument a step further, research suggests a connection between economic development—such as that envisioned by the professors for Newark—and civic life. And, according to this view, a healthy civic life precedes a healthy economy.[21] So while such downtrodden cities as Newark possess hidden potential, these cities may have to find ways to revivify civic life before investors will put their money into risky ventures. Meanwhile, schoolchildren in such locales are held hostage. The chicken-and-egg question has to do with which comes first: civic life or economic vitality? But children need both in order to reap social capital.

Some enhancements written about in this book seek to better the lot of students by improving the communities that have so much impact on them. For instance, New York City began in 1991 to set up a network of programs called Beacon schools. The creation of these institutions was predicated on the conviction that the destiny of a school and its immediate neighborhood are inextricably linked. External agencies working in conjunction with each school provided an array of social, recreational, and educational services. This model of using an outside partner to marshal and coordinate services characterizes most of the programs dealt with on these pages. "[T]o remain a

great city, New York must ensure the safety and vitality of neighborhoods and community life, and it must ensure that young people
develop the skills and attitudes and practice the behaviors that will
lead to their becoming competent and responsible adults," said a
report on the Beacon schools. It continued:

> The Beacons Initiative seeks to link community-based youth organi-
> zations with schools to increase the presence of supports for youth
> to meet their needs and to assist them in building academic and
> social competencies and adopting values that will enable them to
> become economically self-sufficient and successful parents and
> citizens. It also seeks to engage youth in making contributions to
> their families, their peers, and their neighborhoods as the vital
> resource for the present and future that they are.[22]

In another era, community schools arose to serve the needs of
families and neighborhoods. These schools, many of them inspired
and supported by the Mott Foundation in Flint, Michigan, opened
early in the morning and remained in operation long after dark,
providing child care, adult education, recreation, and a host of
activities available from few other agencies. This kind of relationship
between school and community was not restricted to urban areas.
Historically, some of the schools that identified most closely with their
communities were those in rural settings. It was not unusual as
recently as the 1940s, for example, for small country schools scattered
across the Midwest to add a month of, say, "German school" or
"Norwegian school"—depending on the origins of the local community—after the regular school term.[23]

Needs even greater than those that existed earlier in the century
are prodding schools in disadvantaged settings to refashion themselves
as modern versions of the former community schools. And the needs
are so intense that advocates of a new kind of community school
would like to see the evolution of an even more encompassing
institution. Today's aspirant to the title of community school, especially in America's impoverished neighborhoods, is transforming itself
into a comprehensive enterprise that involves agencies and organizations that devote their energies to all aspects of human endeavor. This

approach places the school among groups concerned with housing, health, the environment, employment, and civil rights, for instance. By connecting itself to these functions, the school can try to help save the neighborhood upon which its students depend for their personal development. One name for the idea of rebuilding neighborhoods in this way is *community sustainability*.

Sustainable Seattle, a civic forum founded in 1990, developed 40 indicators of sustainable community by which to measure the environment, population and resources, the economy, youth and education, and health and community.[24] The Johnson Foundation of Racine, Wisconsin, which in 1995 made community sustainability a centerpiece of its work for the remainder the century, argued that this approach focused "on the development and strengthening of the social capital, institutions, and process that enable communities to grapple with, and prosper from, change." The foundation pointed out in its quarterly publication, *Wingspread Journal,* that community groups in the past carved up separate sectors of interest. One group might concern itself with jobs, another with social equity, and others with, say, environmental protection or growth management. The resulting fragmentation impeded the development of long-term solutions to problems with interlocking challenges.[25]

The implication for contemporary schools is that they must regard themselves as part of a larger landscape and, like trees radiating roots, extend linkages in many directions at once. In building social capital for their students, schools can contribute to the youngsters' well-being by enlisting in a grand scheme to make the streets safer, housing more pleasant, the local economy more bustling, and the air and water cleaner. Additionally, the social capital of young people will increase if their parents can find gainful employment and members of their family enjoy good health. Hints that children yearn for a sense of community to bolster their lives were contained in a bulletin board display at Intermediate School 218 in Manhattan's drug-riddled Washington Heights, where youngsters who had been studying ideas of community posited their definitions of community:

- A place where families celebrate
- A group of people who help one another

- A group of people that spends time together having fun
- A group of family or friends that live in the same neighbor-hood
- Community is all for one and one for all

Interestingly, so prominent a figure as John W. Gardner, a former cabinet secretary, head of Common Cause, and president of the Carnegie Corporation, proposed a definition of community that in its essence was not significantly different from that of the children at I.S. 218. He said that among the characteristics of community were caring, trust, and teamwork; participation; development of young people; a reasonable base of shared values; and institutional arrangements for community maintenance.[26]

Learning has a chance to prosper when communities are friendly to children and to schools. Normally, young people should be learning all the time, not only in school. The entire community should be a classroom, with informal experiences in the out-of-school hours contributing to productive growth. The development of social capital is tied to what children do with their free time. In healthy communities, young people gather experiences that promote their learning when they travel to and from school, visit the homes of classmates, play outside, use their home computers, make trips to the store for small purchases, ride their bikes to nearby neighborhoods, talk with adults on the block, and spend time in the park. Imagine, if you will, the response of parents in an affluent community if these pleasurable and valuable experiences were denied to their children, as, in effect, they frequently are to children in poor communities.

Children who live in the worst neighborhoods pursue their out-of-school life at some peril. Conscientious parents in such neighborhoods may lock their children inside as their only way of protecting them. Is this any way to promote intellectual, social, and emotional development? Probably not, but at least it keeps kids safe and alive. Think of the unfortunate black child who was doing nothing more than exploring the community on his bicycle when he was savagely beaten by white youths in Chicago's Bridgeport neighborhood as spring was about to begin in 1997. "Leisure time becomes more negative than it was for the old-time poor who at least had the neighborhood to stimulate them," said

Michele Cahill. Then poverty may have meant a shortage of food on the table, but did not mean getting assaulted on the streets. Cahill, a vice president of the Fund for the City of New York, was a moving force in the establishment of the Beacon schools, which included neighborhood renewal in their mission.

One of the new-style schools that exemplifies the trend toward a contemporary version of the community school is El Puente Academy in Brooklyn, New York. The school evolved from an organization founded to bring about a cultural rebuilding of the Latino community in Brooklyn's Williamsburg section. "The school is an extension of the larger community," said Frances Lucerna, its director. For years the El Puente group ran an after-school program to imbue young Latinos with self-respect and knowledge about their culture. Eventually this mission led to the founding of the school, which was recognized as part of the New York City Public School System in a network of what were called New Visions schools.

The school opened in 1993 with a single class of ninth graders and added a new group of ninth graders each year, reaching an enrollment of 130 by 1996-97, the first time at which it contained all four grades. As an alternative high school with roots in the Puerto Rican neighborhood from which it sprang, the school owed its uniqueness to the support of the El Puente organization, which provided the funds for personnel who supplemented the ten members of the staff paid and licensed by the Board of Education. Students were largely unaware of who worked for the school board and who was employed by the organization, a situation that the school encouraged by designating all who dealt with students as "facilitators" and letting the students call everyone by their first names.

The largesse of the El Puente organization allowed for the continuation of the after-school program, thereby extending the school day into the evening. Furthermore, El Puente added a Saturday program. The extended offerings were open to youngsters from the entire community; students who attended other schools during the day could enroll during the added hours. A parents' component in the extended day program was eliminated in 1995 because of financial constraints, although El Puente lamented the loss and vowed to reinstitute the program. El Puente underscored its tie to the Williamsburg community by expecting that all participants in the organization's activities would each give a day of service to the neighborhood. They had to sign a pledge to strive "for excellence in body, mind, spirit, and community." This emphasis on bolstering the community was the proper approach if the lessons of the Annie E. Casey Foundation's New Futures project are to be heeded. New Futures focused its funding on schools in five mid-size cities, striving during the late 1980s and early 1990s to coordinate health and social services and to promote school reform. Yet after reviewing the five-year program, the foundation concluded that "in some environments, system-reform efforts must be augmented by social-capital and economic-development initiatives that target the whole community."[27]

The Rheedlen organization tried to build a sense of community at P.S. 194, situated in central Harlem between Seventh and Eighth avenues, surrounded by burned-out buildings and abutting blocks where drug dealers openly sold their lethal products. Rheedlen brought changes to the block, introducing hope and building a feeling of community. At the heart of the effort was an after-school program that began after the regular school day and extended well into the evening, acting as a magnet to children of all ages as well as to adults. It served a large swathe of the neighborhood, reaching roughly from bustling 125th Street to 155th Street, although those connected to P.S. 194 were the core group. At the end of the school day, the program opened with snacks to sustain children through the afternoon. Then the students turned to their homework, getting help if they sought it. Recreational activities followed homework help, but children knew that the academics came first. Once an hour or so of homework was out of the way, they could play basketball and participate in a variety of activities.

This program gave the participants a sense of community that would otherwise have been missing. Marooned in the middle of the metropolis, constrained in their movements by poverty and crime, youngsters at P.S. 194 had only their school to provide them with some of the basic amenities of childhood, experiences that their counterparts in suburban Chappaqua, New Canaan, and Hewlett, for example, could take for granted every day of their lives. A school embedded in its community recognizes that almost anything that can affect the lives of children has some relationship to their education. Thus the enhancements featured in this book, to greater and lesser degrees, linked themselves to programs and agencies providing health care, youth development, and a wide array of family and community services.

The theory of youth development that underlies the Beacon schools in New York City, for instance, holds that young people require positive ways to meet such basic needs as safety, a sense of belonging, a sense of contribution and mastery, and legitimate opportunities to build skills and make contributions. "In the absence of positive supports and opportunities, youth will often engage in risky or negative behaviors to meet their survival and developmental needs," said a report on the Beacons Initiative.[28] The philosophy of the Beacon schools was to reinforce the child in ways that presumably would make it easier for him or her to function as a student. This approach involved supporting these five protective factors for youth: (1) caring relationships, (2) high expectations and clear standards for behavior, (3) high quality activities, (4) opportunities to contribute, and (5) continuity of supports.[29]

All children require such protective factors as precursors to educational achievement. For some, especially poor children, this kind of protection can come only with outside intervention. Some of the programs struggling to enhance schooling in these ways are described on the pages that follow.

PART

A Sense of Connectedness

ONE

Linking Students to Schools

It happened on the campus of the University of Southern California, an immaculately manicured chunk of real estate that stands in regal contrast with the modest dwellings of its Latino and black neighbors on the other side of the fence that surrounds the institution. On this particular day, two minority teenagers—obviously too young to attend USC and apparently of the neighborhood—approached some adult visitors who seemed unable to find their way. "Can we help you?" asked the youngsters, who readily pointed the visitors toward their destination.

Impressed by the teenagers' aplomb and by their familiarity with the campus, the adult visitors issued what they thought to be a compliment: "You seem almost like you belong here," they told the two lads.

"We do" was the quick and unexpected retort.

And, indeed, they did belong at the university, even though they still attended high school and lived with their families outside the gated campus. The young men were members of the USC-sponsored Neighborhood Academic Initiative, a program that brought students from local secondary schools onto the campus six days a week to pursue a rigorous program intended to qualify them for entrance to the university, where they would be eligible for full-tuition scholarships.

That incident embodied the kind of connectedness that helps students wend their way through the system. Connectedness operates in several ways to equip young people with the social capital they need to negotiate their success. Students build a network of connections that makes them feel a part of something larger. On one level, connectedness means gaining a feeling of belonging so that they regard themselves as a part of an academic enterprise. On another level, it means developing ties that students can use to thread their way around obstacles. Beyond that, the sense of connectedness is strengthened by bonds that the school establishes with home, family, neighborhood, and community. Mary K. Boyd was the principal of an alternative high school in St. Paul, Minnesota, that enrolled mostly students who had had unfavorable experiences in regular high schools. She saw part of her role as building the connections that would make students want to attend the school. "We have to invite kids to choose us as their school," said Boyd. "In effect, we have to get them to hire us to be their school. They won't give up their old habits until we prove worthy of their trust." That is the essence of a healthy connection between school and student.

The Neighborhood Academic Initiative at the University of Southern California exemplified the sort of program that developed a sense of connectedness among students to fortify and enhance their academic achievement. The participants, all students at junior and senior high schools in the neighborhood, spent extensive time together, undergoing common experiences that bonded them to each other and to the program. The closeness and the mutual support promoted their academic success and created a subcommunity in which scholastic striving was acceptable. Even gossiping about each other was verboten. Weekly group counseling sessions helped bring to the surface undercurrents of disaffection that might otherwise have marred the cohesiveness. The sense of connectedness was further solidified by rituals that were built into the program and by pledges that students recited on various occasions. In much the same way, the REACH program, operated near Cleveland, Ohio, during the summers for young black males, began each morning with an assembly that concluded with the singing of James Weldon Johnson's "Lift Ev'ry Voice and Sing," a kind of unofficial black national anthem.

The yearning for connectedness serves a fundamental human desire. Psychologist Abraham Maslow posited a theory holding that human beings will not grow emotionally to higher levels until very basic needs are met in regard to their psychological makeup, their security, their belonging, and their self-esteem. Only after fulfillment in these areas, according to Maslow, will someone be receptive to meeting his or her need to know and understand and other needs further along the hierarchy that he envisioned.[1]

A student's connection to a school begins with the feeling that he or she is a part of it, a point illustrated by the tale of the two youngsters in the Neighborhood Academic Initiative. Many students never attain that sense of oneness with their schools. An overwhelming barrier to connectedness is the large size of so many schools, especially at the secondary level. "In a big high school, teachers don't pay that much attention to you," said Alexis Gonzales, who attended ninth grade at a high school with thousands of students before transferring to Brooklyn's tiny El Puente Academy. "Some teachers don't even know you when you come to class at a big high school," said another student at El Puente. "Our teachers know everyone by name."

The size of the school matters less for elementary-age children because they spend most of their time in a single classroom; what counts most for them is the size of that class. In high schools and many middle schools, though, students melt into anonymity, a particularly vexing problem for youngsters who already suffer the disenfranchisement of poverty. High schools have to be small enough for teachers to know students and for students, in turn, to know teachers. *Breaking Ranks,* a report on high school restructuring by the National Association of Secondary Schools, recommended that every high school student have a personal adult advocate to help him or her personalize the educational experience.[2] The goal was to combat the loneliness that frequently engulfs adolescents. Educators must strive to understand the day-to-day circumstances under which young people and their families live. The educators should come to appreciate the extent to which neighborhood culture shapes students and demands their allegiance. Moreover, students must see that the school is not alien territory to them and their parents, regardless of the family's social stratum. Finally, connectedness should lead to actions to affirm the school's intent to strengthen prospects for academic success.

The Communities in Schools (CIS) program predicated its very existence on the idea that connectedness enhances the potential of young people who would otherwise go into freefall with no safety net to catch them. CIS strived to increase the number of adults in the child's world, whether this meant providing counselors, mentors, volunteers, health professionals, or tutors. CIS fashioned itself as a dropout prevention program; the ultimate bottom line against which the program measured itself was its impact on keeping students in school long enough to get their diplomas. The students who felt the program's effects tended to react like Milton, a seventh grader at Louise A. Spencer Elementary School in Newark: "Before the program, I was in a lot of trouble and I didn't like coming to school. Now I like coming to school. We have a better teacher and a lot is getting through to me this year. I used to come and just talk to the other kids. Now I come and I'm ready to learn. Mr. Guyton [the teacher] makes it exciting; he makes me want to learn. I'm doing homework and my grades are up." A classmate added: "I like the teachers and I like the trips. We're different from the rest of the school; we get more attention. I like having to work harder. My mother said if I want to be a vet[erinarian], this way I'll have a better chance."

Some enhancement programs capitalize on young people's desire to feel connected. The programs build a community of which the students want to be a part. This, for example, made students in the Neighborhood Academic Initiative different from other students in their high schools who did not participate in the program. This same feeling dominated the ambience of El Puente Academy. "We develop a sense of community within these walls," said Director Lucerna. "It starts with clear statements about the fact that we respect students as people." Their sense that they were connected to a community led to intense bonding among most students at El Puente, a school where youngsters willingly spoke to each other of their problems and provided support to one another. "A school is pretty much the relationships between teachers and students," said Mark Lopez, a student there.

Cynics might deride this aspect of schooling, insisting that school should be solely about book learning and that feel-good programs have no role in such settings. What they overlook, though, is that young people from disadvantaged backgrounds may have no other place to deal with their feelings in a healthy manner and that without the embracing atmosphere of the school, they might not be able to open themselves to learning. "We cannot make real progress until we recognize that cognitive and social processes are neither separate nor separable—that learning is inherently social," the Institute for Research on Learning said in a report.[3] Thus connectedness promotes learning by addressing students' social and emotional needs. Lucerna said: "For a lot of young people at the Academy it's very hard to focus because their daily lives are so chaotic and in many ways so wanting."[4] El Puente built connections by personalizing education, dealing with students as individuals. The director met two or three times a year with every ninth grader, the newest students to the school. "I pretty much know each of their personal situations," she said. She followed the meetings with conferences with staff members who prepared individual learning plans for each student. The staff members—facilitators, as they were called—kept tabs on the youngsters by serving as informal mentors.

Creating social capital for students at El Puente meant plugging them into a network of contacts that enhanced their learning and gave them access to people who could help them move in ever-wider circles. Youngsters whose economic situation limits their horizons and opportunities need these kinds of associations to construct ladders that they can climb to ascend from impoverishment. Internships of all sorts got El Puente students into offices of businesses and corporations throughout New York. The school's participation in the American Field Service let some students take trips to other countries, where their bilingualism—most El Puente students spoke both English and Spanish—was a distinct asset. Students also traveled to conferences, such as an AmeriCorps Leadership Seminar in Maine. Some of the trips were closer to home, as when students sailed down the Hudson River on the sloop *Clearwater,* a vessel supported by folk singer Pete Seeger for the study of marine biology and water pollution. The social capital of students at El Puente grew as their world expanded. For the most able and assertive of them, the provincial impoverishment of Williamsburg loomed less and less as a barrier.

To comprehend just what a school like El Puente represented to those enrolled there, one must understand that most students from Williamsburg attended the zoned neighborhood school, Eastern District

High School. It was housed in a modern structure that replaced a building so decrepit and inadequate that pillars obstructed the gym floor and the ceiling over the basketball court was so low that a ball could hit the ceiling if the player put too much arc on the shot. The new Eastern District High School provided better facilities for its students but did little to overcome the anonymity that was a function of its size. Students felt unconnected to each other, and the school still seemed unconnected to the community it served. The educational achievement of its students, not surprisingly, languished as it had in the old building. The graduation rate of 25.5 percent at the school in 1996 was the third-worst in New York City.[5] El Puente Academy, on the other hand, was able to build connections with its small student body. It had an educational vision, and the community activism embedded in the program lent purpose and provided a vehicle for learning.

Connectedness also was made palpable in some of the programs in which the Children's Aid Society was involved elsewhere in New York City. So many children participated in the voluntary extended day program that visitors wondered if attendance was mandatory. It was not. "The kids want to be in our centers," said Martha Cameron, director of Youth Development Services for the society. "They come because they want to be there. They derive their main sense of belonging when they are there. They don't want to be on the street or at home."

And at another program in New York City, the Beacon that the Rheedlen organization mounted at P.S. 194 in Harlem, connectedness figured prominently in a special dropout prevention effort to deal with the absenteeism of 50 to 75 children whose families lived in homeless shelters. "Kids that age want to be in school," said a Rheedlen worker, "and so if they are not there the problem is probably with the parents, not with the kids." The challenge was to work with a group of students whose members kept changing as the shelters' population turned over. The program began by closely monitoring the students' attendance. If a youngster missed two or three consecutive days of school, a program representative would go to the shelter to investigate. No excuse for missing school—one of the few constants in the lives of these children—was acceptable. If a student needed an alarm clock, he or she was given one; if someone had to pick up a student and walk him or her to school, the program provided someone. Program workers won the confidence of the parents in the shelters and built relationships with the families that led to discussions on many of the issues affecting the students' school success. "When they see I'm so concerned about the welfare of their children," a program worker said, "they feel more free to discuss all kinds of problems with me."

The Educational and Community Change (ECC) project began because many children in poorer areas of Tucson, Arizona, seemed as they grew older to think that going to school was a waste of time. Teenagers wanted to stop attending school just as soon as they were legally able to do so. One reason for this disconnection was that school seemed to be a place that did not value what they knew. They were asked to learn new material but were seldom invited to use what they already knew from their neighborhood and culture. The ECC project was launched with the idea that the schools would engage students by doing more to build their education on their prior experiences, an approach from which needy children everywhere could benefit. A brochure for Educational and Community Change proclaimed: "The project seeks conditions that can bring about changes in the educative process of these children to keep them interested in learning so they will complete their education and have greater opportunities as adults."

Clay High School, in the heart of impoverished Appalachia, was housed in an immaculately kept building nestled against a river, across the highway from a cemetery. Graffiti hardly ever appeared at Clay, and the wide, well-lit halls, with their yellow-painted cinder-block walls, evoked a cheerful atmosphere. "We want to give kids positive reasons for being here," said Kenneth Tanner, the principal. Students' favorable attitudes toward the school were constantly reinforced by the upbeat mood of a dedicated faculty. Teachers displayed pride in themselves and acted as role models for students by dressing as if they worked in a corporate office, almost never wearing the jeans and informal clothes that teachers wear at so many other schools around the country. The male teachers, for instance, all voluntarily wore neckties. Their loyalty to Clay High was such that faculty and staff members seldom took sick days. For several years the head custodian missed only one day of school, and that was when a grandchild was born. "I wouldn't teach anywhere else," said a history teacher who went to Clay after growing up in Philadelphia. "It's safe and there are good kids. They look to us, the teachers, as role models. It is very self-satisfying."

Taking their cue from the educators, students at Clay were paragons of good conduct whose attendance verged on the exceptional. Students voluntarily took on many of the clerical tasks involved in running the office, which could afford only one paid employee. Thus at almost any hour of any school day several students would be hard at work in the office—answering phones, running the copying machine, greeting visitors, taking messages to teachers' classrooms, preparing the calendars listing the coming weeks' activities.

The accent on attendance was unremitting. Clay had a computerized system that phoned each home during the day with a recorded message if a student was not in school. In the evening, someone made a personal follow-up call to inquire into the reason for the absence. Students who attended every day of school through a grading period earned points that were added to their scores on final examinations. In addition, each teacher had his or her own attendance incentives. In some classes, for instance, students who were never absent had their lowest test scores dropped from consideration in determining their grades. And those who missed only one or two days of school had points added to their test scores. Along with the trophies in the main hall that teams won in sports and music competitions was a display case containing lists of the names of students with perfect attendance. During one marking period in the 1996-97 school year, 30 percent of the freshmen, 36 percent of the sophomores, 37 percent of the juniors, and 49 percent of the seniors attained the distinction of attending every day of school.

Gangs and Uniforms as Sources of Connectedness

In its most baleful form, the yearning for connectedness accounts for the inclination of young people to join gangs. Find a gang member and you have uncovered a young person trying to gain a sense of connectedness. For all their negativity, gangs fulfill a need for youngsters who otherwise feel disconnected. What is a gang if not an extended family? That certainly is how the members view themselves. Luis Rodriguez, a former gang member in Los Angeles who eventually became a community worker with gangs, recalled the motivation for his joining. He had emigrated as an infant with his family from Mexico, learned to speak Spanish proficiently, but was prohibited from using the language in elementary school, which he said made him feel powerless. When he was 11 years old, he was intrigued by the bravado of the gangs he saw around him. He said: "I wanted that power. Soon after that, I got into my own little gang, although it was more like a club. It wasn't about fighting as much as it was about ourselves and who we were. It was about a respect we couldn't get anywhere else. It was about love, because if you talk to enough gang kids they will talk a lot about love. And it was about belonging somewhere."[6]

Just as gangs are about making a connection, so are uniforms. Some advocates of dressing students in uniforms speak primarily of the impact on discipline. President Clinton seized on the school uniform as a symbol of orderliness during the 1996 political campaign, declaring in his State of the Union Message that public schools should require uniforms "if it means that teen-agers will stop killing each other over gang jackets."[7] A main function of having students dress alike, however, is that it underscores their unity and their oneness with the school. Young people show connectedness by wearing gang colors; they also can demonstrate that connectedness by wearing a school uniform. If, as a result, their conduct improves, it is not because they want to keep the uniform clean but because they feel better knowing they are a part of something larger than themselves.

Parochial schools mandated the wearing of uniforms generations ago. Even today, 84 percent of the children in Catholic elementary schools throughout the United States still wear uniforms and most of the rest adhere to a dress code of some sort. Robert J. Kealey, executive director of the National Catholic Educational Association, declared in 1996 that the uniform was "a symbol of our Catholic identity . . . an outward expression of our brotherhood and sisterhood in Christ."[8] In today's consumer-conscious society, the wearing of uniforms also counters some of the unhealthy attitudes that impel young people to compete materially, from the expensive Michael Jordan–endorsed sneakers they put on their feet to the designer eyewear frames that rest on the bridges of their noses. The link between uniforms and connectedness may be open to question, but desperate school officials will seize on almost any practice that they think can have a salutary effect on students.

The students at Giants Academy, a Communities in Schools program in Newark, wore school uniforms. Program officials hoped that the self-discipline and unity associated with wearing a uniform would carry over to everything that the youngsters did. Many of the children chafed under the requirement that they wear uniforms, but their parents liked the idea of the youngsters not competing to be fashionable. Thus it was that the 55 students in the Giants Academy were distinguishable from the other 1,300 children in the kindergarten through eighth-grade elementary school not only by the deep purple of the girls' skirts and the boys' pants but also by the plastic shopping bags that many of them carried to and from school. These bags contained the clothes that allowed the students to make themselves look like other kids before heading home at the end of the school day. They would duck into the lavatories to change into regular street clothes, stuffing the uniforms down into the bags and out of sight, to be donned again the next morning.

But during the day, attired in uniforms that included white shirts and blouses, shiny black leather shoes, ties, and—on cool days— purple sweaters, the students of Giants Academy had an outward identity that set them apart from others at the school. Housed in three self-contained classrooms at the corner of one wing, dressed differently from everyone else, these students could not help but feel linked to their own special program. Students in other classes referred to them derisively as "the Catholic kids," likening them to the only other students around the city known to wear uniforms to school. Unlike many others in the vast school, however, those in the CIS program knew they were part of something, and the uniform went a long way toward affirming that connectedness. More recently, during the 1996- 97 school year, the Giants Academy underscored its special status by moving out of the building altogether to accommodations next door at the Boys and Girls Club.

Connectedness as an Antidote to Truancy

Once achieved, by whatever means, genuine connectedness imbues students with a sense of wanting to be a part of the school. Where so many programs go wrong in their efforts to combat truancy and increase attendance is in failing to recognize the role that a lack of connectedness plays in keeping students out of classes, away from school, and uninvolved in learning. Students, like people of all ages, tend not to want to go to places where they feel like outsiders and where few of their needs are met. Requiring students to attend schools is simply not enough to get them there—or to keep them enrolled— once they reach an age when they can exercise free choice. And such mandates certainly cannot force them to learn, however frequently they sit in classrooms.

Wisconsin, regarded as a model for welfare reform, instituted a Learnfare program under which the families of teenagers who did not attend school regularly were threatened with reduced payments through Aid to Dependent Children. Empowered by new authority from Washington for welfare policies, other states considered enacting versions of the Wisconsin law. Connecticut toughened its school regulations in 1995 to define students as truants for having four unexcused absences in any month or ten unexcused absences in any school year, with a provision to refer cases to superior court if parents failed to cooperate in attempting to solve the truancy problem. The Maryland General Assembly tried unsuccessfully several times in the mid-1990s to enact a proposal that would have required students to remain enrolled in school until the age of 18. Would it not be better in such cases to foster circumstances in the school that make students feel so connected to it that they want to be there? A study of potential dropouts by Gary G. Wehlage of the University of Wisconsin and his colleagues argued that a goal of dropout prevention should be to help students achieve "a sense of school membership."[9] This is quite different from the prescriptive approaches that rely on sanctions of one sort or another.

The intractability of the school attendance problem could be seen at Canton Middle School in Baltimore, which was plagued by the chronic absenteeism of a hard-core group of students that the school seemed unable to reach even after implementing extensive reforms. The commitment to reduce truancy stemmed not only from a desire to see children get the education to which they were entitled but also from the school's wish to generate every possible dollar it could from the State of Maryland, which—like most other states—allotted funds based on average daily attendance. In one effort to bolster attendance as the 1996-97 school year began, Canton identified the 70 or so students with the worst attendance records and set out to get their parents or guardians to come to a meeting about the problem. The school made phone calls to the homes and the principal wrote the following in a letter to the homes: "We have tried a variety of attendance incentive programs to motivate your child to come to school but still your child is often absent. Why? What are we doing wrong? Why does your child continue to stay home? You and your child are invited to come to a very important meeting to discuss these questions." A note at the bottom of the letter reminded recipients that several of the worst truancy cases had been referred to court.

Realistically, the school conceded that, with luck, the families of perhaps 20 students would be represented at the meeting. Finally, after all due preparations, the day of the meeting arrived. Three parents came. "You have some parents who care and some who don't," said April Jones, a parent who worked at Canton as a hall monitor and playground supervisor. "Some parents will even walk their kids to school to make sure that they get here." But others, apparently, would not even take the time to attend a meeting in their children's behalf.

School attendance is not an independent variable unrelated to the attitudes that students have about schools. "What causes dropouts is isolation, a sense of worthlessness, not seeing where education leads, lack of a personal relationship with the school," said Jackie Robinson, executive vice president of the national Communities in Schools program. This alienation prevails especially in low-income communities, where youngsters see few people whose lives demonstrate the positive results that going to school can produce. The children in these communities often are cut off from role models and situations that would impress upon them the importance of pursuing education. Isolation among such children is exacerbated by a lack of travel and a paucity of enriching experiences. "The question," said Patrick Coyne, an inner-city teacher in St. Paul, Minnesota, "is how we hook them on education when just surviving is a problem for them." At his school, if a student had perfect attendance over a given period of time, a staff member showed up in class with a basket of candy for the youngster.

Another program, School Success, set up by Minnesota's Amherst H. Wilder Foundation in Dakota County, south of Minneapolis, aimed at hard core truants from the ages of 12 to 16 whose cases had been referred to the courts by the county's 11 school districts. The court filing was enough to get most students back to school, but the youngsters identified by the program were such persistent truants that even the courts were stymied. The program took a four-pronged approach—using counseling, teaching life skills, providing parent education, and referring some youngsters for mental health evaluations. Services were provided both in the students' homes and in their schools. Counselors met with parents and siblings as well as with the truants. Students were taught about conflict resolution and how to deal with their anger as well as how to manage their time and avoid distractions. Like the students at P.S. 194 in Harlem, they were even given alarm clocks so they could no longer offer the excuse of having overslept. Parent education focused on the steps that mothers and fathers could take to help their children get to school on time.

School Success representatives met with the staff at the students' schools, discussing how best to deal with the children and trying in each case to find an adult in the building—anyone, a hall monitor, an administrator, a janitor—with whom the child could form a relationship. Often the student indicated that that adult most cared about whether he or she showed up at school. "The school has to be more positive with these kids," said Lesley Yunker, a therapist who directed School Success. "You can't have one of these kinds of kids walk into the building and the first thing they hear from an adult is 'It's about time you got here.'" Also attempts were made to get the school to change the youngster's schedule if that was thought beneficial. This could mean putting the student in some classes with friends, freeing the youth from classes with teachers who the student thought did not like him or her, or allowing the student to participate in a work-study program that called for being in the building only part of the day. In its first four years, School Success dealt with more than 300 students. Seven out of ten attended school at least 80 percent of the time after completing the program, and 85 percent had no further contact with the justice system six months after leaving the program.

The ways in which schools are organized for teaching and learning also have a pivotal effect on whether students want to attend. The numbing lectures that typify instruction in so many high schools drive some students out the doors. Expectations for passive learning that call for regurgitating facts, however valuable the information, leave some students unconnected to the learning process. The Unidale branch of the St. Paul Area Learning Center in Minnesota, dedicated to alternative approaches to teaching and learning, made its home in a small shopping mall in a seedy section of the city. Its next-door neighbor was a thrift store operated by the Disabled American Veterans. The unorthodox locale symbolized the school's offbeat approach to education. This was education as few of its students had known it in their previous schools. Unidale turned away almost no one and awarded academic credits mostly for life experience and independent study. The 300 students, ranging in age from 16 to 20 and many of them poor, had mostly transferred from or dropped out from their previous schools because traditional approaches to learning simply did not work for them. Unidale was part of a network of alternative high schools, called area learning centers, established as a result of enabling legislation passed by the state legislature. These schools enrolled more than 50,000 students throughout Minnesota by 1997.

This was a mix of students who had parented children, experimented with drugs, suffered physical or sexual abuse, experienced homelessness, and been altogether lacking in the kind of structure, support, and motivation to prod them to attend school regularly. Now they had decided they were ready to go to a high school that tried to induce changes in their behavior through relaxed requirements. It was the elixir that some needed. One student, for instance, who had been absent for 72 days the previous year in a regular high school, said that he missed only one day at Unidale. Another praised the flexibility that allowed him to arrive at school in the afternoon instead of at 7:30 in the morning, as required in his former school, and he liked the idea of being able to stay and get assistance beyond 2:30 in the afternoon, if he chose. Unidale was open from 8:30 A.M. to 6:30 P.M., Mondays through Thursdays, and from 10:00 A.M. to 3:00 P.M. on Fridays. Each student developed a learning contract—committing himself or herself to a specified number of hours per week—and decided when to attend in fulfillment of the contract. Independent study accounted for one-third to two-thirds of the contractual time.

Unidale tried to eliminate most formalities so that students could feel a natural sense of connection to the school. The flexibility meant that every week as many as a dozen new students enrolled in the school, replacing about an equal number who left—having completed enough credits to get a diploma, having transferred to another school, or having been asked to leave for excessive absence. To deal with the transiency of a student body steadily in flux, the school maintained for each youngster a large yellow file folder that acted as a kind of homeroom-in-a-folder. Notes and responses from teachers, scheduling information, and other pertinent materials were stored in the folders. At first, students were permitted to pull their own folders on arriving at school, but the school altered the arrangement when officials discovered that some students were examining materials in others' folders. After that, the file cabinets were moved behind a counter and students had to request their folders from a clerk.

Its revolving-door approach led Unidale to offer orientation sessions for new students at least twice a week. One afternoon at such a session, eight teenage girls sat around a table in a conference room. The group, half white and half black, listened attentively as the teacher handling orientation, Martin Appelbaum, spoke to them in his infor-mal way. "I'm Martin," said Appelbaum, a wiry man with a ponytail, who never bothered mentioning his last name. He told them that the school had no buzzers or bells. "No one's responsible for your education but you," he said. "Everyone's treated with respect; if you give it, you'll get it." They learned that it was up to students to maintain contact with teachers and that child care was available for students' preschool children. They also found out that they could not fail a subject; they would just stay with it until they finally completed the course requirements. They could come and go as they liked, and the school would give them free breakfasts and lunches.

"I want to emphasize that this place is really different; you don't sit in class and you don't go from class to class all day," Appelbaum said. Each student would be asked to sign a contract promising to put a specified number of hours into his or her studies and recognizing that he or she would be dropped from the active rolls upon not showing up more than 15 consecutive days, although remaining eligible for readmission after going through reorientation. The contract also declared the school to be "neutral territory," where gang colors, weapons, alcohol, drugs, tobacco, headphones, pagers, and cellular phones were banned. Unidale moved swiftly to engage new students in their studies and to forge ties with them. The enrollees immediately received two assignments, one in English and one in social studies, to carry out for graduation credit.

The English assignment called for the student to write about an event that he or she had been a part of or witnessed firsthand. The school provided a one-page outline listing suggestions for doing the assignment in eight brief steps. The modest level of academic expectations for this assignment was revealed by the fact that the paper had to be only three to five paragraphs in length, including an introductory and a concluding paragraph. The first social studies assignment, similarly undemanding, awarded credit for an autobiographical sketch of 500 words. Devoid of any research demands, the paper was to provide four elements—a brief description of one's family and "what life was like growing up," a list of prior schools attended and what one liked at those schools, a description of the current status of one's life, and what one would want his or her life to be like in one to three years.

What was the significance of assigning work containing such minimal demands to students of high school age? Perhaps the content was not so important in this case as the effort to forge an initial connection between student and school. The autobiography also enabled the teacher to get to know the student. Given the unfulfilling scholastic experiences of so many of the students, the idea was to make failure almost impossible. Would it have been better if the first assignment were so daunting that few students could carry it out successfully? Unidale was the last chance for most of the students to get diplomas from the school system. It would serve little purpose to erect an unreasonably high first hurdle in front of young men and women still willing to persist despite their unsatisfactory scholastic histories. Making a connection with the student was what was initially at stake. Unidale hoped that the rest would follow.

THREE

Linking Communities to Schools

Central Harlem is a place where young people say they have little to do with their time but hang out and court trouble. A goal of the Rheedlen program, part of New York City's Beacons Initiative, was to convert hours that might be spent negatively into constructive time that engages children usefully and connects them to meaningful activities. Some of the worst off of the neighborhood's children had no place to go at the end of the school day except for one of the four homeless shelters that housed them and their families. Rheedlen's program at Public School 194 changed this by offering such activities in the late afternoons as videotaping, drama and public speaking, martial arts, dancing, leadership training, and job development. The program did not restrict itself to students enrolled in the school. Any child who came through the school's doors after school could participate. Rheedlen, a community organization, operated centers for children and families throughout Manhattan. Its Countee Cullen Community Center at P.S. 194 was set up in collaboration with the citywide Beacons Initiative.

Rheedlen's goal when it entered the neighborhood was to persuade people that the program was installed for the long run, that it was not going to leave. Residents of central Harlem had been disillusioned by a succession of programs that had ended almost as soon as they had committed themselves to participate. Harlemites grew to resent what they called "carpetbagging," the practice of outsiders with no ties to the community launching a program and then pulling up stakes before it gained a toehold. Rheedlen's presence in P.S. 194 was underscored by the permanency of its cozy office, a former classroom that it converted to a headquarters.

The local community school district had wanted Rheedlen to operate out of the best school in the district, but the organization insisted on going where it was most needed, which turned out to be P.S. 194, on a block surrounded by boarded-up buildings. Rheedlen wanted to demonstrate its commitment by concentrating its efforts on one of central Harlem's most troubled schools and then persevering. When Rheedlen personnel arrived at the school, they found four different posters on the block seeking witnesses to four separate murders. Each Beacon program was supposed to get $1 million, an amount that was slashed even before the venture at P.S. 194 was launched. Rheedlen began making friends in the summer of 1991 by investing $10,000 in upgrading the school library. Rheedlen wanted to show that it was interested in altering even the school's dreary aesthetics. The redecorated library was a source of pride, but Rheedlen had to accept as the price of doing business the theft of the kente cloth that had been draped on a wall.

The library, a pleasant room with a relaxed ambience, was put under the supervision of a librarian who was paid to offer an after-school program. On one particular day, the youngsters were rehearsing a play from Ghana, The Monkey Without a Tail. The program, as exemplified by this activity, was more than simply a way to while away the hours. Its purpose was fourfold: to improve reading, to give the youngsters more confidence in their speaking abilities, to teach them to work cooperatively, and to teach them about their cultural heritage. "When I get their parents to come and see them in a play, they see their children doing something they never expected to see them do," said the librarian. "I had one young man in here who had a serious stutter. I had him play the spider in Charlotte's Web. The other kids poked fun at him, but he prevailed. This was a kid who had to struggle to overcome a lot. I walked him to his home one day and it was difficult to deal with the stench. He lived in an apartment house in the middle of a drug market. He had to walk into the midst of it every time he left the building. But his mother wanted something better for him. She came to see him in Charlotte's Web and was surprised and pleased to see that despite his stutter, he had gotten it together to say his lines and was speaking appropriately. These are children who have to leap hurdles, chasms, if they are going to make it."

The link that Rheedlen built between school and neighborhood was underscored by the fact that the children could look around them and see parents and siblings in the building with them. Programming for adults included such activities as a family poetry workshop and instruction in computer skills. There was even bingo every Tuesday. Rheedlen wanted families to make the school building the center of their social lives. The people's tie to Rheedlen and to the school was cemented by a voter registration booth that the program sponsored and moved around the neighborhood, gathering 2,100 registrations in a single summer. Such accomplishments may appear of small consequence compared with what is achieved in middle-class communities, but in central Harlem—large patches of which look like bombed-out, postwar Berlin—the availability of a school with the attributes of a community center, however modest, was one of life's small blessings.

Rheedlen's efforts at P.S. 194 started from ground zero in a neighborhood bereft of almost every form of social capital. The project's teen youth council of some 40 people, for instance, tried to use its energy and strength to exert an impact on their immediate surroundings. "We lose a few of them," said Jackie Bradley, a community organizer based in the school. "They are the ones who go back to the street corners. The drug dealers end up using them for camouflage." For the majority who remained with the council, the program tried to find constructive recreational outlets during the school year and jobs during the summer. The teens worked with adults to close the school's block during the summer so that it could function as a playground in a neighborhood where safe places to play were in short supply.

The planning committee for the block closing evolved into a block association whose members began taking some responsibility for the upkeep of their immediate surroundings. The very existence of a block association on 144th Street, where so many people had surrendered hope, led to the formation of associations on neighboring blocks. For the first time, some people were sweeping their stoops, painting the trim, and showing concern about the physical environment. The teen youth council and the block association established contacts with the police precinct, telling the officers when events were scheduled so that foot patrols could be assigned. Some drug dealers actually moved off the block and onto the avenues—not a great improvement by suburban standards but a notable event in the inner city. All of this happened because of what began as the work of an enhancement project in an elementary school.

The Beacons Initiative that included P.S. 194 was born of a desire to combat the crime and drugs that were destroying entire neighborhoods in the poorest areas of New York City during the 1980s. There were few facilities in which youths could spend the out-of-school hours. In these neighborhoods, children are not sent for music and ballet lessons after school. Parks are forbidding, just standing in front of one's apartment building can be dangerous. Kids atrophy in such settings. The kind of impact that was envisioned for this new program was noted in a report on the New York City Beacons Initiative: "Beacons directors repeatedly characterized the missions of their programs as community-building. They want the Beacons to serve as a force for building a climate of safety, increasing the number of adults focused on helping children and youth achieve positive educational and social outcomes, building positive peer groups among youth, and stimulating and supporting neighborhood improvement."[1]

Many of the responsibilities that other agencies and organizations and even families fulfill in advantaged settings fall by default to the school in impoverished neighborhoods. And, in the course of taking on this role, the school can position itself as a leader in efforts to revitalize the neighborhood. Families—especially the children—are strengthened immeasurably when some institution acts in concert with them. If the school is not the only player in the game and some other institution accepts part of the responsibility, so much the better. The American Association for the Advancement of Science (AAAS), for example, tried to enlist inner-city black churches and other community-based groups in its effort to improve science learning for poor black and Latino students around the country. "The church was selected because it was felt to be one of the most stable units within the African American community," said Sandra J. Parker, the national project manager. In 1987, with the aid of the Ford Foundation, AAAS launched the Black

Church Project to provide after-school lessons in mathematics and the physical sciences. Then, in 1991, a similar program in life and behavioral sciences, called the Health Connection Project, was started with funding from the National Institutes of Health.

Due to the symbiotic nature of the relationship between families and community, the neighborhood gains when family fortunes rise and families benefit when their immediate surroundings improve. "The two worlds are inextricably linked," wrote *Education Week*. "How can a neighborhood sustain long-term economic health if its children aren't well-educated? How can schools nurture the best and brightest in neighborhoods where children can't work, play, or sleep in comfort and safety?"[2] The school, as one of the last surviving institutions in some blighted areas, can serve as intermediary in community revitalization.

Therefore, a school that stays aloof from its community, especially with a minority constituency that may not trust it in the first place, does its youngsters a disservice. By building ties to parents and to the community, a school makes the work of educators easier. In this technological age, the links may even take new and unfamiliar forms in promoting contact and dispelling isolation. The Newton Street School in Newark installed personal computers in the homes of more than 20 students whose parents agreed to attend training sessions. Using a grant of almost $107,000 from the U.S. Department of Commerce, school authorities encouraged the participating parents, called "captains," to set up an electronic network among themselves to promote mutual support and to bolster their children's learning. All of the families lived in the low-income housing of the New Community Corporation, a Newark self-help group whose 3,000 units were home to 85 percent of Newton Street's students. Another partner was the University of Medicine and Dentistry of New Jersey, across the street from the housing project. Each captain was responsible for training four other parents on computers. The computers were networked to the public library, the Internet, the school, the central office of the Newark Public Schools, a local church, and the medical school. A main goal of the program was to provide the capacity by which the families could seek and receive health information to prevent illnesses and to recognize alternatives to the emergency room as a source of primary care.

A neighborhood's connection to the school in its midst can bind children to education and lend cohesion to the community. With this sense of connectedness comes a feeling of ownership by the people whose support the school needs in order to thrive. The captains in the Newton Street network, for instance, had a proprietary attitude toward their electronic network and found that it led them to form close personal ties with each other. Schools that take seriously their role in fostering such relationships can begin constructing links even where other institutions have failed. "Part of the problem facing blacks and Latinos in America's inner cities is that they lack 'connections' in the most literal sense," wrote Robert Putnam of Harvard University.[3]

In forging the Neighborhood Academic Alliance, the University of Southern California, in effect, provided some of these connections to its black and Latino neighbors. To be sure, the university had a vested interest in rendering this assistance. The 'hood begins literally across the street on any side of the verdant campus. The riot that rocked Watts in 1992 raged right up to USC's front door. As recently as 1996, reconstruction continued on a fast- food restaurant that had been torched on the Vermont Avenue side of the campus, facing the 36th Place entrance. The riot rudely reminded the university of how few blacks and Latinos were enrolled. The Neighborhood Academic Initiative was fashioned as a pipeline to funnel more minority students into USC, a recognition that if the institution, indeed, thirsted for minority students it had only to look across the street to find a reservoir of potential candidates.

Rachel Smith, whose granddaughter Maiya Rae Winston lived with her and participated in the USC program, considered it a godsend for inner-city children. "The program means everything to her life and her future," Smith said of the Neighborhood Academic Initiative, which assured her grandchild of a full scholarship if she completed the program and met USC entrance requirements. "I live in this neighborhood and couldn't afford to send my kids here. This is an incentive to her. She wants to be a doctor. She likes it, but sometimes it seems to me to be all school and no play. What we're looking at is the reward. This is a way to break out of poverty."

Canton Middle School in Baltimore emphasized the need to build connections in the effort to improve its educational program. Elaine

Urbanski's job at Canton was not just to oversee relations with parents but also to reach out to community organizations. Her preparation for this role was the 21 years she spent in the community relations department of Baltimore Gas & Electric, a position that included involvement in the company's school outreach programs. Urbanski said she decided to put more meaning into her life when she took a pay cut and went to work for Canton Middle School.

With her help, the school's connections took many forms. Fidelity & Deposit, a bank, assisted the school in writing applications for grants. A lawyer from Semes, Bowen & Semes intervened to facilitate a grant from the state that was caught in the thickets of the bureaucracy. The Maryland Business Roundtable helped make it possible for the school to send a team of teachers to participate in team-building training offered by Perdue, the chicken people. The 1st Mariner Bank provided a sponsor for the school's Girl Scout troop. By 1996-97, the school was operating on a budget of $2,760,000 in local, state, federal, and private funds. A school improvement grant from the state and a grant from the Carnegie Corporation under its middle school program allowed Canton to do much that it could not otherwise have afforded. The money, however, was not the key: the school had a vision for spending it.

Even the Edison Project, a profit-making enterprise that won contracts in 1995 to operate public schools in several districts around the country, realized at the outset that community connections were desirable, presumably for public relations reasons as well for educational ones. Whatever Edison's motivations, its blueprint for community partnerships could serve as a worthwhile model for other schools. Included in the multipronged approach for each school were plans for community engagement, a consortium of local social service providers, and a board of friends. A community resource director was to oversee these outreach efforts at each Edison-run school. Deborah McGriff, an Edison executive, said that in appointing the board of friends, principals were supposed to reach beyond the parents to find people in the community "who would help us understand the local context." In instances in which Edison operated charter schools, the charter board would become the board of friends. Based on surveys of the students and other assessments, the community resource director was to find partners among social service providers in order to broker services. While the mandate for community engagement was the vaguest part of the outreach effort, at least it was a reminder that an Edison school could benefit by identifying and tapping community resources.

Connections to Rural Communities

The enhancement program in rural northwestern Wisconsin involving six public school districts, a tribal school for Native Americans, and a small private college sought to improve education in tandem with efforts to bolster the community. An area populated almost entirely by whites, the region is ostensibly very different from Harlem or inner-city Baltimore. Poverty, however, is the common denominator. By the mid-1990s, small dairy farms were dying as milk prices fell and the government phased out federal subsidies for the dairy industry. At the same time, nonfarm jobs grew so scarce in the northwest part of the state that a manufacturer of window frames and doors laid off 500 unionized workers and replaced them with lower-paid, nonunion workers so eager for work that they would accept part-time employment without benefits. Hoping to link school improvement to community betterment, the coalition of small school systems formed the New Paradigm Partners and in 1996 won an Annenberg Rural Challenge Grant of $600,000 to be spread over three years. In large part, the grant recognized the coalition's contention that schools, especially in rural America, have the potential to make significant contributions to community building and to community development.

The six public school systems—which together enrolled only 5,000 students—planned to concentrate on four elements with the grant money: community discussions and consensus building around rethinking the purposes of schooling; community education programs for people of all ages; project-based learning in the community for students; and the preparation of materials for dissemination. In working toward consensus in the community, the New Paradigm schools wanted to bridge the gulf between school and community so that those on both sides embraced the same goals and pursued them with equal vigor, not an easy task in an area in which citizens did not readily see how better schooling would alter their children's destinies. The region's isolation added to its economic woes but beneficially accentuated the sense of community.

This was a place where poverty was not accompanied by the overlay of crime and violence that usually plague poor urban communities. Furthermore, the churches, as one of the few viable institutions in the area other than the schools, figured prominently as potential partners in community building. On Monday mornings, for instance, discussions in many public school classrooms readily referred to church activities in which students had participated the previous day. These were schools that resembled those in small rural towns in New York State, where a computer analysis suggested that poverty did not have as profound a negative impact on student performance as it did in big cities. Experts attributed the difference to the fact that rural schools were a focus of social life and the beneficiaries of greater family involvement than schools attended by similarly poor children in urban areas.[4]

The support for community education in northwest Wisconsin revolved around the goal of making lifelong learning a reality for a modestly educated population. The people, it was thought, could use opportunities for more schooling to improve the region's lagging economy. Project-based learning for youngsters was seen as a vehicle for connecting education to the real world in tangible ways that could lead to productive work. By disseminating their experiences, the New Paradigm schools could keep each other abreast of their progress and inform schools elsewhere of developments that had wider application.

The spark that lit the fire for New Paradigm was the community education program in the Flambeau School District, one of the partners. Chuck Ericksen, as director, built a community education program in Flambeau that was so exemplary that it could support itself almost entirely on outside grants. Ericksen said: "We believe our public schools have a responsibility to be responsive to community needs and demonstrate leadership in helping build the capacities of individuals to mobilize community assets and improve community life. Community education, to us, is all about connections." Examples of this philosophy abounded under the aegis of Flambeau's community education program. For instance, a group of 17 students worked with the new owners of a movie theater to renovate and retain one of the only such sites in all of vast Rusk County. Other students spent four summers working with the Department of Natural Resources to develop a community park. Workshops were offered to area employers and their employees in partnership with the county's economic development committee. A program was launched to assist the families of children who were at greatest risk of failure in the district's two elementary schools.

The Ivydale Elementary School served one of the most impoverished parts of the population in the second poorest school district in the nation's poorest state, West Virginia. This was the Appalachia against which Lyndon Johnson waged one of the prime battles of his War on Poverty. By 1997, however, almost 80 percent of the 120 children in this school were still so desperately poor that they qualified for federally subsidized lunches. Ivydale Elementary School was housed in a small one-story building wedged onto a narrow strip of land between the railroad tracks and the Elk River. Dotted throughout the rugged, wooded hills overlooking Ivydale were the plywood shacks and trailers in which many of its students lived. Welfare was a way of life for many residents of Clay County, where jobs at the coal mines had grown scarce and the lumber industry had reduced its cuttings. There was every reason for the educators at Ivydale and the families they served to despair. But this school chose to link its fortunes extensively to the community, trying to bolster the struggling families and their children.

Nancy Updegrave, the dynamo who was principal of Ivydale, scratched and scraped for every extra dollar she could obtain for the school, staying up to all hours of the night writing grant proposals and firing them off every which way, like shells from one of the ever-present shotguns in the nearby hills. She supplemented the grants with money she obtained for the school from the county health department and from other agencies. As a result, Ivydale Elementary offered one program after another to its otherwise bereft community. Various grants paid for a preschool for 23 children who otherwise would show up for kindergarten utterly unprepared; a reading tutor; a summer camp that was one of the few recreational opportunities available in this isolated area; a program to keep the gym open on Sundays for teenagers; an after-school child care program; a high school equivalency class for the adults at a school in which one-third of the parents had not even finished high school; a program to clean up the sewage that oozed from a faulty septic tank right outside the school's back door and to add a playground on the reclaimed plot; and the construction of the only tennis court in all of Clay County. These ambitious efforts gave new meaning to the phrase "community school."

The nine teachers in the school, which offered classes from preschool through fifth grade, constantly were assisted by parent volunteers who did more than simply tend to clerical tasks. Parents read to children and children read to parents. Parents also joined teachers on a school improvement council that set educational goals for the students. Parental labor was donated for repair and construction work around the school as well. One parent installed a ramp to make the school accessible to people with disabilities. Another parent partitioned off an end of the portable in which the kindergarten was housed to create a 10 by 22-foot room. Half the new space was devoted to creating a library for a school in which many students never saw books or newspapers at home; the other half was turned into the office of a fledgling family resource center.

"We want this to be a place where they can come and sign up for welfare and get everything else they need," said Loretta Conley of the family resource center, a parent with a son attending the fifth grade at Ivydale. Conley and Karen Vaughn, who had two boys attending the school, were paid through a parents-as-teachers grant to go into homes to help parents of preschoolers learn how to provide their children with developmentally stimulating activities. On one such visit they came upon a family living in a decrepit trailer with wind and snow blowing through uninsulated walls and broken windows. Now they were calling every agency they could think of to get the family help to weatherize the home. The homes of some families were so substandard that the school qualified for "homeless" assistance.

Updegrave made sure that Ivydale operated according to her philosophy that education depended on providing a healthy base for each child. The school attended to every need, from alleviating hunger to—when necessary—cleaning and clothing the children. The school acquired a washer and dryer and changes of clothing to accommodate the students who habitually showed up in dirty clothes. Almost two dozen of the neediest youngsters ate supper at Ivydale most days so the school could ensure that they got fed. When the school ran out of space, the indefatigable Updegrave converted her office into a room for the reading tutor. She also assumed responsibility for teaching the preschool class in order to obtain an extra position for the school. In an attempt to raise achievement, she assigned that salary line to a certified math teacher who handled all of the school's math instruction. So boundless was her energy that Updegrave, a wiry, gregarious woman, took a break from her hectic schedule to hike up a nearby mountain almost every day.

Connections to Public Housing

For some inner-city youngsters, the neighborhood is the housing development in which they dwell. Living amid hundreds if not thousands of families in publicly subsidized housing, the younger children may leave the project only to attend school. In such cases, connectedness between school and community should mean that the school builds links to public housing. Yet despite the fact that certain housing projects may provide a large portion of the enrollment of a particular school, usually little effort goes into forging such connections. Signs of change are emerging, however. An example of this new kind of cooperation was seen in Houston, where the school district, the housing authority, and Texas Southern University collaborated. The housing authority provided a site in the housing project for a laboratory school for the university, which is located across the street. Texas Southern provided student teachers, tutors, professional development, and other support.[5] Earlier, on Chicago's South Side, a private donor enabled the Beethoven School to create a relationship with mothers and mothers-to-be in the sprawling Robert Taylor Homes, from which it drew its students. At the higher-education level, San Antonio College paid a staff member to recruit students from nearby public housing projects and assist them in the seemingly arcane process of gaining admissions and choosing majors.[6]

Another example of change in the relationship between schools and housing projects was seen in the I Have a Dream program. What the students in each local program had in common during the first eight years of I Have a Dream was that they entered the program as sixth graders who had been in the same class. The program promised to pay their college tuition if they completed high school, meanwhile giving them social, emotional, and academic support during the middle and high school years. In 1993, however, I Have a Dream launched some new programs that started with not a single classroom of sixth grade students but a group of younger children who lived in the same public housing project and attended various schools. This direct connection to home and family was a crucial change in direction for the program. By selecting the dreamers at younger ages, during the early elementary years, officials hoped to heighten their chances for success.

One such program began in 1993 at the Chelsea-Elliott Houses, a project for low-income residents. Chelsea-Elliott comprises 12 boxlike high-rise buildings erected in the 1950s to fill the area between 9th and 10th avenues, from 25th to 27th streets, on the West Side of Manhattan, a short walk from bustling Penn Station. Like most other public housing sites across the country, it was populated largely by single mothers and their children. The few men living in the apartments tended, by and large, to be unofficial tenants, who may or may not have been the fathers of the children with whom they lived.

To embark on this new venture, I Have a Dream forged an alliance with the U.S. Department of Housing and Urban Development (HUD) and with the local operators of the projects, which for Chelsea-Elliott was the New York City Housing Authority. Headquarters for the Dream program was a ground-floor apartment in the housing complex. For the first time, I Have a Dream required each local program also to have a university partner, a step that had less to do with the housing-based approach than with the fact that program officials thought that the university could provide help and expertise to advance the program. Chelsea-Elliott formed a partnership with the New School for Social Research, an institution of higher education in Greenwich Village, a neighborhood with its northern boundary just a ten-minute walk south of the housing project.

The Chelsea-Elliott program designated every second and third grader living in the 12 buildings, some 77 children in all, as dreamers. Most attended Public School 33, the Chelsea School, on Ninth Avenue, adjacent to the housing project. But more than 20 percent of them went to one of at least a half-dozen other elementary schools, including two nearby Roman Catholic schools. All of the families, of course, rode the same elevators, heard the same noises outside their windows, and walked the same neighborhood sidewalks. Under the traditional I Have a Dream program, after a class of sixth graders was adopted, they eventually scattered to different secondary schools and had little in common other than having attended the same elementary school together. This, of course, was not the case with a housing-based project like Chelsea-Elliott, where the students would continue to live side-by-side. The dreamers gathered four afternoons a week and on Saturdays as well as during the summer for homework assistance, tutoring, and recreation at Public School 33, at the housing project's community room, or the at Hudson Guild, a century-old settlement house situated in a Chelsea-Elliott Building.

When those in a housing-based program arrived home they were at the program site, so no further traveling was required for tutoring or homework help. This was an interesting switch on the effort in some locales to relocate schools into housing projects so that children would not be put at risk having to travel to and from school. Another advantage of a program operating at a child's place of residence is that it can make connections more readily to the rest of the family. It was not unusual for siblings of the dreamers to accompany brothers and sisters to after-school tutoring sessions, cultural outings, and other activities. The number of dreamers grew to 90 during the first three years because children who moved into the project were automatically added into the program if they were in the same grade as those already participating. This policy of accepting additional students prevailed as the original group advanced to sixth grade. At that point, however, participation was to be restricted to those already in the program, with all of them guaranteed college tuition if they completed high school.

In other dreamer programs a single coordinator handled most of the work, a policy that was easier with the typical sixth-grade class of 25 or 30 students. But the size of the Chelsea-Elliott group was so great that Mindee Barham, the project coordinator, needed help. Her major assistance came through two federal government programs, Ameri-Corps and Vista. AmeriCorps participants, paid by Washington, were the backbone of the Dream project at Chelsea-Elliott. In addition, Vista paid for two full-time staffers, and the program obtained local funds to hire a social worker on a part-time basis.

Barham tried to leverage the program's impact by collaborating with other organizations such as the Hudson Guild. The partnership breathed fresh life into the Guild, which had suffered from dwindling participation. The dreamers used the Guild facilities and held joint events with the organization, making Hudson Guild a more integral part of the lives of Chelsea-Elliott residents. Curiously, the dreamer program found it could not as readily elicit the cooperation of the tenant association of the Chelsea-Elliott Houses, which would have seemed to have been a natural ally. But some residents resented the omission of their children from the program simply because they were of the wrong age.

A series of incidents characterized the schism that arose between some tenants and the dreamer program. The dreamers tried to plant a garden in a courtyard at the project, but it never took hold. Some residents threw rubbish and garbage down onto the garden at night. The students finally gave up on the garden and went on to other activities. Apparently the tenants' grievance stemmed from the housing authority's refusal at an earlier date to let them plant a garden on the same site.

Nonetheless, the dreamer program was inextricably attached to Chelsea-Elliott Houses and served to bring together some families in ways that no previous venture had done. The most active parents formed bonds that extended beyond the dreamers, helping each other in various ways. Furthermore, some became volunteers and a few even were hired into the program with Vista money. James Harris, the father of a nine-year-old dreamer, was one of the small number of fathers involved in the program. At first, he was paid by Vista and later, from the program's own funds. He said that the program made a great difference to some families at Chelsea-Elliott. "The children get to know each other and the program gets them to bond," he said. "It brought parents together too. There is a sense of community. I know that if I am not around and one of the other parents is, they will look out for my child. This program benefits the whole neighborhood." Another parent, Lisa Fuentes, said that she moved into Chelsea-Elliott Houses in 1993, after eight years on the waiting list for an apartment, just as the project was beginning. Her daughter was the right age to become a dreamer, and Fuentes said that the program gave her a way to get to know other parents.

A school enhances the education of its students when it forms ties to the community. When this process draws together members of the community, chances increase that the network of support for youngsters—part of their social capital—will grow stronger. Affluent families find their own ways to make connections to the schools their children attend. Less advantaged families, no less in need of such connectedness, usually require some help.

FOUR

Linking Activism to Schools

Frances Lucerna of El Puente Academy said that a school's legitimacy in the community comes from the community having the attitude, in effect, that it owns the school. Affluent people take this feeling for granted; poor people do not. El Puente and the community group that sponsored it were rooted in the borough's Williamsburg section. The school strengthened its bonds with the community by using the neighborhood as a living laboratory for its environmental science offerings and as a vehicle for cultivating the spirit of social action that it tried to imbue in its students. This approach ties in with the philosophy of the Institute for Research on Learning, which has argued for a view of learning that emphasizes a relationship between learning and social engagement, between knowledge and identity.[1] This notion of having the social problems of their daily lives serve as material for learning can bind students to their community. Outsiders may worry that this approach constitutes a form of indoctrination, but officials at El Puente maintained that the school drew credibility by seeking to embed itself in the neighborhood in this way. Furthermore, students liked the idea of having to learn a portion of their subjects through community-related projects that found their way into the curriculum as topics for field experiences.

The historic Williamsburg Bridge that connects Brooklyn and Manhattan loomed literally outside El Puente's front door. So, when sandblasting the bridge to remove old paint was being considered, students and faculty alerted the community to the dangers of filling the air with fragments of lead paint. The students and their allies won the battle when a judge halted the sandblasting, a ruling that eventually was expanded by the State Supreme Court to include all of New York City's bridges. Another time El Puente underscored its community connections by actively opposing the construction of a 50-story incinerator planned for the nearby Brooklyn Navy Yards. The students also participated in CAFE, the Community Alliance for the Environment. This interest in environment and community led students to seek to beautify a lot two blocks from the school that had become an eyesore. Students worked with an architect to design a park for the lot, and some of them did the actual work, receiving pay through a summer youth employment program. They planted 100 trees and built a garden with a meditation corner.

For people who are powerless, the idea that education and, specifically, schools can serve as routes to empowerment has definite appeal. The social capital of the affluent ensures that schools in their communities operate on their behalf and according to their dictates. The intricate network of connections that links suburbanites to the schools is as prevalent as the barbecue grills on their patios or the crabgrass in their lawns. Parents in poor areas, however, sometimes wonder if the interests of their children are of paramount concern to the schools. During the 1995-96 school year in San Diego, for instance, some parents and their supporters sought a role in contract negotiations when teachers struck for five days. Complaining that there was not "an independent parent voice," Walter Kudumu led a citizens' group in trying to win recognition as a parents' union that would have a place at the bargaining table.

The Center for Parent Involvement in Education that Kudumu directed played a role in galvanizing parents and others. The district responded by forming a parents' council as a consultative group, a move that Kudumu called a step forward but "not enough because it is an advisory body that has no policy impact." The parents probably could not have joined the bargaining even if the union and the district agreed to allow them to participate because California law seemed to bar third-party representation in collective bargaining. Kudumu's ongoing dissatisfaction with the ways in which the school system related to minority people had led him to form the parent center in 1989—with private grants—to offer training for parents so that, as he said, "they could hold schools accountable." Kudumu's five children attended the San Diego public schools, and he apparently exacted enough accountability to make it possible for three of them to go on to become graduates of Stanford, Duke, and Berkeley. As of 1997, the two youngest were still enrolled at the University of Rochester and North Carolina Central.

The specific issues in San Diego aside, it is clear around the country that a shortage of social capital among poor people creates the need for them to organize in some way to obtain for their children the attention and services provided by a plethora of groups and agencies in advantaged communities. This need underpinned the collaboration called Neighborhood Education Watch that in 1996 brought together such groups as the Quality Education for Minorities Network, the American Federation of Teachers, the National Council of Negro Women, and the Urban League. Neighborhood Education Watch set out to marshal support for children's learning by unifying the resources of local organizations, businesses, and residents.[2] Clearly, it is to the advantage of schoolchildren for schools and community activists to combine forces on behalf of improving the neighborhoods that exert so much influence over young lives.

When, for example, Intermediate School 218 in Manhattan wanted to enhance safety inside the building and on adjacent streets, the school reached out to the police as a part of its effort at community-building. Officers from the local precinct were made to feel welcome at I.S. 218, so much so that students eventually thought little about seeing uniformed police officers in the building. The police went into classrooms to teach students about the legal aspects of their jobs. The students, in turn, tried to promote understanding by instructing the police in the customs and habits of the Dominican community in Washington Heights. The relationship that developed even led to a basketball game in which the school staff squared off against the police. The game was taken so seriously that the police, noticing a 6-foot-8 staff member, asked to reschedule the contest at a time when the tallest precinct employee would be available to play.

Parents liked having the police around the school because their presence tended to cause the drug dealers who clustered on nearby streets to lower their profile. When the police were not in view, the dealers hawked their wares openly and sometimes amused themselves by provoking students to fight. Despite periodic police crackdowns, Washington Heights has been held in thrall by an estimated 150 drug organizations employing 5,000 dealers working out of 500 locations.[3] The situation grew so threatening at one point that a contingent of mothers began accompanying the children to school. I.S. 218 welcomed the police presence in the building for another reason as well. Each afternoon at five, the school opened its doors to neighborhood teen-agers as a part of the extended day program. Many participants were alumni of I.S. 218 who were imbued with the school's mission and acted responsibly in the building. But some other teens brought with them the harsh attitudes of the streets. Having police on the premises ensured a peaceful atmosphere.

Social activism tied to community concerns through the curriculum, as the program at El Puente showed, can position a school to identify more closely with the lives of its students and their families. Clay High School in Appalachia, for instance, included a component to foster community-oriented learning in its plan for spending a $186,000 federal grant for math and science education. One such project involved analyzing the water quality in some of the county's many mountain streams. Another called for interviewing parents of students and senior citizens about the traditional use of herbal medicines in the area. When possible, these science projects were infused with a strong dose of mathematics. Youngsters who study conditions in their own neighborhood should not doubt the relevance of education to the everyday world. Lessons in math, science, social studies, English, or almost any other subject can serve to make these connections.

In one case, students from El Puente went into the neighboring Satmar Hasidic neighborhood to learn about the Orthodox Jews who live there. These families resided along Lee Avenue and its cross streets, as if caught in a time warp—conversing in Yiddish, dressing in a distinctive Old World mode, and largely shunning outsiders. The teacher told the students to think of *Star Trek* and to imagine that they had arrived in spaceships, beamed down among the Hasidim.

The students, notebooks in hand and observing without asking questions of anyone, dutifully recorded all that they saw: Bearded men in long black frock coats, girls and women in dressy outfits that covered them neck to toe, carriages with babies left unattended outside of stores in the midst of this close community, mothers with many children in tow, big families everywhere. And streets filled with vans. Everywhere the El Puente students looked, there seemed to be another van. Back at school, the students reflected on what they had seen. The living lesson in community was important for them, and they searched for relevance to their own Puerto Rican families. As for the multitude of vans . . . when a Satmar rabbi visited the school to answer questions as the final part of the lesson, the students could not resist asking: "Is it part of your religion that you all drive vans?" The answer, of course, simply had to do with the need to accommodate all those large families.

Canton Middle School linked the education of some of its students to the conditions of the Outer Harbor, just blocks from the school's southeast Baltimore site. Molly White, a science teacher, organized her students into what they called the Chesapeake Bay Club. Using a $5,000 grant from the Chesapeake Bay Trust, the students set out to learn all they could about the body of water that they saw almost daily but to which they seldom gave a second thought. They tested the water for the effects of pollution and gauged the extent of the growth of algae. They ventured into the harbor in boats. Altogether enthused, the students gained an awareness about a part of their immediate environment that they came to believe they could take a role in improving.

One result of the project was a glossy booklet that the students published to disseminate what they had learned. The introduction stated: "We pollute the bay when we pour chemicals into the storm drains or down the sink. Dirt from vacant lots, construction sites, and other unplanted areas is eroded by the rain and carried to the bay along with any fertilizers and chemicals we have added to it. Every time it rains, the oil, soap, and trash we leave on the streets and sidewalks are washed right into the bay. The Chesapeake Bay Club was formed by Canton Middle School students who care about the Chesapeake Bay and want to keep it healthy for their future."

Bringing Adults into the Equation

Even the adult education programs that some schools in lower-income neighborhoods use to bind themselves closer to their communities can contain an activist dimension, enhancing people's feeling that the school relates to their concerns. At Rogers Elementary School in Stamford, Connecticut, where this connection could be seen, an English as a second language course veered off in a way that underscored the tie between adult education and neighborhood betterment. This happened one morning when most of the adult students were absent. The class proceeded with only three students, all immigrants still honing their English. The low turnout on this pleasant day was puzzling. Only a couple of months earlier, on a morning after one of the worst storms in years, the entire class had shown up, disappointed to discover that the heavy snow had caused cancellation of adult courses. Class began on this particular day as it always did—with the students standing, facing a flag that hung in a corner of the room, each covering his or her heart with a hand and reciting the Pledge of Allegiance.

The teacher quickly initiated a discussion of current events. Guillermo, from Colombia, said that there was "bad news" for Stamford that morning in the daily newspaper. A 19-year-old was shot as he drove a car on a local street. A woman from Haiti, who had brought her toddler with her to class, said that there was also "bad news" in the international report and proceeded to relate the sad tale of a gunman in Tasmania who had slaughtered some two dozen people. The teacher used the woman's recitation of the shooting to seize on one of the words mentioned from the news report. "Do you know the word 'hostage'?" the teacher asked. They did. Since the shooting was in Australia, the teacher referred to the locale as an introduction to another topic, mentioning the film *Crocodile Dundee*. She talked of the accent used in Australia and heard in the film, making the point that English can be spoken with many different accents, which greatly pleased the immigrant students. Furthermore, to make the point that words can have different meanings in countries that use the same language, she cited the words for popcorn as used in three Spanish-speaking countries.

As the class progressed, a woman from Mexico digressed to ask a question about an offensive smell she had encountered lately on her way to school. The teacher used the opportunity to encourage the students to discuss, in English, the suspected origin of the offending aroma. Eventually the class decided that the smell was probably emanating from a nearby garbage dump. "Does Mr. Malloy, the mayor, know about this?" the teacher asked rhetorically. "If you want to have someone solve this problem, what's the way to go about it?"

The man from Colombia was leery of complaining to the mayor because, he said, "In Colombia, people complain and nothing happens."

"Maybe the class can write a letter to the mayor," the teacher suggested. She immediately assigned such a letter as homework for each student and volunteered to assemble the thoughts they produced into a single letter and send it to the mayor. This was clearly a lesson in activism at a community school that used a class as a device for raising community consciousness as well as for learning English. This approach was not dissimilar from what occurred in Baltimore when a group of students at Northwestern High School, with the aid of the law school at the University of Maryland, worked to force absentee owners of vacant buildings in the neighborhood to refurbish derelict housing.[4]

Another example of school and community uniting on behalf of action occurred in Arizona at the Ochoa School in the Barrio Libre section of South Tucson, a town of one square mile surrounded by Tucson. The 75-year-old tan stucco building, renovated several times over the decades, was tucked among small one-story adobe houses, some so modest that they had dirt floors. The view from almost anywhere on the school grounds with its open-air campus of covered walkways afforded a captivating panorama of the distant mountains. Inside, the clean, neat corridors and classrooms spoke to a sense of caring about the 350 children who attended the school, which ran from preschool through the fifth grade. The large Latino presence in the neighborhood was underscored by the fact that only 10 percent of the enrollment was non-Latino—30 Native Americans, 6 African Americans, and 3 Anglos. Notices in the front hall were posted in both Spanish and English. Paired posters with an identical rafting scene, for instance, encouraged girls to join the scouts with the words "Adventuras Por Vida" on one and "Adventures for Life" on the other.

These students were poor—more than 90 percent qualifying for subsidized lunches—but came from striving families that made certain that 94.6 percent of the youngsters were in attendance at school each day. This was a place where every morning at 8:45 one or another of the classes gathered around the pole in front of the building for a flag-raising ceremony. Many of the students' families lived with relatives, and the slightest downward shift in the economy would drive them back across the border into Mexico, where the child might or might not continue to attend school. No more than 30 percent of the students completing fifth grade at Ochoa spent all of their elementary years in the school.

Just around the corner was the Shamrock Bar, known throughout the neighborhood as a place not only to get a drink but to find drugs and prostitutes. It attracted a host of unsavory types who clustered on nearby streets. The denizens of the bar intrigued the children of Ochoa, who could watch the comings and goings from the vantage of their play-ground. The students were fascinated to find used syringes and con-doms outside the school, not to mention an abundance of empty beer cans and liquor bottles that rattled around their playground. Once some blood-soaked clothing was abandoned on school grounds. Sometimes wayward activities overflowed onto the school's grounds and even into the corridors, where drunk and drugged vagrants used the school's drinking fountains as makeshift bathing facilities.

"I no longer felt the kids were safe and called a parents' meeting so that I could let them know that I was not able to assure the safety of their children," said Elsa Padilla, then the principal of Ochoa. The assembled parents readily agreed that the Shamrock Bar should be closed down. But they doubted their ability to compel such action, even in the face of the perils and negative examples that the bar posed for their youngsters. Seeking to strengthen their hand, the parents decided to join forces with the Pima County Interfaith Council, a grass-roots social action group. By coincidence, a police investigation of the Shamrock was also under way, and law enforcement officials shared information with the coalition of parents, community activists, and educators. The principal began storing as evidence the used syringes that students and teachers picked up around the school.

Members of the coalition started phoning the police every time they saw what they thought was a violation that could provide ammunition to use against the bar. Until then, many neighborhood families were afraid to call the police because they did not want to draw attention to themselves. An estimated 40 percent of the school's enrollment consisted of children whose families had entered the United States without legal documents. Their reluctance to report incidents was overcome by an arrangement to let them call the police anonymously from pay phones.

The parents and their allies gradually built their case against the bar, using research to ferret out the facts about violations. Receiving sympathetic assistance from a member of the City Council, they circulated a petition that 800 residents signed. Finally, a delegation that included representatives from the interfaith council, educators, parents, and other neighborhood residents—accompanied by some students—went to a City Council meeting to press their case. Principal Padilla took along her box, which by then was overflowing with syringes. The owner of the bar was trying to sell it and the community group presented arguments for not transferring the liquor license. They said that the would-be buyer was a former manager of the Shamrock who had done little to alter the bar's objectionable influence on the neighborhood.

Eventually City Council voted unanimously to recommend that the state deny the license transfer. The next step was a trip to Phoenix to attend a meeting of the State Licensing Board. This time a City Council member provided a bus, and 40 people from the school and the neighborhood made the trip to testify once more against the Shamrock Bar. Victory came with the denial of the license transfer at the state level; the bar was closed down. The families of the Ochoa School and the surrounding neighborhood were elated by their accomplishment, which they achieved by using the school as the focal point for their empowerment.

The sense of oneness between school and community had manifested itself earlier when students in one class were assigned to write about something in the community that they would like to change. Many decried the filthy conditions in their neighborhood, complaining that outsiders considered them "pigs" who did not care about their surroundings. The young essayists lamented that even if the neighborhood somehow got cleaned up, it would simply get dirty again. Their teacher thought that the youngsters felt despair over the situation. She enlisted two other teachers and, together, the three classes launched a crusade to address the problem in an organized and deliberate way.

Community betterment was deemed of such critical academic importance that class time was given over to the campaign to remove the blight of trash from the neighborhood. Lessons included exercises to make maps dividing the neighborhood into sectors for which individual students could take responsibility. The youngsters were assigned to figure out how to solve the trash problem and how to win the compliance of their neighbors. Children from the three classes made flyers and distributed them to each home. The flyer called on residents to sweep their yards and curbs clean and deposit the trash for pickup. A homeless shelter provided garbage bags for distribution in the neighborhood. The children decided to encourage people to dispose of the abandoned rotting furniture and other junk that many had kept behind their houses for years.

And so at nine one morning, when the students normally would have been busily engaged in their classrooms, they were on their way to canvass houses in the neighborhood, ringing bells and delivering carefully rehearsed speeches imploring residents to gather up the trash from their property and take it to the curb for pickup. Accompanied by parent chaperones, the youngsters felt a keen sense of connectedness to their school and to their neighborhood and were exhilarated by the idea that they were making a meaningful contribution to improvement.

From out of this enthusiasm grew the determination to clean and beautify an empty lot near the school that had become a dumping ground. Initially the teachers and students conducted an urban archaeological expedition and analyzed the trash. Then research of county records revealed that the property was owned by the city. The students, with the aid of teachers, prepared a proposal to turn the land over to the parks and recreation department so that it could be converted to a park and environmental habitat. One of the school's teachers, a member of the Audubon Society, directed the students to an organization that could help them document their case. Plans were discussed with a landscape architect, and meetings were held with the agriculture department at the University of Arizona and with the League of Women Voters. Soon the students were learning about varieties of trees so that they could help decide what to plant in their proposed park. These activities involved classroom lessons that required reading and arithmetic to measure the lot properly. The students finally presented their idea to the City Council. The payoff came in 1996, when the saplings were in the ground and an incipient park replaced what had once been a blight on the community.

Activism with Outside Allies

Another kind of connectedness was evident in the Fair Haven neighborhood of New Haven, Connecticut, where Christopher Columbus Elementary School and Centro San Jose faced each other across Grand Avenue. More than 80 percent of the school's enrollment was Latino, largely Puerto Rican; Centro, a community-help organization, devoted itself to promoting Puerto Rican culture. The sense of simpatico between school and neighborhood center was strong without detracting from the separate missions of either. Migdalia Castro, the family education advocate at Centro, began her career as a parent volunteer at Christopher Columbus. Representatives from Centro San Jose even sat on the school management team. Centro was created in 1957 in another part of New Haven as a church-related group but severed its religious ties in the 1980s to concentrate solely on its social mission.

Centro provided space for after-school and summer recreational activities for children from Christopher Columbus and sponsored sports teams and other activities. But the larger vision of Centro San Jose was devoted to something grander—altering the circumstances in which the children lived by changing the neighborhood itself. Families from the school were the most direct beneficiaries of these efforts. Onell Calveras, then the school's family liaison representative and later an assistant teacher, said: "The premise is that you can't have a kid educated without a good environment—housing, food, jobs." Although the center's mission stretched beyond the school's immediate feeder area, many of the parents most involved in the center were the ones most active at Christopher Columbus. The center did much to encourage those parents to become advocates on behalf of both the school and the neighborhood.

In 1990 the director of the center, Peter A. Noble, and the principal of Christopher Columbus, Carmen Y. Polanco, presented a joint proposal to Connecticut's Department of Children and Families, requesting a grant to help the two entities work together on behalf of the neighborhood. The proposal won a five-year grant from the state, permitting the school and the center to mount a host of projects for neighborhood children and families. Much of the thrust during those years was on helping people learn to help themselves, including assisting them to become more savvy about the political process that affected them. Christopher Columbus, a bilingual school, presented programs in English and Spanish, and Centro San Jose followed with another program in Spanish, targeted toward yet another part of the population that the school had not reached.

Program participants tried to deal with neighborhood problems that impinged upon the lives of children and affected their schooling. This effort, called the parent empowerment program, offered workshops on such topics as parenting skills, lead poisoning, public speaking, and time management with an eye toward cultivating people as neighborhood advocates. Food and prizes were an important part of most events, used as magnets to attract people who might otherwise have not attended. A portion of the grant provided salaries to pay program participants to train friends and neighbors in the skills that they had learned. Migdalia Castro found herself helping parents register at community colleges, writing referral letters to aid families in their quest for better housing, and accompanying neighborhood residents to public meetings where they could lend support to positions they favored.

At Ochoa, the community activism was a part of a larger movement that connected the schools of the Educational and Community Change (ECC) project to the community. ECC tried to live up to its commitment to effect community change—as well as change inside the school—by collaborating with groups outside the schools. It was in this connection that ECC forged a relationship with the Pima County Interfaith Council (PCIC). This organization pursued an old-fashioned, grass-roots approach to community organizing, working through ECC and other groups to help poor people gain power over their destiny. The efforts were bound together through what PCIC called its family and community preservation strategy. Local groups like PCIC have stirred poor people to action in cities around the country under the coordinating influence of the Industrial Areas Foundation, an organization that traces its origins to one of the twentieth century's premier organizers, the late Saul Alinsky.

"What educators are beginning to realize," said Ernesto J. Cortes, Jr., the southwest regional director of the Industrial Areas Foundation, "is that, without the support and engagement of the parents and community leaders at the grassroots level, any attempts at improving the public schools will be ineffective."[5] PCIC sought to build an activist base in Tucson that was supportive of children and youths. Without such organizations as PCIC, according to Cortes, common people are not connected to genuine political power and lack social capital, which he defined as "public relationships of trust and collaboration."[6]

Frank Pierson, the PCIC organizer in Tucson, was paid from funds raised by some 50 participating churches and several businesses. Paul E. Heckman, the project director of the Educational and Community Change project, saw a connection to PCIC as a way to keep alive the momentum for school reform after outside funding expired and ECC ceased to exist. And so it was on a mild winter evening that about two dozen representatives from neighborhoods throughout Tucson, including those from which ECC's schools drew its students, gathered in the basement of Prince Chapel AME Church for a leadership training session. The meeting hall, directly below the sanctuary, was paneled in wood, much like a recreation room in someone's home. The faint sounds of a choir rehearsing upstairs could be heard, and a ceiling fan turned slowly as people arrived to fill the chairs at two long tables that faced each other.

When PCIC began operating in Tucson early in the 1990s, it solicited support through one-on-one sessions, hundreds of small meetings in people's homes, neighborhood meetings in larger places of assembly, and training sessions. The organization asked people to direct their attention to the future of the city's children. This led to attempts to try to mobilize support for programs for children and youths involving summer employment, recreation, and after-school activities. PCIC activists conducted research on various programs in the community and on the agencies that sponsored them, hoping to arm themselves with facts that would let them speak with authority in meetings with public officials and agency executives.

Even though it was still winter, the conversation that evening at Prince Chapel dealt with building an apparatus to ensure that during the coming summer jobs would be available for teen-agers and recreational opportunities for younger children. Everyone was concerned about impending cuts in the youth employment program. One woman said that the previous summer her church had signed up 150 youths for jobs and could place only 95 of them, but she believed that with better coordination, activists could have obtained jobs for most of those who registered. "You start off learning," she said of her experience in trying to promote summer employment. "We learned that we have to involve the parents in the applications. We have to explain to them what it means to build a community. It takes more community leaders to identify these jobs for kids. We could have used 550 jobs. We have to keep perfecting the system so that it meets our needs."

A representative from another church said that her group had struggled for more than a year to mount an after-school recreational program for neighborhood children. The city had refused to aid the effort on the basis that it was improper to house such a program in a religious institution. Finally the city relented after the church agreed that any child—whether a member of the church or not—could participate in the program. The principal of one of the area's schools and the director of a youth center told of the after-school program on which they were collaborating, providing youngsters with homework help, recreational activities, and snacks between 2:30 and 6:00 every weekday afternoon. Budget cuts loomed and they worried about what would happen to children suddenly turned out on the streets in a gang-infested neighborhood. As it was, 300 children had to be put on a waiting list because no funds were available to expand the program.

PCIC was laying plans to focus citywide attention on the plight of young people in Tucson. The organizers wanted to attract 1,000 people for a march through the city that would be held in a few months. Many of those in the room worried that without greater support for programs for children, more of the neighborhood's young people would fall prey to gangs and get pulled into the cycle of violence that had raised the number of deaths of youths to a new record level the previous year. Of the 94 people killed in Pima County that year, 1995, 23 were 19 or younger, and 20 of the 73 homicide suspects charged in those crimes were in the same age group.[7]

Gloria Manzanedo, a representative of St. Margaret's Catholic Church, took the situation very personally. She said: "I have two teenagers. A lot of other kids their age have problems with the law, getting involved with drugs and violence; their neighbors fear them. I want to help bring them back. We're losing these young people. Summer jobs is an important part of this. It will get them working and interested in pursuing their education. The youth are a resource; we just don't realize what talent we have here. We have meetings about this in the church and we hear shooting outside. We don't know where the bullets are coming from. We don't know where the bullets will land."

FIVE

Linking Homes to Schools

Recent attempts by schools to do more for children in need have included the creation of more programs to reach parents. These efforts are underpinned by the belief that a parent better connected to a school is more likely to reinforce scholastic goals in the home. Yet parents, at the same time, may look to the schools to perform many of the tasks that the schools think ought to be handled by parents or some outside agency. In poor neighborhoods, where the schools may be the most visible and most viable institutions remaining, families— lacking social capital and the knowledge and ability to work the system—depend heavily on the schools. Even a dispute between neighbors may wind up at the schoolhouse door. One day at Canton Middle School in Baltimore, for example, a student's mother came to complain to a guidance counselor about the mother of another student who she said had tried to kick down her front door during an argument. The guidance counselor told her that she should be talking to the police, not to him. "When neighbors argue around here," he explained later to a visitor, "their disagreements sometimes end up playing themselves out in the school building."

While few enhancement programs advocate that schools should mediate neighborhood disputes, the programs nonetheless strive to get parents into the schools so that closer ties may be forged with them. Such links between school and home can be instrumental in advancing the fortunes of children in impoverished neighborhoods. And one way that schools try to build this relationship with the home is by creating what they call family or parent centers. These centers offer various programs to adults and often have a physical presence in the school, housed in a former classroom in which parents can gather. The center becomes almost a home away from home for some parents who speak of the warm atmosphere and the tight bonds that they build with other parents. The programs offered may provide educational opportunities ranging from guidance in balancing a household budget to certificate courses leading to a high school diploma. The center may also provide family members with entree to health services, job placement, and information on housing. Sometimes the centers distribute donated used clothes and canned goods. They also act to bridge gaps in relations between families and teachers.

The value of family centers in schools is heightened by the fact that so often in the past parents in impoverished neighborhoods have had limited contact with the schools that their children attend. This lack of connection between school and home is viewed as an impediment to the academic achievement of children in need. Two decades of research show that children's growth and development benefit from a link between home and school.[1] The President's Advisory Commission on Educational Excellence for Hispanic Americans said in 1996 that the failure of schools to involve parents was closely related to many factors affecting the low educational attainment of Hispanic Americans. "School professionals who are not linguistically, culturally, and socially sensitive to Hispanic students also do not relate effectively to their students' parents," stated the commission's report.[2]

Adults who do not feel at one with the school may take less interest in their youngsters' education. They are not as apt to discuss schoolwork with children or to monitor their progress. The relationships that these adults form with schools tend to be shaky because their own experiences as students may have been negative. They wonder whether the school truly welcomes their involvement. Youngsters, picking up on their parents' ambivalence, may end up putting less value on school and may not acquire the attributes and predilections that contribute to academic success.

A model for parent and family centers was developed in Kentucky as part of the state's Education Reform Act in 1990. Family resource centers were established in elementary schools and youth service centers in secondary schools in which at least 20 percent of the students qualified for free lunches under poverty guidelines. By 1997 the centers were serving 923 schools, 85 percent of those eligible. In some cases, two or three schools joined together to share a center. The state allotted the centers $200 per eligible child, for a minimum amount of $10,000 and a maximum of $90,000. This was enough money to staff each center with at least a director. Most centers were situated in former classrooms, and some were housed in portable units placed on school grounds. A few were installed in vacant storefronts near the schools.

A prime goal was to mitigate the obstacles outside the classroom that stood in the way of school achievement. Thus the mandated components of each family resource center were child care for preschoolers; after-school care for children of school age; training for child care providers; classes in parenting and adult literacy; and health services either on the premises or through referral. At the youth service centers, serving secondary students and their families, the mandated components were referrals to health and social services; employment counseling, training, and placement; summer and part-time job development; drug and alcohol abuse counseling; and counseling for family crises.

Separate legislation previously had provided the state with legal mechanisms for integrating various services to families. Many centers adapted their activities to these coordinated programs, which had a budget of $38 million in 1996. The centers were free to fulfill their mandate through collaborations, contracting for some services and making referrals for others. As it turned out, parents of children in the elementary grades were reached more easily than parents of high schoolers, who—like parents throughout the country—felt less inclined to involve themselves with their children as they got older. The youth service centers in the secondary schools found it more effective to work directly with students than with parents, although they remained receptive to parent involvement.

Families on Two Coasts Get More Involved

Enhancement programs, through their outreach to parents, try to counteract the various factors that put children in need on a slippery slope. A survey of a network of family centers at the Vaughn School and several others in the valley north of Los Angeles identified these five main ways in which family centers exerted an impact on parents:

- Increased self-esteem; provided for more empowerment, greater assertiveness, more security, pride, and enhanced functioning of families
- Greater communication with teachers or administrators at the school
- Increased parent learning as well as general gains in information
- Met diverse needs, including those for food, clothing, and health care
- Served as places for socializing[3]

Outside intervention was vital to the creation of the family center at the Vaughn School and to the spread of the concept to five neighboring schools. The effort at Vaughn began with the FamilyCare Initiative, a joint project of the Los Angeles Educational Partnership (LAEP) and the United Way. This venture was the basis for a strategic plan that eventually brought state funds into the school in support of a family center under the Healthy Start program that California created for preschool children. The centers for parents at Vaughn and other schools tightened connections between school and home. The resulting networks enlarged the social capital of children from participating families by providing entree to linkages that otherwise would not have been as readily available. The centers in some of these places, however, were not fully integrated into the schools they served. They stood apart, as entities that teachers and administrators sometimes did not fully trust or understand. This separateness may have given the family centers a necessary aura of independence, but because many students' academic lives remained untouched by the centers, their ultimate impact on scholastic outcomes is debatable. The link between parental involvement and student achievement, therefore, is forged to some degree simply on faith that it will make a difference in student learning.

The program at Vaughn became a linchpin for the network of school-linked family centers that the Los Angeles Educational Partnership and its allies tried to establish across part of the San Fernando Valley. The LAEP got into this sort of work in the first place out of its desire to promote children's school readiness, which depends immeasurably on what transpires in the home. At about the same time as the founding of the family center, Vaughn was emerging from a state of ethnic ferment and the neighborhood itself was changing with a large infusion of immigrants from Mexico and Central America. Before long, a school that had had an enrollment about equally divided between Latinos and blacks would be 90 percent Latino. Meanwhile, a new principal, Yvonne Chan, whose Chinese origin lent her an air of neutrality, took up the reins. Vaughn converted itself into a charter school and moved into school-based management, thereby increasing its flexibility.

The Los Angeles Educational Partnership had designed a program for families with children younger than age five, but the program was expanded even before implementation to include the families of pupils of all elementary-level ages. The family center offered activities ranging from classes on parenting for pregnant mothers to trips to a museum, where some parents said they saw abstract art for the first time in their lives. LAEP provided a budget that reached $350,000 so that the family center could hire its own staff members, who, eventually, would work side by side with regular school district employees. The funds made it possible for the center, situated in three rooms at the school, to hire two family advocates and five community liaisons. Family advocates made home visits and, when appropriate, referred family members to a counselor at the school. The links to the community grew even stronger as the family center jobs went almost entirely to neighborhood people, most of whom had a vested interest in the school because their children attended it. Parents began working for the center as volunteers and had the opportunity to begin receiving wages that grew with their responsibilities. Those in the most demanding jobs were paid as much as $8 to $10 an hour.

Marcos Zelaya, who ultimately became Vaughn's bilingual coordinator, started working for the school in this way, hired by the family center to be an assistant teacher. He took the job after he enrolled his children in the school, sat in on a meeting, and was asked if he had any education. "A little," Zelaya said in his understated way, not elaborating. He liked being in the classroom with children so much that he earned a teaching credential and then got a master's degree in educational administration. It was not until he was well established at Vaughn that Zelaya quietly let it be known that he had attended medical school in his native Bolivia, preparing for a career that he later decided not to pursue.

As it hired more and more local residents, almost all of them women, Vaughn turned into the kind of place where neighborhood "Mamas," as they were called, kept peace on the playground and around the schoolyard. Attired in distinctive vests, the women hovered like mother hens, ensuring that each child who fell get an affectionate hug and that every fracas was quickly broken up. The children came to take it for granted that their mothers and other women from the neighborhood were fixtures at the school. Vaughn Family Center won acceptance as a neighborhood institution—so much so that every weekday at lunchtime the wonderful aromas of homestyle Mexican cooking wafted through the family center as the Mamas collaboratively cooked a delicious lunch for themselves and anyone else who happened to be around.

Elsa Rojas became an involved parent at Vaughn near the beginning of the school's transition because she was disgusted with what she saw happening there—or not happening during the days when it was still dysfunctional. The oldest of her three children, a girl, still could not read after completing the third grade. Rojas had heard that Vaughn was the worst school in its part of the city, but she and her husband bought their home in the neighborhood anyway because they could afford it. Rojas was considering transferring her children to a Catholic school—although it was unclear how she would pay the tuition—when she went to Vaughn to talk to a teacher. It was halfway through the school year and Rojas felt frantic. Her desperation was exacerbated by her recent layoff from a job in an electronics plant.

What Rojas anticipated as her final visit to Vaughn led to an unexpected encounter. Yvonne Chan, who had just assumed the principalship, introduced herself. "Nice meeting you, but I want my daughter out of here," Rojas said. Chan, a persistent woman, persuaded Rojas to leave her daughter in Vaughn for another six months to see if a new principal and revamped policies would make a difference. Rojas relented and six months later was delighted by the child's progress. As part of the agreement with Chan, Rojas also became a volunteer at Vaughn, putting her six-month-old son into the child care program that the Los Angeles Educational Partnership had helped start at the school. Rojas, who had emigrated from Mexico after coming of age as the nineteenth in a family of 21 children, served as a volunteer tutor in the school's bilingual program and gradually was given increasing responsibilities. She fought, though, to keep her own children out of bilingual education and gathered signatures from other parents of Latino background who also wanted to ensure that their children were taught entirely in English. "I don't believe in bilingual education except for the newest arrivals, but schools like to have the classes because it brings in money for them," she said. Eventually she was hired as a family advocate by the family center.

The formation of the Pacoima Urban Village, a nonprofit corporation meant to build a self-help enterprise for the parents, using the family centers as a launching pad, symbolized the personal growth of the parents at Vaughn and the other participating schools. "The basic premise here is to break the cycle of poverty," said Kay Inaba, a semiretired industrial psychologist who worked as a United Way volunteer to help advance the urban village concept. He continued: "The capability resides within the people themselves. It can't be done from the outside. Even creating a perfect school won't do it because the kids go back to dysfunctional homes and neighborhoods." And so parents and their supporters devoted themselves to figuring out how to continue the momentum beyond the inevitable point when the United Way, the Los Angeles Educational Partnership, and other supporters of the family centers terminated their financial support.

A goal was to get Vaughn and the other schools in the network to divert some of the money they received from the board of education to support the family centers so that they eventually could become self-sustaining. The issue, in many ways, revolved around a test of whether the family centers could win a vote of confidence from the schools that they sought to help. What was happening in Los Angeles was probably a harbinger because most of the enhancement programs described in this book ran on soft money; eventually they would need other funds—preferably from ongoing school budgets—to continue their work. Vaughn itself broke ground in 1997 for a $2.2 million facility on its campus that would contain a community library, ten additional classrooms, technology and science labs, and a teacher training center that would collaborate with California State University at Northbridge.

* * *

attempts to lure parents into the building. Jackson-Keller also wanted to ensure that parents would show up for conferences about their children. Thus, although report cards were sent home after the first six-week marking period, parents had to go to school and have a conference with the teacher to get subsequent report cards. "We hound them and stay after them until they come to school," said Alicia Thomas, the principal. "If the teacher can't get the parent in, she asks me to try, and I am relentless."

A different approach to enhancing connectedness between home and school originated in New Haven, Connecticut, where the School Development Program, conceived by James P. Comer, was predicated on a high level of parent involvement. The program assumed that at least half of a school's parents would attend parent-teacher conferences, reinforce learning at home, and participate in the school's social activities. Another 10 to 50 percent of parents, the program believed, would engage in the school's daily life by being in the building and involved in student learning activities. And the program assumed that 1 to 10 percent of parents would participate in the school's collaborative decision making in one way or another, with some serving on the planning and management team that coordinates the entire school.[4] For most schools around the country, though, the level of parent involvement is considerably lower. These other schools struggle mightily to win parent involvement. At one point, Onell Calveras, who worked with parents at Christopher Columbus School in New Haven, Connecticut, decided that he could make the most impact by concentrating his efforts on the families of 40 of the school's 365 students. And his efforts even with that defined group were constrained by moves the families made back and forth to Puerto Rico and by the energies that parents had to divert toward looking for employment or dealing with other aspects of their impoverishment.

At Expo Middle School in the inner-city Frogtown neighborhood of St. Paul, Josie Ahartz, an Iroquois, headed the multicultural community outreach program that sought to connect families to the school. Expo was housed in a three-story classic brick building that began life in 1924 as Woodrow Wilson Junior High School, a name that remained carved in stone over the front entrance. By the mid-1990s, when it had taken on a new name and become a charter school, the school had an enrollment in which 60 percent of the students were eligible for subsidized lunches. About half of Expo's 420 students walked to school from nearby small working-class houses; the remainder, having chosen the school over those in their neighborhoods, arrived on buses. About 25 students volunteered to be bused to the school from the suburb of Roseville, outside the district. Half of the school's enrollment was made up of children of color, the largest portion of whom were blacks, followed by Asians—mostly Hmongs from Cambodia—Latinos, and Native Americans.

Its reputation for caring made Expo popular among the parents of disabled students, so much so that their children came to make up one-third of the entire enrollment. As a charter school with open enrollment, Expo was obligated to take all applicants in a random fashion. "We're more nurturing here than other schools and the school works better culturally," said Ellie Elmquist, a parent who was a part-time staff member at the school. "I see some tough kids here and if they give us half a chance they succeed better here. They would be out the door at a traditional school." So strong was the sense of nurturing at Expo that critics accused the school of "coddling" its students. In fact, 24 percent of the students responded to a schoolwide survey by saying that they did not feel challenged by their classes.

Traditional Expo was not. All students—the school contained sixth, seventh, and eighth graders—spent the day largely in self-contained rooms, as they had in elementary school, rather than having a different teacher for each subject. This added to the sense of personalization, as did the practice of letting students address teachers by their first names. Of the main subjects, only mathematics instruction was handled by specialists. Much of the rest of the curriculum was taught through thematic teaching that integrated subjects. Classrooms were organized on an interage basis, mixing equal numbers of sixth, seventh, and eighth graders, and a new group of sixth graders replaced the eighth graders who graduated each year. Connections were strong because a student remained with the same teacher and most of the same classmates for three years.

Expo's policy of holding conferences with parents three times a year increased ties with the home. In addition, written narrative reports—instead of grades on a report card—were provided at the end of each semester. Teachers would even meet parents over coffee in restaurants if that was what it took to get them to a conference. Expo teachers used the conferences as occasions for discussing and displaying the student's work. The student participated in the conference, talking about his or her studies while leading the teacher and the parents through a portfolio of work. Conferences included the negotiation of a contract calling for separate actions by the student, the parent or guardian, and the teacher. The student pledged to complete all academic work, take responsibility for his or her behavior, know and obey school rules, and attend school on a regular and timely basis. Among other matters, the parent promised to provide a quiet place for study, communicate a positive attitude toward education, encourage learning in such places as the library, planetarium, and museums, and attend parent-teacher conferences. The teacher agreed to respect individual differences among students, make clear what standards of behavior were expected, and contact parents about any concerns or work not completed by the student.

Elsewhere, the Rheedlen project at P.S. 194 in Harlem tried to collaborate with parents to head off substance and alcohol abuse among their children and to get parents to set the stage for preventing the students from dropping out of school when they got a little older. The road to dropping out of high school, after all, is paved with attitudes and behaviors that develop during the elementary and middle school years. Because home life and relations between parent and child have so much to do with determining a youngster's propensity to use drugs and to drop out, the program offered workshops and retreats for parents. In addition, a program representative made home visits. Family counseling and teacher-parent conferences were available too. Yet parents did not readily accept invitations to participate in the program. And, in most cases, if a student's mother did not come to an event, there was no second parent available; fathers were absent from the lives of so many of the children in central Harlem. Door prizes were offered at events to get parents to take more interest in the lives of their children. "You have to spark their interest," said a family worker from the school, as if their children's well-being were not sufficient reason for parents to take an interest. One Rheedlen representative put a positive spin on the absence of parents, saying that they did not come because "they knew they could trust the program."

Whatever kinds of programs a school fashions to reach parents of children in need, a special kind of problem often thwarts the attempts: student mobility. Youngsters and their families simply may not remain in residence long enough for the tenuous link to the school to solidify. Americans of all economic groups are among the most mobile people in the industrialized world. And, in general, poor Americans move the most. One of six of the nation's third graders changed schools at least three times since starting the first grade, and 41 percent of those who moved were low achievers, according to a 1994 report by the federal government's General Accounting Office.[5] Homeless people have received considerable attention from the media in recent years, but people with low incomes also frequently have housing problems, chiefly involving an inability to pay the rent. Thus they are forced to move with some regularity.

The impact of this transiency on students and on schools can be devastating. In examining mathematics records of sixth graders in Chicago, David Kerbow, a researcher at the University of Chicago, found that advantaged, stable students achieved the highest level of skills; advantaged but often-moving students and disadvantaged but stable students achieved levels similar to each other; and disadvantaged students whose families moved frequently achieved the lowest level.[6] Students who relocate—especially during the school year—enter new classes in which the work often is not synchronized with their previous studies. Their school records and their special needs are not immediately known to school personnel. Furthermore, their entry into a school may disrupt an entire class as the teacher has to invest time in getting them situated in a host of ways. In schools were mobility is especially high, teachers may try to cope by slowing down the curriculum and reviewing frequently to let the newcomers adapt. Critics of achievement levels in schools with high concentrations of students from economically disadvantaged environments should ponder the implications of conducting an educational program in the path of a revolving door.

Manhattan's P.S. 5 and the Children's Aid Society

Public School 5 at the intersection of Dyckman Street and 10th Avenue in the northern tip of Manhattan strove mightily to build links with parents—even those who were part of a continual inflow from the Dominican Republic. The school, on the shore of the Harlem River, was housed in a handsome, four-story brick structure, completed in 1993. It had classes from prekindergarten through fifth grade for 1,200 students. A bronze sign at the entranceway announced: Children's Aid Society Community School. And it was this relationship between P.S. 5 and the Children's Aid Society, an organization founded in 1853 to care for New York City's poor and abandoned children, that made all the difference in the world for parents. Underscoring the closeness of the relationship was the location of the society's headquarters in the school, a spot adjacent to the principal's office. The mood of P.S. 5 was set in the front hall, where carpeted risers served as magnets to children, who sprawled on them—reading, conversing, or just waiting to meet someone. This was a school where everything stopped every day at 9:00 A.M. so that everyone, students and teachers, could take out a book and read.

It was almost impossible to walk through the front door of P.S. 5 and not encounter a parent. Some were volunteers, some were former volunteers who rose to part-time paid positions, and some came to the school for the sheer sake of companionship. Parents even had their own family room, which bustled through the day as a site for groups to meet and for one-on-one conferences. The inviting aroma of strong Caribbean coffee pierced the air, and conversations in Spanish and English went on simultaneously in different parts of the room, which was the size of a small classroom. When parents at P.S. 5 said "This is my school," they were talking about themselves, not their children. During nasty weather, a phalanx of parents would don orange ponchos and guide students around the puddles and across the busy streets. In the evenings, many parents attended the classes that the school offered in cooperation with the Children's Aid Society, classes in subjects ranging from immigration laws, to literacy, to sewing, to parenting skills, to preparation for the high school equivalency certificate. The computer laboratory, with its 32 workstations, also had classes for parents, some of whom delighted in sitting in front of the exact same machine that their children had faced during the day.

Using a $1.2 million grant from the Hasbro Children's Foundation, an arm of the toy manufacturer, Children's Aid set up a program to reach even adults whose children were not yet old enough to attend P.S. 5—or not even born yet. The program, For Parents Present & Future or, as Spanish-speakers would have it, Para Padres Presentes & Futuros, helped pregnant mothers start learning parenting skills and organized young fathers into small groups in which they could discuss almost anything. "I talk about the early stages of child development with them and about how they can play a more active role in their child's life," said Richard Polanco, an outreach worker who worked with the men. "The mothers say it's about time we got the fathers involved in something like this."

Much of the effort at P.S. 5 to connect the school to the home evolved from collaborations between school officials and representatives of the Children's Aid Society. The principal, Alice Stabiner, said that the society augmented the work of the school in at least three main ways: by operating the health clinic, by establishing workshops for parents beyond those offered by the school, and by supporting an extended day program that utilized the regular faculty. Perhaps a more lavishly endowed New York City Board of Education might have provided the largesse for the same sort of enhancements, but parents maintained that the atmosphere would have suffered and the sense of connection would not have been the same if the efforts were institutionalized. "I wanted to start putting my energies into the community, and I transferred my daughter here from another school," said Wanda Marquez. "The school was ready for us; the Children's Aid Society was ready for us. And we helped make the teachers ready for us. The Board of Education has always worked separately from parents. They don't know how to work with parents." The Children's Aid Society underscored its commitment to P.S. 5 by helping parents in their successful campaign to get a pedestrian bridge built over 10th Avenue so that children could avoid having to contend with the traffic.

Another enhancement effort, the REACH program at University School in suburban Cleveland, operated principally during the summers and had features that tended to distinguish it from many other enhancements. Race and gender, not income, were the defining criteria for entering REACH, which restricted its enrollment to black males. The status of families that had sons in REACH ranged from those on welfare to those in the professions. Participants came from all economic strata, although fully 62 percent were economically disadvantaged and more than half, from single-parent homes. Youngsters were selected not because they were necessarily at-risk academically but because they were generally strong students of high promise. For the most part, their parents took an active interest in their schooling. So why were these able students, particularly the ones from more affluent households, the subjects of an enhancement program? Perhaps the answer was best captured in the words of a third-year college student who worked as an assistant teacher in the program. He said: "No matter how good you are, you will be looked at by a different set of standards because of your skin color. Someone will always put a question mark by your name. The world is a humbling place. We have to learn to cover all the bases and not take any shortcuts if we are going to make it."

Even in the absence of poverty, the social capital available to families of color may be readily exhausted. Prejudice and other factors can make their place in the mainstream shaky. Many working-class families live from paycheck to paycheck, doing perfectly fine so long as wages flow, but in danger of dropping into the ranks of poverty if a job is lost. "These children are just as much at risk," Betty English, the director of REACH, said in comparing the achievement-oriented, sometimes middle-class students in the program with young black males with fewer advantages. "African American parents think they never will be at the point where they can take it all for granted. If they need $5 to get into someplace, they will take along $10 in case the price changes when they get to the gate."

The majority of students in REACH attended public schools in Cleveland and two inner-ring suburbs, Cleveland Heights/University Heights and Warrensville, all systems with large black enrollments. Teachers in the regular schools referred students to REACH. The program began with 36 students in the summer of 1992; by the summer of 1996, 163 boys had entered REACH, and 14 of them had transferred out of the public schools to become regular students at University School, although officials of the elite preparatory school insisted that the program's purpose was not to recruit students. From the point of view of the parents, the program represented a chance to surround the youngsters with other high achieving black males who could demonstrate that it was acceptable to be bright and to perform well in school. The parents and even some of the students said of REACH: "It is a safe place to be smart." Parents were told about the responsibilities that they had to assume—ranging from postponing summer vacations, to making certain that the lads got up on time in the morning, to motivating them to prepare the night before for their classes. The admissions process underscored a family's connection to the program; it required a written statement from parents about why they wanted to enroll their sons.

Officials at University School said that when the program began they did not fully appreciate the parents' pivotal role. It became clear over time, however, that parents had to be assertive in dealing with their sons and that the families had to remain committed to the program at least for the three summers during the middle school years. Parents had to understand—and impress on their sons—that REACH was not a summer camp to attend only when a child felt like it but a three-year obligation with attendance required daily during the five weeks that the program was in session.

Parents said that they hoped, in effect, that the social capital put in place by the program would sustain the youngsters through the difficult days of secondary school. "It helps him build self-confidence as a young black male," said Alforniece Davis of her 12-year-old son's participation in REACH. "There are so many distractions at middle school. I noticed that a lot of my son's friends got off the track when they reached middle school. These are the most difficult years, the early teens. He'll be all right if he gets by these years and REACH is helping him do that. He was making straight A's so he thought it was like a punishment for him to go to REACH. But once he saw how it was, it was fine." The first group of REACH graduates entered the eleventh grade in the fall of 1997. Plans were laid to offer a monthly event to bring together the students during the regular school year.

Also, coaching was to be offered for the Preliminary Scholastic Aptitude Test, which affects decisions to award college scholarships. Also arrangements were to be made to put REACH graduates in touch with the college recruiters who visited University School.

A Sense of Well-Being

TWO

The School as Community Center

The sense of well-being that America's advantaged children take for granted is missing in the lives of many other youngsters. For those who live in the heart of a big city, for instance, day-to-day existence is a craps shoot in which they can come up losers with no notice. Crime and violence stalk them at every turn, and the availability of health care is sometimes no better than in the countries of the developing world. Little about their lives is predictable except for the unsettled nature of their existence. Yet they are supposed to involve themselves in serious learning and overcome adversities that undermine formal schooling.

One way that a school can affect children's well-being is to envelop them in its protecting arms. In many advantaged communities, families provide children with this kind of security. It is the social capital that sustains young people on the precarious passage across the highwire they must negotiate to reach adulthood. But what safeguards youngsters whose families do not have the wherewithal or the ability to erect such a safety net? Those who expect schoolchildren in need to attain academic success at the same rate as affluent children should endorse the idea of providing the former with the kind of support that accrues to the latter. "We must address the needs of the whole child, and this includes drug and alcohol prevention, mental health issues, and violence prevention," said Roberta G. Doering, a former president of the National School Boards Association.[1]

Although critics maintain that schools should limit their purview to academic matters and not swerve from that mission, students increasingly expect schools to provide them with what they say they do not get at home or anywhere else. This attitude that schools should devote themselves to more than academics prevailed, for example, among minority students enrolled in a class on public policy during the summer before their freshman year at Princeton University. Their teacher, Nathan Scovronick of the Woodrow Wilson School, informally surveyed them about the purposes of primary and secondary education. They said that prominent among these purposes was the need to teach skills having to do with parenting, managing personal finance, deferring gratification, and managing one's temper. Clearly these young people thought schools should assume a role beyond what has been traditional. And, in fact, the enhancement programs, by and large, recognize similar needs.

The range of services that enhancement programs offer students to promote their well-being amounts to a fully-stocked supermarket replete with choices. Students make their way down the aisles, picking some items and leaving others on the shelves. They can select from among health services, counseling, drug prevention sessions, tutoring, homework help, mentoring, after-school recreation, Saturday workshops, summer programs, and a host of other activities. Even other members of their families—parents and siblings—can choose from a range of offerings. Society's more fortunate children enjoy the benefit of similar support from the network automatically available to them by virtue of birth.

All children need access to such support to ensure their well-being. Thus one Wednesday morning at 7:15 Heather Studwell, an early childhood teacher at Rogers Elementary School in Stamford, Connecticut, was taking the small chairs off the tabletops on which they had been stored for the night and setting them down next to the tables. Not a child was in sight yet, but Studwell went through the daily ritual of preparing for the arrival of the 30 preschoolers with whom she, another teacher, and 3 assistants would spend the next ten hours. She put cartons of Kix on the tables, along with milk, plastic bowls, and plastic utensils. Abundant nurturing was part of this program as well as a strong dose of developmentally appropriate learning, making it possible for most of the participating children to enter kindergarten knowing their letters and enabling some to reach the point at which they could print their names. Rogers received its first child as early as 7:30 A.M. and sent home its last child as late as 5:30 P.M. Many of those who stayed longest in the building were preschoolers in child care whose working parents wanted a safe and reliable place to send their children.

Rogers, just east of downtown Stamford, was one of 18 schools throughout Connecticut that the State Department of Education and the State Department of Human Resources designated, starting in 1989, as model family resource centers. The program began receiving additional funding in 1993 from the federal government. The concept, developed by Edward Zigler of Yale University, envisioned comprehensive, integrated, community-based systems of family support and child development services operated out of public school buildings. The program to some extent fashioned itself as a conduit to reach parents who themselves had not been successful in school. The idea was to "win them back" so as to "increase the educational outcomes for their children."[2]

Each family resource center was to provide full-time child care for preschoolers, training for child care providers, a before- and after-school program for school-age children, parent training, adult education, youth development services aimed at preventing problems for fourth through sixth graders, and referral to other resources and services. These services were welcomed at Rogers, a school of 735 students whose families spoke 15 different languages at home. Predominant among those students were 113 who spoke Spanish; 79, Haitian Creole; 18, Albanian; and 18, Greek. Altogether, 65 percent of the school's enrollment was made up of members of minority groups, most of whom lived in the blocks around the school. The mix at Rogers was further enriched by the 35 percent of the enrollment from other parts of Stamford who voluntarily attended the school under its magnet program.

The school had initially widened its mission in 1975 by creating the Rogers School Community Center Organization, known by the acronym ROSCCO, to write grants, receive funds, and operate a panoply of supplemental programs. ROSCCO was established to seek multiple funding sources for extra programs to make the school more attractive. Among the programs were those that promised to enable the school to help revitalize the neighborhood. At its inception, ROSCCO was one of the first such ventures at a school anywhere in the country. ROSCCO became so adept at its work that it formed satellite programs in 10 of the other 12 elementary schools in Stamford, Connecticut's fourth-largest municipality, and became an umbrella organization for a host of programs that it supported through outside funding sources, including the state's family resource center program.

By 1996 ROSCCO, which housed its staff in rooms on the first floor of Rogers, was collaborating with 15 separate agencies. Driven by entrepreneurial inclinations, ROSCCO was charging fees for participation in its child care and after-school programs. The monthly amounts in 1996 ranged from $135 for a child in the program three days a week to $165 for daily participation. As a magnet school that drew students from throughout Stamford, reaching from its own modest downtown neighborhood to the estates north of the Merritt Parkway, Rogers had enrolled the children of some families that could easily afford the fees. Their payments helped subsidize less advantaged families, who paid reduced amounts. The program ranged from tutoring and homework help, to science projects to arts and crafts and indoor and outdoor games.

An impetus for the creation of ROSCCO was a desire to stabilize the deterioration of the neighborhood of wood-frame houses that surrounded the school. By the 1970s, what had been a tightly knit– blue collar community of first- and second-generation Irish Americans and Italian Americans was changing as aging residents were replaced by African Americans and immigrants from a host of countries. Furthermore, the one- and two-family houses were converted to contain three or four families. The housing stock was clearly deteriorating and the neighborhood's viability was imperiled. Rogers, one of the oldest elementary school buildings in Stamford, was closed in 1973, gutted, and extensively renovated before it reopened in 1975. The founding of ROSCCO after the reopening assisted in the rebirth of the school and its community.

Indeed, by the middle 1990s neighborhood blight had been arrested and white flight had been halted. People could walk the streets again in relative safety. Residents of the Shappan area on Long

Island Sound, an affluent part of Stamford at the southern end of the Rogers catchment district, were even starting to send children to the school after having abandoned it for private schools. It was doubtful whether this turnaround could have been achieved had Rogers not been transformed. Even its instructional approach changed. The school, for all practical purposes, eliminated grade levels and basal reading books, set up interage classes, made extensive use of computers, and integrated the subjects—with literature as the unifying vehicle. Rogers also got a five-year grant that enabled it to hire a visiting artist annually.

Schools like Rogers that provide a wide range of services are starting to pop up all around the country. Miami Beach, a sunny vacation destination for generations of northerners, for instance, may seem an unlikely locale for the development of a community school to serve the needs of poor students and their families. Yet hard times and immigration produced profound changes in the area's population. The gleaming hotels that line Collins Avenue proved less alluring to tourists as crime soared and alternative spots in the Caribbean offered safer, more chic settings. Meanwhile, the middle-class backbone of Miami Beach withered away with age, and block after block of small stucco apartment buildings became home to poorer, Spanish-speaking newcomers from every country south of the United States. A neighborhood school for the children of these immigrants was Fienberg-Fisher, housed in what had been two separate school buildings that faced each other across a street that was closed to traffic, creating a pleasant courtyard. The gentle beauty of the pink stucco school buildings with their red tile roofs, surrounded by palms and tropical flora, gave no hint of the students' poverty within.

To cope with the growing needs of an enrollment in which 91 percent of the students came from families poor enough to qualify for federally subsidized lunches, Fienberg-Fisher evolved into a community school that provided a full array of services to students and their families, almost nine out of ten of them Latino. Links were established with such agencies as the Jewish Family Services, Children's Psychiatric Center, Barry University, Florida International University, Legal Services of Greater Miami, and Stanley Myers Health Center. The city-block–sized campus of Fienberg-Fisher became a place where very young children could be put in child care, older preschoolers could prepare for school. in prekindergarten and Head Start, school-age students could remain for after-school programs, and adults could find classes on topics ranging from parenting skills, through basic skills education, through occupational training. In addition, families' physical and mental health needs could be met. Interestingly enough, the rejuvenation of Fienberg-Fisher through its effort to remake itself as a community school paralleled the rebirth of the South Beach district of Miami Beach. The old art deco hotels on Ocean Drive, just two blocks away, formerly the preserve of Jewish pensioners, had morphed into hot spots for trendy tourists.

One of the after-school programs, Cool School, which served 80 students from fourth through sixth grade each afternoon after regular classes, began as an effort to deter youngsters from gravitating toward gang membership. The program proved so popular that it had a waiting list. Besides offering tutoring and recreation, Cool School had a counseling component, using interns from a master's of social work program at Barry University to work with children and their families. Every youngster spent at least an hour a week in group counseling, and monthly meetings were held for groups of parents. In addition, individual sessions were provided as needed, with the social work interns even going into homes to meet parents. Crisis intervention often dictated the agenda in counseling sessions with families. Many students in Cool School had a propensity to misbehave so the program encouraged them to earn privileges through good conduct and sought to teach them to control their anger. Misconduct would prevent a student from participating in a party or going on a trip, and irregular attendance in the program would cause a student to be dropped.

On a typical afternoon, Cool School, which was housed in a long narrow room the length of about three classrooms, was a place where several children were playing pool at the table in the middle of the room and others were scattered about, doing homework or art projects. In an adjacent smaller room, still more students were watching a film about Shaquille O'Neal, the seven-foot professional basketball star. The students were supervised by four young adults paid through the AmeriCorps program. One of these supervisors,

Moira Aronson, 22, said: "They have a safe place to be and they have positive reinforcement for good behavior. They do their homework first for about an hour before the recreation begins." Bianca Rudge, a remarkably self-assured ten-year-old, liked Cool School mostly because people were there to help her get her homework done before heading home. But sometimes, she complained, "They force you to do things and it's boring."

Almost 100 other students at Fienberg-Fisher, mostly fifth and sixth graders, participated after school in recreational activities offered in conjunction with the Boys and Girls Club. One afternoon, for instance, some 60 children—mostly boys—were shooting baskets in a cavernous gymnasium in which paint was flaking off the walls. The free-standing building had been the gymnasium when one of the other buildings housed a high school. Now Hipolito Rodriguez, a 21-year-old graduate of Fienberg-Fisher and a full-time employee of the Boys and Girls Club, was overseeing the athletic program. Another three dozen children, mostly girls, had been taken to nearby Flamingo Park for other activities. Rodriguez, who came to Florida from Cuba with his family in 1980, said that he participated in the Boys and Girls Club's after-school program as a Fienberg-Fisher student. "In the long run," he said, "I think this saves lives." One of the students in the gym, 11-year-old Alfredo Gonzalez, explained that without the after-school program, children would have nothing to do "but just go on the streets."

The transformation at Fienberg-Fisher proved an inspiration to nearby Miami Beach High School, situated on 20 acres of prime land adjacent to a convention center. The high school was attempting to change itself into a community school in some of the same ways as Fienberg-Fisher. It was striving to meet the diverse needs of an enrollment of 2,690 that included students from dozens of countries who spoke 32 languages. On average, the students scored at the 38th percentile in reading in 1995. Beach High, as it was known for decades, began emulating the collaborative approach of Fienberg-Fisher by creating a health clinic and a companion counseling program staffed by social workers. The high school established a program staffed by a representative of the State Labor Department to provide full-time employment assistance to students and their parents. Two legal assistance programs were created, one to help students and their parents cope with immigration issues—an estimated 10 percent were undocumented aliens— and the other to deal with issues of domestic violence.

In addition, 34 students signed up for an evening diploma program at Miami Beach High founded for gay and lesbian dropouts whose sexual orientation had been a source of travail for them in high schools throughout Dade County. On top of this, the high school forged close relations with the autonomous Adult and Community Education Center housed on its campus to encourage students' parents and other area residents to pursue courses in English as a second language and to earn credits leading to a high school diploma. The adult center operated from 3:00 to 9:45 P.M., Monday through Friday, and on Saturday mornings.

The Community School Reconceptualized

The concept of a school that serves not just its regular student body during the traditional hours but an entire neighborhood during extended hours has a long and honored history. In the middle 1930s, Frank J. Manley, a physical education director for the Flint Public Schools in Michigan, persuaded the city's most prominent citizen, Charles Stewart Mott, to support an effort to keep the schools open for recreation after school and on weekends. The aim during those crushing years of the Depression was to reduce juvenile delinquency, a goal not unlike that of the controversial midnight basketball leagues that the U.S. Department of Justice funded more than half a century later. Manley and Mott collaborated to create a program that eventually allowed for placing a community school director in every public school in Flint. The content of the programs expanded to serve the needs and interests of all members of the each student's family. Gradually the community school concept spread across the country, linking schools with their communities in new ways.

With the passing years, however, functions of community schools tended to shift to the central offices of school systems and schools narrowed their focus to deal more exclusively with matters directly concerned with instruction. Community schools, which never came into being in most places, diminished as a force in the expanding America of post–World War II. Prosperity returned, immigration from abroad abated, and social service agencies jealously guarded the separate turfs that they had diligently staked out.

In the 1990s, driven by new imperatives, the community school has been rediscovered, in concept if not in name. Too many families have been unable to provide adequately for children and too many communities have lost the ability or the will to protect and promote the interests of children and families. Furthermore, schools have found that they can reach students in need better by collaborating with other agencies and integrating services that previously remained unconnected. Exemplifying the trend, initiatives in two very different places have been impelled by the same objectives. Utah developed an array of collaborative services through its Families, Agencies and Communities Together (FACT) program involving the state's departments of health, human services, workforce services, and education, as well as the administrative offices of the courts. Utah's stated goal, incorporated into statute in 1993, was to develop, promote, and deliver child-focused, family-centered, community-based, culturally appropriate services to improve the health, safety, education, and economic well-being of the state's children. And on a more limited scale, in 1996 the Polk Bros. Foundation chose three Chicago schools to receive a total of $1.2 million to provide children and families with more opportunities for recreation, social services, and health care.

William S. White, chairman of the Mott Foundation, said in 1993 that although community education evolved as resources shrank and times changed, the work nonetheless remained rooted in the theories that led to the movement's founding. These theories were and continue to be, he said, that schools often offer the best facilities in a given neighborhood for carrying out such programs, that buildings can be utilized seven days a week, that schools should be at the forefront in stimulating partnerships to address community needs, and that the educational agenda should remain a local responsibility.[3]

Much of the reawakened interest in community education emerges not from schools but from community-based organizations trying to solve community woes. Problems of child care, health and social service delivery, unemployment, housing, teen pregnancy, substance abuse, gang violence, neighborhood destabilization, and community powerlessness are viewed as interrelated, not disparate. And in this theme of convergence the local school is viewed as a front-line institution—perhaps the only one in some inner-city and rural locales—from which to forge new collaborations. Examples of these partnerships present themselves around the country; a common thread in most instances is a desire to provide, directly and indirectly, for the well-being of poor schoolchildren.

The Children's Aid Society of New York City, for instance, in recent years made itself part of virtually everything that happened in Intermediate School 218 in Manhattan's Washington Heights section. The programs and staff members of Children's Aid were so fully integrated into the school that the borders between the agency's work and the larger part of the school's program operated by the Board of Education could barely be discerned. This melding was made a feature of the school from the time it opened in 1992. And because of the model's success, the city's School Construction Facilities Corporation invited Children's Aid Society to participate from scratch in designing three other schools in the same neighborhood. Officials of the child advocacy group wanted to make sure that the facilities would lend themselves to the multiple uses inherent in a community school model. Eventually I.S. 218, for instance, would be operating 15 hours a day, 6 days a week, 12 months a year.

Contractors built space into the new school buildings for health clinics, recreation, and other programs. This meant constructing schools in ways that put certain areas off-limits at specified hours while allowing access to other parts of the building such as the auditorium. The main corridor and other public areas were designed to make them inviting to adults as well as to children. The schools designed with the assistance of Children's Aid Society were among the few in New York City that had air-conditioning. At I.S. 218, the society worked with assistant principals to evolve five separate academies that would allow the school to break itself into small, intimate units for instructional purposes. This pedagogical approach had implications for the building's design. I.S. 218, however, was already under construction when the district superintendent invited Children's Aid to have a role in the school. Therefore, the organization could not influence construction decisions as much as it would have liked and the facilities had to be retrofitted to accommodate many of the extra features. For example, the health clinic ended up smaller than desired because it was added as an afterthought.

Once I.S. 218 was completed and operational, reminders of the threatening neighborhood loomed everywhere. The school's small parking lot was protected from crime by a 20-foot-high wire fence. Heavy iron gates stood at the school's entrance, and gratings covered the first-floor windows. Extensive outdoor lighting made the building safer for evening events. The tough conditions on the outside contrasted with the serenity within the building. The 1,400 children were wrapped in a physically and emotionally protective covering from the time that the doors opened at 7:00 A.M. until they closed at 10:00 P.M. Parents were delighted to know that their sons and daughters had a safe place to spend the hours before and after the regular school day and on Saturdays.

The influence of the Children's Aid Society could be seen upon entering the building. The society's office was adjacent to the school's main office, and the family resource room was across the hall. Nearby, a neon sign marked the location of the school store, which the society established so that children could learn the ways of business by selling each other T-shirts, candy, and school supplies. The modern five-story structure rapidly become a haven for the entire neighborhood. With its curved exterior facing Broadway at 196th Street, across from a rugged outcropping of boulders in Fort Tryon Park, the school was a palpable symbol of hope. One mother said in Spanish, through a translator, that she wished that such a school had been available when her 21-year-old son was in his early teens. Instead, lacking alternatives, he turned to the streets and went to prison. The mother gloried in the fact that her younger children had I.S. 218 available to them.

Each of the school's five academies occupied approximately an entire floor. Every academy—with its own administrators and faculty—had sixth, seventh, and eighth graders. When they enrolled in I.S. 218, students selected from among academies devoted to expressive arts, ethics and law, communications and technology, community service, and business studies. Thus a youngster could spend his or her entire three years in the school in the familiar company of the same students and teachers, avoiding the anonymity that plagues children at so many schools.

Parents felt that they too had an identity at I.S. 218, and that was especially important given the fact that many of them were born in the Dominican Republic. The school, formally named for Salome Ureña de Henriquez, a Latina poet, reached out to parents, trying to make them feel comfortable. "This is like a home to me," a parent said without prodding. The extended day program created by the Children's Aid Society included classes for adults in English as a second language, citizenship, sewing, aerobics, computers, sex education, and a host of other subjects. Furthermore, the physical and mental health facilities of the clinic that the society maintained in the school sometimes served parents as an extension of its work with children. Parents also could visit their children's classes during the regular school day and were recruited as school volunteers. Some joined the payroll of the Aid Society as part- and full-time employees in the program.

Having parents constantly in the building as visitors, volunteers, and employees contributed to the children's sense of well-being and had a moderating influence on their conduct. "I don't have to fight with my daughter to get her to go to school," said one mother of an I.S. 218 student. The mother explained that when her daughter was still in elementary school, in the fifth grade, rousing her out of bed in the morning was a daily struggle because she did not like the school she attended. "Now I have to hold her back or else she would be here at 7 o'clock every day." Other parents told of having to go to the school to retrieve their children in the evening because the kids wanted to remain with their friends. Labeling the-late afternoon and evening portion of the program the "extended day" was part of a conscious decision to underscore the program's connection to the regular school day. At first it was called the "after-school" program, but the name was changed within a few months to denote the seamless connection that officials hoped to establish between what occurred during traditional school hours and what transpired in the afternoon and evening.

At another middle school elsewhere in the country, Canton Middle School in Baltimore, an effort to connect with the after-school lives of students arose from a collaboration with the Police Athletic League

(PAL). In the summer of 1996, the athletic league began operating a recreation center in a building adjoining the school, a structure so much a part of the school complex that one of its doors opened directly into the middle school's gymnasium. The Police Athletic League used the gym, as well as its own facility, for programs during the late afternoons. The PAL was drawn to Canton by concern about drug peddling and gang activity in the neighborhood, which had few recreational facilities. "Kids need a safe place to be so parents don't have to worry," said Mark Homer, the 35-year-old police officer assigned to run the center. He had previously served on foot patrol and as an undercover officer in narcotics. Now, having undergone special training in community relations, mentoring, and child development, he was assigned to the youth center.

Homer counted on receiving close cooperation from the middle school, which had promised, for instance, to move about a dozen of its computers into the recreation center for after-school activities. Grant money was obtained to pay some teachers to help the PAL with the computer program. Each afternoon at the center started with students doing their homework before playing basketball or becoming involved in some other activity. Fifty to 100 children showed up every day, about 40 percent of them girls. A tall, blond, strapping man who wore a holstered gun even as he assembled the equipment in the weight-training room he was creating for the students, Homer dressed in a PAL T-shirt, warmup pants, and a baseball cap. He spoke of how important it was for him to serve as a role model for the students. Homer hoped that the Police Athletic League would be able to promote good citizenship among the youngsters. When he held a Halloween party, for instance, it was free, but students had to contribute canned or boxed food for the poor as the price of admission. "They're not rich, but they have to learn," he said, hoping to imbue them with a sense of caring. He was planning to organize the students to conduct a drive for blankets for poor people during the winter.

Steps to Coordinate Services

Communities in Schools (CIS) attempted to broaden the services available to students in its community haven initiative, which received a grant from the U.S. Department of Housing and Urban Development.

Pilot programs were set for Miami, Florida; Newark, New Jersey; San Antonio, Texas; Wichita, Kansas; Charlotte, North Carolina; Adams County, Colorado; Compton, California; and Greenwood-LeFlore, Missouri. CIS sought to bring together public agencies, human services, business, and individual volunteers to, in effect, build social capital for schoolchildren. As with other programs, a crucial element in this approach involved extending the hours during which the building was open, from earlier in the morning to later in the evening. Services have less impact when they are restricted to regular school hours, failing to take advantage of other times when children and families are available.

As various locales joined the community haven initiative, CIS encouraged them to facilitate access to services not only for students in the school but also for family members and for neighborhood children who attended other schools. This approach, also followed by other enhancement programs, such as the Children's Aid Society and the Beacons schools, represented an effort to recast educational facilities as community schools. The Adams County community haven in Colorado at Kearney Middle School, for instance, provided child care two mornings and two evenings a week. Spanish-speaking adults took courses in English as a second language four evenings a week, and a program for teens served about 80 students in the late afternoon each school day. A health clinic opened in the school, and a food bank was established to assist about 20 families.

In Minnesota, the plan for a network of community learning centers envisioned by Wayne Jennings and his Designs for Learning organization called for schools to form partnerships to share resources with government as well as with public and private agencies, early childhood programs, and colleges and universities. The design sought to overcome the fragmentation that so frequently made the delivery of services inefficient. A new approach of this sort provided for integrating social services with education through agreements for sharing costs, revenues, and sites. One of the first schools to follow this model, Expo Middle School in St. Paul, worked avidly at carrying out a referral program, giving families the phone numbers of appropriate agencies and making the calls when families neglected to follow through. Housing, employment, and health were all included in the referral plan. To expedite the delivery of services, Expo provided space at the school for families to meet with agency representatives.

Despite the interest of enhancement programs around the country in using schools as vehicles for providing social services, efforts at collaboration remain problematic. One study of school sites that coordinated services found that they did so only with difficulty. This study, by the Annie Casey Foundation, stated:

> True integration at the service-delivery level, we learned, requires unprecedented commitments by school boards, child-welfare agencies, and other youth-serving institutions to subordinate their traditional authority over critical functions—including budgeting, staffing, and resource allocation—in favor of collective decision making.[4]

As schools become service providers and service brokers, more professionals will have to learn how to operate in an atmosphere in which collaboration, not insularity, guides their work. Teams of professionals, focusing on the needs of individual students and their families, must make their expertise available in synergistic models that yield more far-reaching results than those achieved when separate entities work in isolation. A prerequisite for this approach is a firm understanding of the roles of other service providers. Some professionals gain these insights on the job, but most do not have the time to learn as much as they would like about how the work of others affects their role.

Institutions of higher education are starting to recognize the need for training that cuts across several service areas. California State University at Monterey, for example, began a program in 1996 leading to a bachelor's degree in collaborative human services. It offered academic concentrations in social work, community health, public safety administration, and parks and recreation management. The course work was combined with practicums in which students would earn part of their academic credits through placements in the field. The Keck Foundation of Los Angeles awarded $600,000 to the university to develop the new program. Communities in Schools would serve as a partner to the university in fashioning the program;

the aim being to develop a model that the CIS could institute around the country.

An Institute of Community Collaborative Studies was created at Monterey to oversee the program. The long-range goal was to build a graduate program as a companion piece to the baccalaureate offering. The newly-created California State University at Monterey Bay was a desirable site for such an interdisciplinary program because it had none of the departmental traditions that frequently complicate attempts to mount interdisciplinary programs at institutions of higher education. The campus, situated on the former Fort Ord army base, opened its doors in 1995, and was not organized into academic departments. While the idea of offering courses in collaborative human services would be attractive almost anywhere in the country, it was expected to have special appeal in California, where in 1996 a law took effect allowing for the expulsion of students the very first time they brought weapons or drugs into a school. Districts had the responsibility of creating alternative settings for the violators, who would then have to earn their way back into the mainstream. Officials at Monterey believed that experts in collaborative human services could play a major role in the implementation of this new approach.

Thus the community school in its new incarnation is beginning to take on an identity that can lend fresh hope to those whose needs far exceed the resources and mission of the traditional school. Teaching and learning are complex transactions deeply affected by the milieu in which they occur. The formidable obstacles associated with poverty impinge with depressing regularity on the ability of teachers to teach and of students to learn. When schools convert themselves into institutions that address issues of well-being and fill gaps in the community they make it possible for formal education to thrive. Yet in accepting these tasks, schools must simultaneously maintain a laser-like focus on ensuring, above all, that students learn the academic lessons without which they will remain bereft of possibilities—regardless of how good they feel.

SEVEN

An Array of Health Services

One of the first steps that Baltimore's Canton Middle School took after receiving a grant from the Carnegie Corporation's middle grade school state policy initiative was to expand the availability of health services for its students. The school's premise was that children could not learn unless they were physically and mentally healthy. As a move in this direction, Canton was among the first schools in Baltimore to use the concept of third-party billing so that it could tap into Medicaid funds to support mental health therapy at the school. Under this approach, Canton formed an alliance with the Bay View Medical Center of the Johns Hopkins University Hospital to station a mental health therapist in the school, although the person was employed by the hospital.

Eventually this idea spread to neighboring schools in southeast Baltimore, and mental health workers from the network of participating schools met regularly with a psychiatrist from the hospital to present cases and discuss ideas for treatment. The issues for which students were referred most frequently involved substance abuse in the family, weapons and violence, grief and loss, and family disintegration. Canton also arranged for Baltimore Medical Systems, Inc., to provide a full-time nurse on site at the school with the backup services of a school-linked clinic at Highlandtown Health Center. Similar arrangements and grant money made it possible for the middle school to expand its staff to include a broad array of health service providers. Canton exploited every possible opportunity to increase services and revenues on behalf of its students. The school, for instance, aggressively solicited applications from families in order to document that the parents were poor enough for the children to qualify for free lunches. "We hustle to get the lunch applications," an administrator confessed, pointing out that the larger the group qualifying for free lunches, the better the chance of getting more federal assistance for disadvantaged students. "We have kids who require tremendous resources and even the extra funds don't make up for the inequities," said Craig Spilman, the principal.

Thus by the mid-1990s the school had a social worker, a nurse, two psychologists, a speech and language pathologist, a mental health therapist, and two guidance counselors. In addition, a pediatrician and a psychiatrist were available for consultations. Most of these professionals gathered every Wednesday morning in the school's conference room, where they sat as the primary assessment committee (PAC) to consider the cases of students, six or eight a week, referred by the instructional teams. Committee members were joined by the school's head of special education and by the person who coordinated special education referrals, although the referrals to the PAC included many students other than those classified as disabled.

Depending on the cases at hand, the meeting also might involve the leader of the instructional team to which the student belonged, the addiction counselor who worked at the school one day a week, one of the two house principals, and a representative from the parent advisory committee. Sometimes the school invited a student and his or her parent to attend the meeting, depending on what input was needed. The process brought together many people who might be involved with the same child and enabled them to combine their various perspectives to paint a composite picture of the youngster's needs.

The weekly PAC meetings allowed Canton Middle School to deal quickly with student problems. Besides discussing new cases, the committee reviewed existing cases that it was monitoring. One morning, for example, the leader of Team A was speaking to the PAC about a sixth grader, a girl we will call Tracy. Someone asked who on the committee knew her. It turned out that one of the guidance counselors had been meeting with her twice a week, and, in addition, Tracy had been undergoing mental health therapy outside school. Tracy was described as a sweet, talkative girl. Someone on the committee asked if she were on medication, and the counselor said he did not know.

Tracy was having academic problems, particularly in social studies and science, and her mother was eager to know what could be done to help her daughter. Tracy struggled with the instructional materials, seemingly unable to understand them. Her mother said she labored unsuccessfully over her homework for about four hours a night, an unduly long time. When Tracy was in elementary school, the teachers had modified the materials so that she could understand them more easily, according to her mother. Tracy had been a special education student—apparently suffering a learning disability—until the fifth grade but was no longer classified as disabled. Her mother thought that Tracy ought to undergo testing in an effort to diagnose her problem.

The school guidance counselor who had been meeting with Tracy said that her out-of-school life was complicated by the fact that she and her mother lived with the mother's boyfriend in a home that he owned. The arrangement persisted on a week-to-week basis, the guidance counselor said, and it appeared that mother and daughter were at peril of being thrown out of the house if either of them had the slightest disagreement with the man. The mother and daughter already had suffered this fate at the hands of one of the mother's previous boyfriends. The guidance counselor said that he suspected that the mother and her boyfriend were both substance abusers, creating the potential for an incident that could at any time end the living arrangement.

Members of the primary assessment committee, probing to see if the mother had any independent sources of income, wanted to know if the couple worked and whether the mother and child were welfare recipients. No one could answer the questions. The girl's problems had been exacerbated by the fact that the man's school-age son was in some kind of trouble. A group of boys, pursuing retribution against him, had confronted Tracy the previous week and held the flame of a cigarette lighter close to her throat as a warning to her "stepbrother." The committee decided to refer Tracy for the full battery of tests that were used to determine eligibility for special education.

Another case presented to the committee that morning involved a boy we will call Charles, also a sixth grader. The house principal said that the teachers were at a loss, unable to do anything to help the child, a special education student who apparently needed the kind of highly structured setting that was not available at Canton. Charles's home life was complicated by the fact that his family lived in the midst of one of the worst drug-dealing centers in the neighborhood. Two schools that might have been able to offer the more structured setting that Charles needed had turned down requests by Canton to accept him as a transfer student. The house principal said that Charles had become a truant; when the police found him on the streets and brought him to school, he would quickly disappear out the back door.

A group of teachers had met a few weeks earlier with the youngster's parents, but they seemed incapable of dealing with their son's problems. The psychologist, who had attended that meeting, told the committee that Charles literally could not sit still in class. He would get on the floor and roll around under the chairs and desks. Some concern was expressed that Charles's behavior was having an adverse effect on other students, who saw that he was "getting away" with misconduct. The psychologist said that the boy's grandparents, who were close to him, tried to be encouraging, but—like the parents—seemed to have no impact on the problem. The committee proposed to refer Charles to the nearby Bay View Medical Center for a thorough evaluation. Cost was not an issue because he was covered by Medicaid. The house principal, however, worried that Charles would not show up for the medical tests. It was decided that the best hope of Charles's keeping the appointment was to involve his grandmother in the arrangement. "The poor woman has already gone through hell with the older brother," someone said of the grandmother's struggle to help Charles's sibling, who had troubles of his own.

Increasingly, schools provide a broad range of services to address students' well-being. Attesting to the need for such services are statistics such as those cited in a federal government report that said that urban children face greater likelihood of "being surrounded by poverty, with all its attendant risks. In addition, they are more likely to be exposed to safety and health risks, and have less access to regular medical care than do other children."[1] Involving schools in the provision of health services does not mean that the school itself must deliver the services. Much of the effort to address the health needs of students involves interagency collaborations that allow schools to draw on a multitude of providers, sometimes in school facilities and other times through outside referrals. The school can, for instance, broker services and put clients in touch with outside providers.

The social capital that provides these services for advantaged children includes informed families with the money and the contacts to access the system. The family usually has health insurance coverage through employment and can afford to go outside the system when deemed necessary. Poor families generally lack the knowledge of and access to this system. Enhancements, however, can work through the schools to help fill the gap. Directors of the various Beacon programs in New York City named health services as the top priority in terms of unmet needs for schoolchildren. Almost all of the first 20 Beacon schools were situated in neighborhoods designated by the New York City Department of Health as "health crisis zones."[2]

Critics of schools' efforts to involve themselves in the provision of health care ignore the fact that children in need, unlike those who are advantaged, may depend on the school to fill their health needs. James Comer, a leader in the movement to get schools to meet the full needs of students, said: "Academic learning must be understood as a product of overall child development and not as an isolated mechanical function determined almost entirely by the child's innate intelligence and will."[3] Where an enhanced approach proves most successful, school personnel work in a collaborative fashion with parents and health providers in the community.

The recent rapid growth in school-based health clinics can be traced from the point in the 1980s, when they "began to pop up serendipitously around the country,"[4] to 1994, when there were in 500 of them,[5] to 1996, when there were 913.[6] Public schools in impoverished neighborhoods struggle to cope with a range of physical, mental, and emotional needs of students that just a few years ago society was prepared to cede to families. This approach—leaving it up to the family—worked so long as the family was ready and able to absorb the responsibility. But, increasingly, families cannot find ways to provide children with the services they need, a fact that undermines students' ability to fulfill their potential as learners in school. Access to health care through the school also tends to reduce absenteeism. Parents who might otherwise keep their children home with slight illnesses know that the youngsters will receive treatment at school. In addition, early treatment helps prevent more serious ailments that might cause a child to miss school over an extended period.

In some ways, schools return to their roots when they attend to the health of their students. Nurses, doctors, dentists, psychologists, social workers, and therapists have worked in schools throughout the century. The flood of immigrants into big-city school systems in the early 1900s necessitated the deployment of health professionals in schools. The citizenry recognized that this was not simply an act of altruism but a way to protect everyone—rich and poor—by controlling the onset of diseases that could spread to all segments of the populace.

Educational historian David Tyack reminded Americans that many key reformers at the turn of the century were motivated by a kind of noblesse oblige, convinced as they were that immigrants were ignorant of the rudiments of proper health and hygiene.[7] This was an era in which recent arrivals from southern and eastern Europe huddled in such settings as the tenements of the Lower East Side of New York, two or three families cramped together in a cold-water flat with windows that opened into dimly lit airshafts. From these origins evolved a system in which nurses became fixtures in schools across the land. The nurse looked after everything from headaches that suddenly afflicted students in the midst of math tests to inoculations to ward off a host of diseases.

Education Week estimated in 1996 that 40,000 nurses worked in the nation's schools,[8] which would average out to not quite 1 nurse per 1,000 students for the nation's public school enrollment of more than 45 million. But the nurses are not distributed equally; some suburban districts deploy a nurse on a full-time basis in each school, while schools in many urban districts may, at best, have a nurse stop by each building once or twice a week. In recognition of the disparities, some of the enhancement programs have made health services integral to their efforts to improve student outcomes.

Different Ways of Providing for a Sense of Well-Being

The Children's Aid Society in New York City operates in a manner consistent with these historical precedents. The society, which early in the twentieth century sent the orphaned children of immigrants from eastern cities to new, ostensibly healthier, homes in the West, involved itself during the 1990s in a panoply of services in several schools in the densely populated Washington Heights neighborhood. With the organization's assistance, these schools provided medical and dental care, extended school days, tutoring, parent education, and community activities.

The clinic at Public School 5, near the upper tip of Manhattan Island, for example, carried out such a mission with the help of the society, working through a subcontract with the visiting nurse service. The school clinic, three small rooms side by side, was situated at the end of a narrow corridor, near the school's main entrance. Each nurse practitioner had her own examining room; the other room housed a well-equipped dental office. Two dentists, augmented by a hygienist and a dental assistant, alternated their hours in the office. In addition, the clinic employed an administrative assistant, and a parent worked part time to escort students between the office and their classrooms and, if necessary, to serve as a translator.

The clinic at P.S. 5 was the primary health provider for 40 percent of the school's students. The clinic largely conducted physical examinations, administered vaccinations, and treated first-aid emergencies. But it also dealt with a host of chronic problems that affected students, one of the most troubling being the asthma that seems to afflict so many inner-city children. "We hope we are preventing kids from ending up in the hospital emergency room with asthma attacks," said Sister Rosemaria Pelligria, a nun who worked in the clinic as a nurse. Keeping in touch with parents was part of the strategy to head off more serious health problems. When a child with eczema came to the clinic with a painful outbreak, for instance, the nurse practitioner hastily scribbled herself a reminder to call the girl's mother to discuss the necessity of making certain that the child took her medication regularly.

The Children's Aid Society spent about $900 a year per student on its enhancement program, including the dental and medical clinic, the extended school day, and the programs for parents. This amount, of course, came on top of regular expenditures for the school made by the New York City Board of Education. Health workers at P.S. 5 sometimes offered lectures on health issues to parents, but the clinic's impact on families came in other ways as well. Students often got free medicine, saving families money, and sometimes the clinic treated siblings who attended other schools as well as an occasional neighborhood child who had no link to the school. The Children's Aid Society felt that it could hardly turn away sick youngsters who were not apt to receive prompt attention elsewhere.

The work of the society extended to Intermediate School 218, where most of the students went after completing P.S. 5. A health clinic operated in that school too. Its dental department, for instance, saw about 15 students a day, five days a week, handling mostly fillings and cleanings but sometimes emergencies necessitating extractions and root canal procedures. Following the pattern at P.S. 5, the office had a hygienist and two dentists who alternated days in the office. The dentists said that the students who came to the intermediate school from P.S. 5, where they had access to the dental clinic, were more likely than students from other elementary schools to have had the benefit of up-to-date dental care. Some of the other youngsters, already entering their teens, had never seen a dentist before reaching I.S. 218. "This may be free to them, but we don't want to deliver second-class dentistry just because they don't pay," said one of the dentists. Since students had to miss classes to go to the dental clinic, efforts were made to schedule the visits when students were not due to attend one of their main subjects.

Given the pent-up demand for health services in poor neighborhoods, school health clinics operating as part of enhancement programs, such as those in Washington Heights, have been used heavily. An evaluation of the clinic pointed out that it struggled to provide preventive examinations because it devoted so much time to children requiring emergency care for mostly minor injuries and illnesses. The constant flow of children complaining about one "emergency" or another severely compromised the amount of time available for physicals. Furthermore, as many as half of P.S. 5's students had Medicaid coverage and were assigned to outside physicians but bypassed them to take advantage of the more convenient school clinic. The evaluation report recommended that Children's Aid and the visiting nurse service develop guidelines relating both to the type of care the clinic should provide and who should receive priority in treatment.[9]

Another approach to caring for students' well-being could be seen in New Jersey, which in 1988 created its School Based Youth Services Program to link schools with health service providers before, during, and after school as well as on weekends. The program, which operated under the aegis of New Jersey's Department of Human Services, strove to ameliorate the risky life conditions that lead poor and working-class students to drop out of school at a disproportionately higher rate than students from advantaged families. After being established in some high schools, the program was extended to middle and elementary schools, eventually operating in 30 school districts with at least one site per district. Every site provided health care, mental health and family counseling, job and employment training, and substance abuse counseling. In addition, recreational facilities and information and referral services were available. Some sites also offered teen parenting education, transportation, child care, tutoring, family planning, and hot lines.

Prior to creating the program, officials in New Jersey ran focus sessions with teenagers to see what they wanted of such a venture. Opinions were solicited from both those who had had emotional problems and those who were by all accounts free of such difficulties. Students said that most important to them would be the availability of caring adults to listen to them without being judgmental and help them with decision making, although they did not want decisions made for them. They asked for activities after school hours, on weekends, and during the summer. The students said that when such activities were not available, they were left only with nonproductive, sometimes destructive, alternatives. The young people wanted the program to be open to all students, not just those who were troubled. This way, they said, participation would not carry a stigma.

Officials of the School Based Youth Services Program illustrated the advantages of coordinated services by citing the case of a student on the verge of running away from home. A staff member discovered that the youngster was plagued by problems, her home life was in disarray, and the family faced immigration difficulties. The student also apparently had been raped by a family member. The teenager felt helpless in the face of such overwhelming travail. The program integrated efforts to help her and her family, coordinating the services of a family counselor, the local health agency, municipal authorities, immigration officials, and school personnel. The family stabilized itself, the sexual abuse issue was addressed, and the young woman remained in school, graduated, and entered college.

The program at New Brunswick High School, serving students in a small industrial city long past its prime, typified those at high schools around New Jersey. This was the sole high school in a town where, by 1996, for the first time, Latinos eclipsed blacks as the largest segment of the enrollment. The gritty town was the site of many small factories that were downsizing or closing by the time that large numbers of immigrants from Latin America arrived. Unlike other small towns that lost their manufacturing base and had to absorb wrenching population shifts, however, New Brunswick reaped the civic advantages of having two bookend institutions that kept it propped up: the campus of Rutgers University and the world headquarters of Johnson & Johnson Corporation. In fact, the School Based Youth Services Program in New Brunswick was a cooperative effort in which two of the main partners were the Rutgers campus of the University of Medicine and Dentistry of New Jersey-Community Mental Health Center and New Brunswick Tomorrow, a civic group in which Johnson & Johnson was a key participant. Besides what it offered at the high school, the program provided participating students with dental care, the services of a comprehensive health clinic that operated elsewhere in town, and access to Planned Parenthood.

Clay County, West Virginia, which spreads over 346 square miles, is a place of mountain roads with hairpin turns, where accessibility is complicated by the fact that many people live deep in the hollows, far from main roads. Transporting sick children to health care facilities is difficult at best and made even worse by the poverty that causes so many families to wonder about whether they can afford medical treatment. Thus the creation of wellness centers at the school district's middle and high schools in 1994 was a step forward in a state in which 84,000 children 18 and younger lacked adequate health care. Almost half of the 1,186 students in the two Clay County secondary schools visited the wellness centers during the 1995-96 school year. They went primarily for general examinations, various health screenings, and sports physicals, but these seemingly routine visits contributed significantly toward maintaining the health of students in a county in which three-quarters of the families with school-age children were poor enough to qualify the students for federally subsidized lunches. In fact, 28 percent of the students using the two wellness centers either had no health insurance or had limited coverage.

The wellness centers owed their existence to a collaboration of several agencies—the Clay Board of Education, the Clay Health Department, Clay Primary Care, Shawnee Hills Mental Health Center, and the West Virginia Bureau of Public Health. Medicaid and medical insurance groups were billed for services, but no child was turned away for lack of insurance or inability to pay. The health care team—a physician's assistant and a nurse—rotated between the two secondary schools, spending a half day at each. Meanwhile, a clerk remained on duty full time at each school. "This cuts down absenteeism," Connie Harper, a registered nurse who was on her tour of duty in the center's tidy suite of rooms at Clay High School, said of the availability of the wellness center. Health education was also part of the mission of the wellness center, which started a club at the high school known as the Teen Wellness Connection, providing speakers on health-related topics.

Serving Students with Disabilities

An impetus for schools to take on a larger share of the health care burden came from the Education of All Handicapped Children Act that Congress enacted in 1975. A portion of the more than 4 million students covered by this legislation requires extensive medical attention that schools now must administer. Federal courts have interpreted the law generously, and schools sometimes have had to assume duties more typical of hospital wards. In extreme cases, for instance, courts have held that schools must provide procedures as specialized as catheterizations for certain students. All in all, as a result of the law, public schools now enroll and care for many children who in earlier generations were turned away. Schools have to find ways to accommodate the medical needs of students with disabilities, however extensive and expensive they may be. A school district's alternative is to pay the cost, sometimes more than $60,000 per student per year, to send a child to a private school that says it can deal with the student's emotional or physical requirements.

In St. Paul, Minnesota, the Wilder Foundation collaborated with the public school system to create a program, called the Eisenmenger Learning Centers, at six of the system's elementary schools. The program provided a rich array of extra personnel to work with students exhibiting the most severe emotional and behavioral problems. The school system paid the regular salaries of the special education teachers in each classroom, and Wilder underwrote the salaries of supplemental support personnel. Wilder staffed each school with a program director, two psychologists, a social worker, a family outreach worker, and two teacher aides for each classroom. A psychiatrist was on call to the program for further counseling and to write prescriptions for medications. In addition, an occupational therapist offered periodic advice on calming techniques, which were deemed vital given the trouble many of the students had in containing their anger and frustration.

An aim of the program was to teach social skills so that children would have positive ways to get along with others and be able to handle conflicts peaceably. The program, which integrated special education and mental health services, linked itself closely to the families of the students to bring about a level of support for special education students unusual in most public schools. Each youngster, in addition to the individualized education plan required nationally for students with disabilities, also had a personalized mental health treatment plan. The program provided individual and group mental therapy for the students and family therapy for parents and guardians too.

Typical of the effort was the arrangement at East Consolidated School, a sprawling elementary school of 900 students, where the Wilder program served 40 children, 10 of them assigned to each of four classrooms. The students, about half of them minority, came mostly from lower-income families. Officially classified as disabled, the students spent most of the school day in the four classrooms, but many moved into the mainstream for up to an hour each day, often accompanied by an aide. A family night every other week at which dinner was served usually was attended by members of one-third to one-half of the families. This ongoing connection enhanced the trust that families had in the program, making parents more willing to discuss the child's out-of-school life with the staff.

Family nights also gave the staff opportunities to see how the students interacted with their families. "Sometimes we see very different behavior from what we've seen in school," said Karen Roschelle, a psychologist. Every school day a note was sent home with each student in the Eisenmenger program. The form on which the note was written allowed the teacher to make a brief comment about the child's work that day and to suggest specific issues and problems for the parent to discuss with the child that afternoon or evening. The parent had space to sign and offer comments. Home visits by the team's family outreach worker supplemented this daily communication, which ensured constant contact between school and home.

The proposition is simple: Children who are ailing or who have some medical impediment to learning will not realize their potential as students. One way or another, they need health services. Those who object to involving the schools in brokering or providing medical services should point the way toward a viable alternative. Right now Medicaid—for whatever reasons—does not deliver these services in a prompt and efficient manner to all poor children who need them. Schools have enough to do without delving into this area, but they are providers of last resort when others do not step into the breach.

EIGHT

The Emotional and Psychological Climate

Top suburban school districts and private schools frequently have school counselors, psychologists, and social workers ready to meet the needs of students. This support network is augmented by the out-of-school private therapists that affluent families hire with the aid of elaborate health coverage plans or simply by having the money to pay out of pocket. Counseling of the sort available to advantaged youngsters is often unknown among poor children. What are these youngsters to do? How is he or she to cope with the demands of formal learning when an uncle is dying of AIDS or a stepfather is sexually abusing an older sister or a mother has a cocaine habit? This scenario cuts all too close to reality for some schoolchildren. On top of these problems, add the devastating effects of poverty, the uncertainties of employment for the family's breadwinner, and the continuous threat of violence on the streets. It is not difficult to imagine why so many poor children need the counseling that so often is not available to them. Yet critics rail about academic standards as if they can be met in a vacuum. Where is the social capital that allows these children to negotiate the treacherous path that they must travel?

Edward G. Rozycki, a 25-year veteran of the Philadelphia schools and an education professor, observed that some people think that raising achievement levels is simply a matter of establishing standards, and, "hocus pocus," students will meet them. Using the example of mathematics, he noted sarcastically: "Barring the effects of disparities in school funding, domestic upheaval, poverty, disease, social disorder, crime, school violence, drug usage, student lack of interest, and parental complacency, these national standards in mathematics will bring students to almost genius levels of math competence." A "lovely dream," he called it.[1]

The mental health counselors ensconced at New Brunswick High School in connection with New Jersey's School Based Youth Services Program addressed a wide array of problems brought by students, ranging from behavioral difficulties, to substance abuse, to depression. Counseling groups—some conducted in English and others, in Spanish—were formed on an ad hoc basis, depending on the topic at hand. Among the subjects addressed were anger management, impulse control, and suicidal thoughts. The groups were limited to about a half-dozen members simply because that was the most who could be accommodated in a counselor's office and no other spaces were available for the gatherings.

Students were excused from classes to participate in counseling groups, which met at different times each week so that they would not miss the same class every time. After-school counseling groups were unsuccessful since so many students held jobs or were responsible for the care of younger siblings. The counseling staff, made up of certified social workers and social work interns from Rutgers University, sometimes assumed responsibilities that went well beyond the counseling sessions. Counselors regarded themselves as advocates; so, for instance, when a student who was involved in a stabbing had to go to court, her mental health counselor accompanied her to offer emotional support.

Such counseling would have been impossible at this school without the school-based services program. New Brunswick High's four regular guidance counselors, paid by the school board, concentrated on academic issues and did not take on the kinds of counseling responsibilities absorbed by the school-based program. "A lot would go unnoticed and unserved without us," said Sarinet Thorne, a counselor with a master's degree in social work, who was a staff member in the school-based program. "Our students are hesitant to reach out for help. They are not the kind to say 'My boyfriend and I broke up and I want to kill myself.'" The regular guidance counselors frequently referred students to the center, and many other students found their way on their own. One reason why students opened themselves to mental health counseling was because it operated under a kind of subterfuge. The center was housed in a large open room that had easy chairs, a television set, a stereo, a pool table, and game tables. A poster on the wall proclaimed: "We Have Better Things to Do Than Drugs."

"When you have a hard day, you can come in here and relax," a student said. "There's always someone here to talk to if you have a problem and they won't treat you like a little kid." The mental health counselors' offices lined one side of the room, almost inconspicuous to youngsters who came for recreational activities. "It gives us an informal kind of cover," a counselor said. Breaking the ice in this low-income community sometimes required that a counselor assure a student that talking about psychological problems was not a sign of being crazy.

Some of the clublike groups formed by the program served as adjuncts to the counseling. One such group was called HI TOPS, which stood for Health Interested Teens' Own Program. The group was an outgrowth of the attempt to prevent student pregnancy. But rather than lecture and harangue youngsters, HI TOPS devoted itself to providing them with interesting, rewarding experiences meant to make them feel so good about themselves that they would not want to compromise their futures by becoming teen-age parents. "Peer leadership is an important part of HI TOPS," said one young female participant. "I'm only a junior and I don't have to wait until I am a senior to be looked up to. I learn things in HI TOPS that I can go home and explain to my mother. It's really fun. We make up skits. Yesterday we want to the Hyatt for a rally for World AIDS Day."

Counseling was integral to another of the enhancement programs, the Neighborhood Academic Initiative at the University of Southern California. Small groups of students met with a counselor once a week in scheduled sessions. In addition, counseling was available to students and their families as needed. One morning, at a regularly scheduled group counseling session, about a dozen youngsters sat around a seminar table for what appeared to be a class like any other. But, unlike any class with which most students were familiar, this session began—as usual—with a "mood check." Each student greeted his or her classmates with an amiable "Good morning" and a statement of how he or she felt that day. "I feel happy because today we're going to sing in the auditorium," said a small girl in wire frame glasses whose hair was pulled back in a ponytail. A few of her classmates confessed to nervousness at the prospect of performing at the assembly.

"How will you deal with that?" the counselor asked one of them.

"I'll just pretend the audience is not there," the girl replied. "You have to do what you can and not worry about it."

Another girl said her technique for maintaining composure was to resist looking into the faces in the first few rows, and, instead, to look toward the balcony, where the eyes were too distant to meet hers.

"I feel kind of mad," a boy said. "I got dressed in this this morning and my mother got up and told me to put on a different shirt. My dad said the shirt was okay." The counselor explored the possibility that the boy's anxiety over the impending performance had left him unsettled in dealing with his mother.

Eliciting such personal feelings from students at inner-city high schools in the rough-and-tumble neighborhoods of south-central Los Angeles is no small achievement. These were young people who cultivated tough exteriors as a survival mechanism. Ordinarily, a show of emotion would be viewed as a sign of weakness. But to the credit of the Neighborhood Academic Initiative, the participants trusted the program and the youngsters and adults with whom they had bonded so much that they willingly let down their guards.

Across the hall, another counseling group had moved into a discussion of moral and ethical decision making, weighing the implications of stealing, cheating, and lying. "What about the death penalty?" asked the counselor, trying to get the students to apply the principles to a major social issue.

"If you take someone's life, you should get your own life taken," a student said.

"I don't think humans have a right to say whether another person dies, only God," another interjected immediately.

The back-and-forth discussion continued, and then the counselor mentioned that differences of opinion can surround many moral and ethical issues. She shifted to the subject of gangs—a ubiquitous force in the neighborhood—and asked whether gangs are all wrong.

"It depends on what kind of gang," said the student. "Basically, a gang is a group of people, like a family. Some gangs shoot people, though, and that's bad."

Another student, picking up on the gang-as-family theme, pointed out that some youngsters "have parents who are messed up, on drugs and without jobs" and that they join gangs in order to find people who care about them and love them.

By the end of the session, the counselor had gotten the students to focus on their belief systems and the process by which they made decisions, helping them gain new appreciation for the reasons why some people take the positions that they do.

Counseling and Pregnancy

Pregnancy is one area in which counselors in enhancement programs across the country tread gingerly. Although hundreds of thousands of teenagers get pregnant each year, counselors approach this subject with trepidation. Their concern about alienating the young people with whom they deal seems to account for this wariness. They worry that if students think they want to preach to them about sexual habits, the youngsters will spurn the rest of the program. "We pick our issues," said one program's representative, commenting on why the issues surrounding teenage pregnancy are avoided. "We don't want to humiliate, embarrass, or shame them. We want them to feel good about participating in the program."

The reticence persists despite the fact that females 17 and younger deliver 175,000 babies annually, limiting their own potential and that of their offspring by reason of poverty and lack of education. Moreover, taxpayers spend almost $7 billion annually on costs associated with this early childbearing.[2] White teenagers in the United States have a higher birth rate than their counterparts anywhere else in the world, and black teenagers have a birth rate three times that of whites.[3] In view of these statistics, teenage pregnancy is a problem that must be addressed more vigorously.

The absence of fathers—whether through divorces or births outside marriage—from the lives of all too many children further attenuates their fragile links to social capital. When parents live apart, for whatever reason, this decision "damages, and sometimes destroys, the social capital that might have been available to the child."[4]

Teenagers with babies were part of the established scene at such places as the Unidale Area Learning Center, an alternative high school in St. Paul, Minnesota, and New Brunswick High School in New Jersey. Unidale, an alternative school for dropouts from other schools, readily accommodated young mothers who wanted to complete the work for their diplomas. The school had a suite certified to handle as many as eight infants and seven toddlers at one time. The child care services were free to students, but, in return, they had to attend a parenting class and assist in the child care program.

New Brunswick High School had a parent-infant care center, where 12 teenage mothers left their children while attending classes. In turn, the young mothers—like those in St. Paul—were required to participate in programs on parenting skills and join a peer support group. The mothers, and an occasional father, helped maintain the facility, folding linens or putting toys back on shelves. The mothers and their children were transported to and from school and ate breakfast together in the center each morning at 7:15.

The spacious, white-painted room had an ample supply of cribs and toys. The facility operated with the assistance of interns from Rutgers University who used the experience to gain academic credit. "We impact on children at two very different developmental stages," said Ann Pretty, coordinator of the infant care center. "One stage involves the infants and the other stage involves the mothers, who, after all, are children too. We hope that by watching the way we take care of their children and the way that we take care of them [the mothers], they will pass it all on." The school-based program at New Brunswick High did not start with the idea of providing infant care, but the service grew out of the program's mandate to prevent dropouts. Officials created the center when it grew apparent that students who left school to have babies could not return to classes due to lack of reliable child care.

One of the less controversial entry points into discussions of sexuality presents itself before youngsters are sexually active, a point at which the admonitions do not represent a disapproval of practices in which they are already engaged. In the I Have a Dream program at

Manhattan's Chelsea-Elliott Houses, where the children were still in elementary school, a class on sex education for the children's parents served as the beginning of efforts to combat teenage pregnancy. Eventually such classes would be aimed at the students, but the hope was to reach the youngsters through their parents, who were learning how to feel comfortable discussing sexual matters with their children. Similarly, the Children's Aid Society offered family life and sex education, not just for students but for parents too, at each of its centers in New York City. Three separate groups were formed for the classes, one for boys, one for girls, and one for parents. Generally, parents who completed the sequence of classes on human sexuality won admission to the City University of New York under a special program. As of 1996, 20 parents were enrolled in the university through this program and 3 parents had graduated from the college.

Despite such efforts, the problem of teenage childbearing continues to confound those who urge young people to wait before becoming parents. Programs directed toward males who would father such children have grown more prevalent. But females, of course, suffer the main consequences of early childbearing and programs aimed at them have, by and large, not succeeded. Researchers analyzed 125 pregnancy-prevention programs and found only 17 programs in which documentable changes occurred in behaviors that might avert pregnancy. And even those programs tended to have only a modest impact on behavior.[5] While almost one-third of the nation's births are to unwed mothers of all ages, the issue for purposes of this book is not simply one of morality. Concern must be focused on the tens of thousands of impoverished young females—hardly out of childhood themselves—whose childbearing most likely seals their fate, making them and their babies destined for a lifetime of poverty and all that it represents.

Engendering Self-Control

Whether the issue is pregnancy or simply the school atmosphere, the well-being of children depends on the ways in which they accept responsibility as well as how they interact with one another in and out of school. The *emotional intelligence* that author Daniel Goleman said in his book was so important for children to develop includes the sort of self-awareness, impulse control, and empathy that can go a long way toward improving life even for children who face adversity.[6] The attempt to build self-discipline permeated the Choir Academy of Harlem, the school from which pupils were drawn for membership in the widely known Boys Choir of Harlem. This school concerned itself with more than academics on the assumption that character development, sense of purpose, and courage all contributed to scholastic achievement. Furthermore, the demanding routines of rehearsal and performance required self-discipline. Walter Turnbull, founder and director of the Boys Choir, spoke of the "Sisyphean" task of instilling self-discipline, conceding that it was "too late for some of these children" but asserting that "in most cases it isn't too late."[7]

The relationship between discipline and school climate is very much affected by the ability of students to exercise self-control. Intruders commit some violent acts in schools, and, certainly, outsiders pose a danger when students travel to and from school. For the most part, however, schools become unsafe when the students who attend them put each other at peril. In communities where violence is the norm, the school tends to reflect the aggressiveness of the larger society. Violent reactions follow provocations and perceptions of insults. Brushing against another student in a crowded corridor or even staring at someone may invite a vicious attack. Programs try to get students to overlook perceived slights. In general, though, students do not check their attitudes at the schoolhouse door, and they are inclined to react to provocations in school in the same ways that they would outside.

Frances Lucerna of El Puente Academy spoke of the peer pressures on students, particularly on the males, many of whom live in housing projects in which a show of weakness puts them at risk. "I sat in a room with 15 young men," she explained. "They said that they have to prove themselves everyday, to show that they are men." Students will strike out at each other less frequently, however, when mechanisms are available to resolve differences and when they believe that they will not lose face by using these alternatives to violence. The well-being of poor youngsters depends on their accepting these alternatives. A show of force in the school building can increase security, but in the long run this will not change neighborhoods and it will not assure youngsters of their well-being when they are beyond the aegis of the schoolhouse. El Puente's philosophy held that profound changes were possible when students incorporated the values of the school and lived by them wherever they went, in effect, inculcating values about dealing with people that affected their behavior outside the school as well as inside.

Thus self-control figures prominently in efforts to stem violence among young people. The motivation to act responsibly must come from within; youngsters have to learn how to exercise self-restraint. Codes of conduct, behavior modification, mediation, and conflict resolution programs appear as regular features in many schools these days. "We struggle to get kids to respect each other," said a school social worker in Minnesota. "There are issues of self-respect to address. How can you have respect for someone else when you have no respect for yourself?" Across the country, teachers and community workers say that peer pressures exerted on young people outside of school make it difficult to curb violence in school and complicate attempts to get youngsters to eschew violence once they leave school grounds. What young people need desperately and often do not have are families and communities in which wholesome values exert a powerful force for good. "You can't talk about self-discipline out of context," said Frances Lucerna. "It goes back to a question of community."

Teaching self-control was so much a part of the mission that one day at Vaughn Elementary School, a teacher used a class session to talk to the students about the evils of fighting. "How do you feel when you fight?" she asked.

"Sad," one student said.

"What can happen to you when you fight?" the teacher asked.

"Get hurt," a child said.

"What can you do instead of fight?" she asked to a chorus of responses.

"Tell the teacher."

"Stop fighting."

"Talk about it."

After some discussion, a boy said that "if you fight you won't have friends." Another boy quickly added: "You might not want to come back to school."

* * *

A town meeting format was used at Intermediate School 218 in Manhattan to recruit students to serve as peer mediators. Previously, some students had taken parts in a role-playing activity in which they acted as participants in an argument. The next week the teacher asked students to select classmates to serve as peer mediators. Using an overhead projector, he listed on a screen the five steps of peer mediation: opening statement, fact finding, open questions, moving toward a solution, and agreement. He told the students that he wanted them to list the names of students whom they thought ought to be mediators, obviously a way of ferreting out the youngsters most respected by their classmates.

Then he reviewed the five mediation steps. "The opening statement means that the mediator introduces himself," he explained. "One person talks at a time and you don't insult each other. What's the slang for that?"

"No dissing," a student responded.

"Right," the teacher said. "The mediator doesn't take sides. I want you to remain—." He paused, waiting for a student to supply the word.

"Neutral," one said.

"What does 'neutral' mean?" the teacher asked.

This exchange continued until the teacher projected another slide, this one listing what a peer mediator was and was not. The attributes included being a good listener, a good team worker, a fair person, a helper, a dependable person, and a flexible person. He told them, on the other hand, that a peer mediator was not a disciplinarian, a person who interrupts or focuses attention on him- or herself, a judge, a person who gives orders or advice, or a person who talks to others about the peer mediation session.

The students, particularly the boys, were inattentive. They squirmed in their seats, occasionally shouting to each other and sometimes punching one another in the shoulder, as young males entering puberty are apt to do. Two teachers' aides, paid by the Children's Aid Society, stood in the aisles, quieting the outbursts. The teacher stressed the need for confidentiality on the part of the mediator. "The worst thing a mediator can do is leave and talk about the students' problems. Then they won't trust anyone to mediate."

Finally, the image of the form that the students were being asked to fill out appeared on the screen. There was a line on which to nominate a classmate to be a mediator. Students also could write their own names on the bottom if they wanted to be mediators. Prospective mediators would be trained, mostly through role playing. "If you become a mediator you will miss some classes to conduct mediations," the teacher explained. "You will be responsible for talking to the teacher and making up the work."

Security and Safety

One of the main tests of a school's success in engendering self-discipline among its students has to do with the security of its environment. Teaching and learning require tranquility. Some schools across the country, however, are places where neither students nor teachers feel safe. These schools are attended by children who know of others their age who have been murdered. Students talk about kids who were shot on the street as if describing scenes from a movie. Some even mention plans for their own funerals. "You can't expect them to be typical kids," said an elementary school teacher in Newark. "It's amazing that they deal with what they do and keep going. They deal with what children should never have to deal with."

One in four teenagers, and one in two in high-crime areas, stated in a national survey that they did not always feel safe in their own neighborhoods. A pervasive fear of violence and crime affected their behavior, expectations, and school performance, causing these teenagers to miss school, get lower grades, and carry weapons.[8] A striking part of this phenomenon is not simply that such fears exist but that they are so prevalent in high-crime neighborhoods—where, of course, poor kids are most apt to live. "From a policy perspective these figures say to me that kids really long for and need adult connections," John Calhoun, executive director of the National Crime Prevention Council, said in commenting on the situation to The New York Times.[9] These connections help constitute the social capital that enhancement programs strive to put in place.

The search for ways to make schools safer prodded the staff of the Wilder Foundation to look to Scandinavia, where social scientists had developed a multifaceted plan. The approach was dressed in an American name, Cool 2B Safe, and Wilder hoped that it would alter the climate in an inner-city middle school in its headquarters city of St. Paul, Minnesota, which was plagued by violent behavior. A critical element of the program was the formation of staff teams of teachers and administrators to work to reduce violent incidents. The underlying theory held that adults carried the main responsibility for setting standards of conduct by example and, by direct intervention, for teaching kids how to behave.

Wilder instituted the program in 1993; three years later the level of serious misconduct in the school had hardly changed. Considering the fact that problems of this kind had increased in schools throughout Minnesota during those three years, Wilder found some satisfaction in its work because at least conditions had not worsened. Yet foundation representatives believed that a serious flaw had prevented Cool 2B Safe from having more effect. The school teams that were to be the basis for carrying out the program never jelled. The school did not allot ample time to train teachers for their new responsibility, which prevented the teams from developing fully. "It was a basic failure in our model," said Sarah Snapp, the Wilder social worker who headed the program. "We did not get the kind of face-to-face time that we needed with the staff."

Students require the security of safe, accepting places that offer them emotional and physical reassurance. Before they can learn, they need a sense of well-being. Responding to the annual Gallup Poll on the public schools, 92 percent of Americans said they favored removing troublemakers from classes if that was what it took to maintain order.[10] Schools confer a sense of well-being on students when their atmosphere supports youngsters' physical, social, and emotional development. In such a locale, youngsters can not only feel safe but can enjoy the company of peers. Some youths have few other opportunities for this kind of socialization because of the dangers that await them on the streets. A teacher in Newark told of a day when the school dismissed students at noon in recognition of an impending snowstorm. "I had seven or eight kids who wouldn't leave the room," she explained. "They said they would have nothing to do once they left the school building, got home, and had to remain in the house. Here they have someone they can talk to."

El Puente Academy prided itself on being a safe haven from the threatening streets of Brooklyn's Williamsburg section. This high school, unlike many in New York City, had no metal detectors or security guards at the door, though crime and drug-dealing were common in the neighborhood. It was clear that the prevailing sense of community inside the school was a source of protection. Small and personal, El Puente was the kind of place where even the presence of a stranger was obvious. Students who live in trouble-prone neighborhoods treasure their good fortune when they are lucky enough to attend schools of this sort. "Students want that sense of trust," said Mark Lopez, a student at El Puente. "Everywhere else they see their friends jumped, killed, and shot. Here there is a sense of having a dream and seeing it fulfilled."

Another student at El Puente, Nitopia Walker, said that the school stood in stark contrast with other, less rewarding parts of life; as testimony to its reassuring influence, she sought to build a life for herself that revolved around school. She explained: "In the streets you learn nothing. You get locked up, die, or get involved with drugs. You see what's outside and you know it's not worth paying attention to it, that it's a step backward. I try not to involve myself with negative people because I don't want to become negative." Walker tutored at the Boys and Girls Club besides involving herself in school. She found that when she told students at other schools about El Puente, they would say: "Stop lying—there isn't a school like that."

As the school's director, Frances Lucerna derived satisfaction from the students' attitudes because she believed that El Puente had to convey a sense of well-being if the students were going to enjoy the peace of mind to study and achieve. She said that the staff had to focus, before anything else, on helping students feel safe, respected, and cared for.[11] "For a lot of young people at the academy," Lucerna said, "it's very hard to focus because their daily lives are so chaotic and in many ways so wanting." In other words, if the school could bring order out of chaos and give young people a safe, orderly place with some predictability, the result might be a better climate for learning. The staff at El Puente started the process of building trust by leaving their own coats, jackets, and other belongings on pipe racks that were in full view of everyone. The students, made wary by bitter experience, gradually learned that they too could store their belongings unattended with some degree of assurance that members of the school community would not steal from one another.

During the 1980s, the unruly scene at Baltimore's Canton Middle School resembled that at many inner-city schools. When a commitment to school reform was made and a school improvement team was formed, the first order of business—not unlike that awaiting a new sheriff in Dodge City—was to establish discipline. Climate is everything in education. Teachers and administrators must set out, as their first objective, to minimize disruption and to make everyone in the building feel safe. For Canton, this meant inducing students to accept responsibility for their own behavior and getting teachers to reorganize instruction so that it engaged students' interest.

A half decade later in 1996, Canton Middle School was a peaceful oasis in which the one uniformed security guard seldom had to break up fights or contend with serious disturbances. A legacy of the school's concern about decorum was the continuing practice of requiring students to line up at the doorway of the classroom that they were about to enter for the next period. The first student in the queue stood on the third tile from the door, and others lined up behind him or her. Each teacher, once satisfied that the line was straight and the students were orderly, invited them to enter—single file—into the classroom.

In fashioning themselves as safe havens, such schools as Canton Middle School and El Puente Academy resembled the successful neighborhood youth organizations that Milbrey W. McLaughlin and her co-authors identified in a book they entitled *Urban Sanctuaries*. Those organizations for youth tended to have strong sets of rules and codes of expected behaviors. Such organizations visualized themselves in terms of a family and created a place where young people always had something to do and someone to do it with.[12] Schools would do well to emulate these organizations and to form alliances with them. People often tell of the influence of youth organizations in shaping them—the Y summer camp where nature first came to be understood on its own terms, the scouting adventure in which learning to tie knots was secondary to human bonding, the Boys and Girls Club where serving as an officer provided an initial taste of leadership, an after-school basketball league that filled otherwise idle moments with hours of satisfying recreation. Youth organizations enhance a young person's sense of well-being, the very goal that schools increasingly set for themselves. "Academically successful children from non-mainstream backgrounds" are those "who have widened their net of social partici-pation" to encompass these activities outside school or home.[13]

Children who participate in the activities of youth organizations often end up feeling better about themselves. Self-image is not as easily bolstered in school if a record of low achievement has been estab-lished, or at home if parents have created a climate of criticism. While school is seen primarily as a place for teaching and the family is viewed as a purveyor of guidance and direction, youth organizations can augment both, and sometimes in more benign ways than either the school or the family can. A report on the Beacons project in New York City considered it "good sense" to link community-based organiza-tions and schools because "in many neighborhoods, schools are often not only the best, but also one of the only decent and safe places for children and their families to be."[14] In fact, the first Beacons were established in 1991 in response to the recommendations of a study group headed by Nicholas deB. Katzenbach, the former U.S. Attorney General, that envisioned the creation of safe havens for youths and families in poor neighborhoods, the very function of many youth organizations. Officials in the network of Beacons acknowledged that an extension of the school day into the late afternoon and evening could not succeed unless a secure climate was established. This supportive environment is part of the sense of well-being that ought to characterize the everyday school experience.

At some Beacon schools, security officers employed during these after-school hours were community residents trained specifically for the task. About half of the Beacons hired youths as security assistants and trained them in security procedures and conflict mediation. Rheedlen, which ran the Beacon at P.S. 194, organized the security assistants into a group called "peacemakers." One such assistant, Ray, a 22-year-old student at Borough of Manhattan Community College, spent 30 hours a week in the school as a paid service worker with AmeriCorps. Ray knew the territory well, having grown up on W. 144th Street, near P.S. 194 in Harlem. He watched one of his friends get shot to death down the block, at the corner of 8th Avenue. Now he doubled as a security assistant and program aide at the school, taking responsibility for assembling 120 youngsters into a basketball league of 12 teams.

Ray and his fellow peacemakers enlisted the school's oldest students, the sixth graders, as "junior peacemakers," training them in conflict resolution. Ray's emphasis was on teaching kids to avoid trouble by instructing them in the "right" ways to talk to people. Staying out of trouble is especially vital in a neighborhood in which the slightest misstep can lead to the brandishing of weapons. "I try to tell them how not to anger people and cause people to think they've lost your respect," Ray said of the life-preserving instructions he imparted. "These kids have to learn they can't just go around saying whatever they want." Ray's goal upon completing community college was to leave the city "so I'm not pulled down by people I know."

Rheedlen's effort to foster a safe climate did not stop with the training of the security assistants. Beacon staff and the students' parents were encouraged to think of themselves as having security responsibilities during the extended hours. In neighborhoods with turf issues, where gangs compete for territory, officials enlisted teen youth councils, youth outreach workers, and recreation staffers to broker the school as neutral ground. The Beacons sometimes hired youth staff from rival neighborhood groups as members of the same work teams to set the stage for better relationships in the community.

A major security issue arose between 6 and 10 P.M. Most centers doubled their security forces during these hours. Some deliberately scheduled programs for 14- and 15-year-olds earlier in the evening and programs for older youths later as a precaution, trying to keep the younger children out of harm's way. Intergenerational programming also helped make buildings safer. Parents and grandparents were often on the premises for their own programs and to serve as coaches and volunteers for youth programs. Directors of individual Beacon programs said that young people acted more responsibly when their parents and the others' were in the building. Some Beacons did outreach through their community advisory councils and youth councils to persuade drug dealers and other potential troublemakers to move away from the area around the school. In addition, some Beacons worked with local police precincts and, in particular, with community policing officers, to establish safe corridors to and from the school.

The programs most successful at creating an aura of safety did not rely exclusively on security forces but also sought to build feelings of neighborliness so that people would regard the programs in the buildings as their own. With this attitude of ownership, neighborhood people who used the school felt personally violated when troublemakers and drug dealers intruded. Inculcating this feeling was part of the continuing struggle to win back the streets. The sense of community ownership was heightened when parents and siblings participated in programs. The Beacon program at P.S. 194, for instance, tried to draw entire families into the building for afternoon and evening programs. Members of the teen council assisted by informally scrutinizing everyone who entered. People grew willing to tell the staff about those who had carried weapons into the building.

The predispositions that students bring to school with them go a long way toward determining their receptivity to learning and the quality of the learning climate for everyone around them. Youngsters who live in poverty suffer under pressures that frequently prove unfriendly to events in the classroom. Without access to counseling and guidance, they may not be able to maintain the focus that serious learning requires. Students with disabilities have additional needs. The stakes extend beyond the individual. Almost anyone who has spent time in a school can relate stories of youngsters whose conduct disrupts classes, threatens teachers, and makes a shambles of education.

Schools must do all they can to engender self-discipline in children. In an America that glamorizes violence, the inner cities—populated largely by poor people and their offspring—may have reaped the worst excesses of this harvest. Schools have to take seriously their responsibility to promote a climate for learning and to ensure the safety of students and teachers. The examples of schools that have done this successfully should be widely replicated.

NINE

Developing Human Potential

Asked by their teacher to list "five things I really like about myself," a number of students in one enhancement program tended to limit their lists to such physical attributes as "my hair." The teacher believed that the students had cultivated within themselves so little of a substantial nature that they thought that having attractive physical features made them complete as human beings. Their sense of well-being was limited by their inability to appreciate the worthiness of desirable traits of character in themselves as well as in others. As a result, their self-image rested on qualities and accomplishments of questionable merit. Young people with this kind of attitude weaken themselves by building their self-worth on flimsy structures.

The solution is not to fill their heads with hot air about how great they are but to afford them opportunities for positive experiences that will enable them to discover and cultivate genuine inner strengths. Many enhancement programs recognize this need and try in various ways to build self-assurance in students as a foundation to learning. At one high school where many students had spotty academic records, the principal said that the youngsters had to be taught to take baby steps along the path to self-development. "You have to treat them as if they were toddlers and take them through a process that they have never been through," she explained, cautioning that "we never let them know we're treating them like toddlers."

Teachers at the Ochoa School in Tucson maintained that one of the most important results of their attempts to change the school was the cultivation of a climate in which youngsters felt more confident. After the school underwent several years of reform that encouraged student initiative, the students, once reticent and withdrawn, more readily expressed their opinions. Changes in the curriculum and in pedagogy meant that students probably found school a less judgmental, less threatening place. Chances of success grew as students got more support to overcome hurdles to their learning. They also were buoyed by the school's more assertive attempt to involve parents, which created a familial aura that raised children's comfort level. Teachers' attitudes toward both students and parents changed. By the time the Educational and Community Change Project had been operating for four years, a neighborhood coalition had replaced a traditional parent-teacher organization and the coalition concerned itself with a host of health, educational, housing, and safety issues affecting children and families. Teachers were "seeking the parents and the community as resources," and "parents were invited to work alongside children in activities where the parents could provide expertise." Teachers no longer saw parents "as incapable and unsupportive."[1]

Even students who had seen few tangible results from their efforts in school began to attain recognition. Ochoa held monthly ceremonies to award students for improvement, citizenship, and attendance as well as for achievement in reading and mathematics. The principal called the names of honorees, summoning them to the front of the room, handing a certificate to each, and shaking their hands—all to the applause of fellow students. The Rheedlen program at P.S. 194 in Manhattan also sought to involve students in activities that led to greater fulfillment. Turned loose with video-tape recorders, youngsters worked together to record and edit films. Others participated in the martial arts, gaining confidence in themselves as they mastered the various levels. And some students wrote poetry, discovering that they had something to say and taking pride in their ability to manipulate language for their own purposes and for the edification of others.

An underlying issue for youngsters when it comes to self-regard has to do with respect—the degree to which they respect themselves and to which they believe other people respect them. These issues played themselves out in a classroom one morning in the REACH program at University School. The students were about to enter sixth, seventh, and eighth grades in the public schools that they attended during the regular school year. The reason for the discussion was a feeling by some students that the program director had "dissed" them in reprimanding them for ill behavior without asking what had provoked their conduct. Now the classroom teacher had written some key words on the chalkboard—parents, God, authority, teachers. The students were pouring out tales of how they thought they had suffered from disrespect in the past. One, who had a part-time job in a shoe store that allowed him to buy footwear at a discount, told of a teacher in regular school who, upon seeing him in a new pair of expensive sneakers, said: "Your brother probably sold drugs to get you those shoes." Another told of a teacher who said that they—the students at an inner-city school—were stupid but that suburban kids were smart.

The discussion veered onto the issue of authority and whether it always should be respected. Some students said that they did not respect authority figures, even their parents and grandparents, who did not earn their respect. A student asked why adults "get mad when you catch them in something they say"?

"You mean being hypocritical?" the teacher asked. That was exactly what the youngster meant and the teacher wrote one word on the chalkboard: "Pride." Soon the class was talking about the program director's failure to ask their side of the story after the group misbehaved at the swimming pool. The teacher led them through a discussion about respect being a two-way street. "Communication is the linchpin," he said, quickly asking them if they remembered what a linchpin was. They did. "To feel respect," he said, "you must feel like you're being heard. Another way to get respect is to be the best," he added, segueing into new territory.

"Like Michael Jordan," a student blurted.

"Be the best if you want someone's respect," the teacher continued. "Some kids get respect just from playing basketball, some from being wizards—being smart."

"Some don't get credit for that," a student observed about the lack of respect for academic excellence.

"Students will want him when they get together to do a project even if they think he's a nerd," the teacher said.

* * *

The positive development program, aimed at girls in the fifth grade at Rogers Elementary School in Stamford, Connecticut, began with teachers identifying students they judged to be at risk of falling through the cracks during their final year of elementary school. The program operated in conjunction with the family resource center that the school created with state funds. These were not youngsters who were causing problems, but they needed help with social skills and their homework in order to succeed. The program organized the girls into two separate groups, one called Girls II Women and the other known as RAP, standing for Rogers Adolescent Program. Some of the girls who had started in one or the other of these programs at Rogers moved into a teen pregnancy prevention program when they reached middle school, getting an added dose of the same kind of medicine. The program for the Rogers girls operated largely during the after-school hours, giving youngsters wholesome late-afternoon activities of performing arts and discussion groups.

In Miami Beach, at the Fienberg-Fisher Elementary School, after-school classes with the explicit goal of building self-esteem were held for children from 3:00 to 4:30 in the afternoon and from 7:00 to 9:00 P.M. for parents. Each children's session had a specific theme. One day when the topic was learning how to take responsibility, the youngsters watched the theme played out through a puppet show. A puppet talked about taking charge of their lives and gave them ideas for achieving that goal. Parents, on the other hand, were assigned readings and delved into their own parents' parenting styles, trying to understand why they acted as they did with their own children. A self-confessional style was encouraged in the class for the parents; once they passed around a heart-shape object, and the person holding it was expected to speak from the soul.

Officials of the Neighborhood Academic Initiative at the University of Southern California maintained that it was students' sense of achievement in the program that kept female participants from getting pregnant. Leaving little to chance, however, the program not only helped students to feel better about themselves but reminded them regularly that they were too young to be sexually active. Females were warned that they would be under pressure for sex from older males. "I talk to them about not ruining the opportunity that awaits them for the sake of three minutes of pleasure," a program representative said.

More than most enhancement programs, the Neighborhood Academic Initiative took an "in-the-face" approach, getting involved in the most intimate parts of the students' lives.

In one instance, an eighth grade girl who was trying to act grown up around the friends of her 18-year-old sister took to stuffing her bra and flirting with older boys. At one point she told some of the youngsters in the enhancement program that she—a 14-year-old—was going to go out with a boy who was 17. A program official, hearing about this, asked her mother to confront the girl over her behavior. The older boy, it turned out, was a figment of the girl's imagination, invented to impress her friends. The following week, at one of the program's regularly scheduled group counseling sessions, the counselor brought up the episode and asked the girl in front of classmates why she thought this kind of behavior would win the admiration of others. Fellow students told her during the counseling session that not only were they unimpressed, but that she had acted stupidly. A discussion ensued about what older guys want from younger girls.

In many of the enhancement programs, efforts to develop human potential as a way of ensuring students' well-being begin by helping them to develop and appreciate their strengths so that they do not dwell on their shortcomings. It is easy, amid the ravages of poverty, for children to stop believing in themselves and to view the future not in light of possibilities but in terms of impending deprivations. Youngsters have to learn to care about themselves, to have enough concern to strive to change the circumstances in which they live. At the same time, they can grow as human beings and contribute to their community if they care about others. Community service has a place even among those accustomed to being on the receiving end of largesse. And, finally, human potential should be incubated in a milieu that encourages students to contribute toward a civil society—a not inconsiderable task for those who have witnessed and suffered from incivility in all its many forms.

Self-Image in an Impoverished Rural Setting

As the dairy industry has declined and economic pressures have increased in Rusk County, Wisconsin, the fabric of family life has been torn asunder, hastening changes similar to those that have ripped through society generally. Efforts to revive the local economy have clashed with the double reality of the region's locale—too far north for a good summer growing season and too far south for winter tourism. The specter of poverty lurks just behind the facades of the trailer homes that sometimes lack the most basic amenities of modern American existence—electricity and telephones. Even an occasional outhouse may still be seen.

One can drive for miles through Rusk County's Flambeau School District without seeing a person or any structure other than an occasional home, barn, or silo. It is a place where a sweep of the radio dial provides mostly country music and religious broadcasters. In general, the most successful students leave the area for greater opportunity; the others remain behind to emulate the arduous lives of their parents. This is a place where houses that cost $30,000 would fetch triple that amount three hours away in Minneapolis-St. Paul. The low cost of living is one of the most attractive rewards for contending with the isolation of northwest Wisconsin. Some people eke out a livelihood by combining subsistence farming with part-time jobs that pay modest wages. As a result, certain residents of Rusk County resent teachers simply because they regard educators, whose salaries in 1996 started at $23,535 and ranged up to $40,071, as an economically privileged class.

Hunting, however, is one of the pleasures that poverty cannot obliterate in Rusk County. People regard it as unexceptional that the cars and pick-up trucks that students drive to school have shotguns reposing within them, at the ready for stalking game. This also is a place where students may marry while still attending high school even though the female partner is not pregnant. A teacher remarked of one such wedding that involved a student who remained enrolled to obtain her diploma: "Her husband is a recent graduate of the high school, and they will both work in the turkey processing plant, make $28,000 a year between them, and be happy with that." This is Appalachia without the mountains. The poverty is so basic that a few Flambeau students are continually plagued by pangs of hunger. Eager for free meals, these students eat heartiest, according to their teachers, at the free lunches on Mondays and Fridays—gorging themselves before and after weekends at home without sufficient food.

A teacher who had taught in Detroit and Racine before arriving in Flambeau compared urban and rural poverty: "I thought that lots of the problems I saw were distinct to black Americans, but they are not. Many of those same problems exist here." She recalled meeting with a father in Rusk County who was raising his children alone. In the course of the conversation, she enumerated three steps that she suggested the father, who was clearly having trouble carrying out his parental duties, ought to take for his children—have two or three sets of clothing for each, provide them with the food and implements to make their own breakfasts and lunches since he spent long hours working next door in his shop, and establish a set time for them to go to bed. "He looked at me like I had just invented something great," the teacher said. "These things had never occurred to him. He thought it was enough for him to go hunting, shoot a deer, cut it up, and put it in the freezer for them to take when they were hungry."

Many of the children in the Flambeau schools, especially the older ones, recognized the oppressive economic conditions under which their parents, frequently with limited education, labored on the farm or in one of the area's few factories. "When the parents have no hope, the children don't either," said Pauline Lundgren, a teacher of remedial education at Glen Flora Elementary School. A high school student said that his father had been working almost a dozen years at one of the window frame factories and that "he absolutely hates it, but he doesn't have the training for anything higher paying."

The grim economic circumstances lowered the self-esteem of the parents and, in turn, sometimes made students doubt their own worth. A high school senior in a one-parent family said that her mother worked as a seamstress for a small manufacturer. "She's getting nowhere and they pay her hardly anything," the 17-year-old said of her 42-year-old mother. "There's no way she can raise three kids on that and, yet, she's the family income provider. She would try to go to work in one of the window factories, but pushing that pedal on the sewing machine for seven years has left her hip constantly hurting. So she can't do the factory jobs. There are some sewing machines there that let you stand up and put less stress on the hip, but they won't let her use one of those."

Critics scoff at the notion of schools striving to lift students' self-confidence. They assert that if schools restricted themselves to making substantial academic demands on students, then the youngsters, by virtue of gaining dominion over knowledge, would have more than enough reason for feeling good about themselves. Intellectual mastery does, in fact, lift one's sense of worth. The problem, however, is that students with low self-regard may resist learning in the first place. They may feel so downcast that they don't care about formal learning or they rationalize their refusal to learn.

Some educators in places like Flambeau proceed on the assumption that until kids have more regard for themselves their attitudes toward learning and almost everything else will suffer. Dick Varsho, the guidance counselor for the district's two elementary schools, saw as one of his main tasks the bolstering of students' confidence. His bywords, recited repeatedly, were "Make school fun." Varsho visited each classroom in both schools at least every other week. He spent his time speaking to children about such matters as getting along with each other, thinking about careers, avoiding drugs, making friends, cooperating, and following school rules. During the limited time he had available for intensive individual counseling, he took on the most pressing cases.

In one instance during 1996, for example, Varsho counseled a third grader who had reacted sharply to a child of Asian background who had transferred into the school. The child had never before knowingly encountered a member of a minority group in school and therefore had no firsthand negative experiences with such people. Yet he refused to sit near the Asian youngster and voiced his objections to "black people, niggers, and everyone else who was no good." It became apparent quickly to Varsho that the third grader's father, a ne'er-do-well who felt better only by trying to believe his whiteness made him superior to others, had inculcated this attitude in his son.

"The best thing we can do is produce a citizen with self-esteem, kids who are self-directed and sure of themselves," Dave Johnson, an administrator at Flambeau High School, said by way of explaining what the students needed most. "There are not enough opportunities here for students to succeed. It's a stacked deck." Thus signs, literal ones at that, of this effort showed up consistently in the schools of Flambeau. In an elementary classroom at Glen Flora School, for example, the "I Am Creed" hung on the wall. Its tenets were "I am unique in the world, I am capable of learning and growing daily" and several other similar expressions that culminated in the statement: "I pledge allegiance to myself, to try my best, to believe that I can do a good job . . ." Nearby hung another sign, listing "101 Ways to Praise a Child."

The search for self-confidence took Flambeau students on overnight trips—kayaking, rope climbing, and other challenges that required teamwork to succeed. In the winter, expeditions included dog sledding and camping. Students arranged for the transportation and the food and raised funds to pay their expenses. The idea was for students to learn to cope with challenging situations in which they could assume responsibility and bolster their self-confidence. "Some of them haven't experienced much success in the classroom, in athletics, or in a job," said Doug Spielman, the high school's guidance counselor, who pointed to the first-time success that can be enjoyed on such outings. "Not everyone has paddled a kayak across Lake Superior in four-foot waves."

Some academic courses, too, were developed with these goals in mind. A course in television production techniques, using an array of state-of-the-art equipment, was launched at the high school in 1991. The chance of Flambeau graduates landing jobs in the broadcast industry were about as likely as getting sunburned in a Wisconsin winter, but the school had other intentions. "It is a chance for students to present themselves," said Bob McMahon, the teacher. "They stand in front of a camera and get experience in public speaking. This builds confidence. I tell them that if they can do this they can go out and interview for a job, any job."

The Role of Caring

Students, for the sake of their sense of well being, need both to feel cared for and to cultivate a sense of caring about others. Such feelings can help them develop into empathetic adults. Robert N. Bellah and his colleagues in their noteworthy book *Habits of the Heart* observed that the ability to engage in caring nurtures interconnectedness.[2] If they feel uncared for during their growing-up years—a particular problem for children subject to the iniquities of poverty—young people may act in antisocial ways that impede their learning and undermine the atmosphere in the schools that they attend. Given the high levels of violence among today's children, it should be clear that society desperately needs to explore what can be done to engender feelings of caring. This imperative points to the need for young people also to develop healthy feelings of caring about themselves, not selfishness but feelings of worthiness.

For one youngster at I.S. 218 in Manhattan, knowing that others cared about him made all the difference in the world. When he arrived at the school as an immigrant from the Dominican Republic, he wore a bandanna and five earrings. He terrified teachers, classmates, and anyone else who crossed his path. He seemed to be fighting all the time and hardly attended classes. People throughout the school feared him. Then some parents involved with the Children's Aid Society and some teachers took him on as a reclamation project, flooding him with personal attention. The caring was intense, and he responded.

Less than a year later, the hostility and the constant battling had ceased. The bandanna and the earrings were gone. He even started wearing a necktie to school. Children's Aid arranged for the youngster to work in the store that it operated in the school, giving him a key to open the store each morning and letting him run the cash register. On days he was late for school, the store manager called his home to make certain he was okay. He struggled with English, but the caring and confidence that others showed in him spurred a transformation. He also was admitted into the school's intensive care education program that gave him extra attention without labeling him as disabled.

Caring, in effect, is a value rooted in relationships and takes on real meaning only in terms of how a person interacts with other people. Studies of the effects of caring are relatively new. The Lilly Endowment launched a research program on youth and caring in 1990 through the Chapin Hall Center for Children at the University of Chicago. Researchers found that caring and connectedness have a positive impact on the lives of children, protecting them against specific risk factors or stressful life events. "The experience of being cared for and the feelings of connectedness resulted in demonstrably greater well-being (and correspondingly less risky, health-

compromising behaviors) among teenagers in general and particularly among those one might expect to come to harm," the research
revealed. "The perception of a meaningful, caring relationship with
one's family was the strongest of the various factors that correlated
with emotional health."[3]

The family plays a key role as a provider of social capital and as a
buffer in this regard. It is, after all, a form of social capital when a
seven-year-old has someone to tuck him or her into bed and provide a
good-night kiss or when a 15-year-old has someone to hug him or her
and say "I understand" when the rest of the world seems on edge.
Some kids have no one to perform such acts for them. Is it any wonder
that they, in turn, show little caring for classmates and teachers?
Sometimes those working in enhancement programs despair of the
plights in which they find needy children. A representative from an I
Have a Dream project took home one particular student some nights
in the hope that she could provide the child with the caring that she
was not getting from her mother. The child had so many siblings living
at home that she received little attention. In addition, the child, still in
elementary school, was pressed into service regularly as the caregiver
for her younger siblings, hardly allowing her to enjoy her own
childhood. Taking the youngster home was a questionable act, but the
girl's plight certainly could not help but evoke sympathy.

Researchers have found that poverty is "the most pervasive,
persistent, and devastating" impediment to the development of caring,
pointing out its association with depleted neighborhoods, crowded
and unhealthy living conditions, limited access to health care and
other services, and single and/or teen parenthood.[4] Children's needs in
this regard were made abundantly clear to an I Have a Dream mentor
who got a call late one night from the mother of a student with whom
she had built a special bond. "They're going to take away my kids," the
single mother of three blurted in a panic. It turned out that the mother
had fallen behind on the rent on the two-room apartment in public
housing in which she lived with her children. The family was, in fact,
scheduled for eviction. The problem began when the mother's boss
accused her of breaking the stove in the fast-food shop in which she
worked. He was withholding most of her $95 in wages each week in
order to pay for the repairs, leaving the woman without enough money

to pay her rent. She could no longer afford even the bus fare and was walking the two miles to and from work.

The family was so poor that there were no lamps in the apartment; the only light emanated from the ceiling fixture in each room. There were only two chairs in the entire apartment, so the family could not even assemble around a table for a meal together. The mentor from I Have a Dream and a representative from the state's child advocacy office steered the mother to an office of the State Department of Labor, where she found sympathetic ears for her tale. A labor department representative intervened and got her pay restored, and the employer agreed to pursue the matter of the broken stove no further. The woman later obtained a new job, in a pizza shop. Such are the circumstances under which children of poverty live each day; yet people wonder why they do not do better in school.

The compassion that leads to caring need not be thought of as coddling. The Neighborhood Academic Initiative in Los Angeles took a tough-love approach toward the secondary students that the program was preparing to compete for entrance to selective colleges. "In general, we have to recognize they have a disadvantage in terms of where they live," said a counselor in the program. "But we won't accept this as an excuse for not achieving. They have to get past that. We get into their business in the most intimate way. We'll put it in their faces." In addition to the once-a-week group counseling sessions that students attended, counseling was available to their parents on Saturdays and sometimes on other days. The program helped to cushion the students over the bumps that beset their educational journey while continuing to hold them to high expectations.

Counseling sessions for the students boldly confronted every topic, no matter how uncomfortable it might have been for them. Counselors, for instance, would lead students through the intricacies of dealing with sex abuse in their families. Counselors also could be counted on to show up for funerals, all the while reminding students that the hand-holding did not relieve them of the responsibility to study. The lengths to which the program went to keep students from harm's way knew no bounds. One night, for instance, when a parent called a program representative to say that she feared that her daughter had run away, the program immediately mobilized people to search for the youngster. Early the next morning, people from the Neighborhood Academic Initiative began contacting other students, seeking leads to the girl's whereabouts. They visited 16 different homes until they found her. Caring was a palpable part of the program.

Caring, by improving relationships, provides building blocks for fashioning a better sense of community. Evidence gathered over more than nine years by the Developmental Studies Center in Oakland, California, indicated that a school can re-create itself as a caring community where students feel valued, a sense of connectedness, and responsibility to others. The center's child development project followed an original group of children from kindergarten through eighth grade and was then expanded to 12 elementary schools in six additional districts.[5]

A summary statement of the project concluded: "These results support the utility of an approach to education that attends to children's developmental needs; that tries to create school and classroom environments that are cohesive, supportive, and involving; and that engages students' intrinsic interest in academic activities and in promoting pro-social interpersonal relations."[6] While the approach did not work in every classroom, and some classrooms that were not part of the project showed gains as great as those in the project classrooms, the project demonstrated that caring can make a difference.

A report issued in 1996 by the National Association of Secondary School Principals urged educators to change high schools to make them more caring places that meet students' personal needs. One of the report's more than 80 recommendations proposed that "teachers will convey a sense of caring to their students so that their students feel that their teachers share a stake in their learning."[7] A result of such a policy was clear: In the words of a student at one school, Alexis Gonzales of El Puente Academy in Brooklyn, "By making you feel good, the school helps you learn more." Teachers of poor children especially need empathy to reduce the emotional insecurities that often interfere with the children's learning.[8]

There are two sides to caring. On the one hand, students who feel uncared for can respond favorably when they start thinking that others care about them. But some enhancement programs predicate

themselves on the idea that youngsters—even those from needy
circumstances—can stir good feelings within themselves also by
caring about others. In other words, they become givers of care, not
simply recipients. As long ago as 1989, the Children's Defense Fund
urged youth service programs to enlist disadvantaged students as a
way to improve the youngsters' self-worth and chances for success.[9] El
Puente Academy took this matter seriously in its admonition to
students to "give back" to the community. The director and staff
members saw themselves contributing through their work at the
school and they tried to inculcate among students a similar feeling for
service to community. "Giving back to the community is expected as
an obligation of membership in El Puente and of enrollment in the
Academy," observed an evaluation report on the school, noting that
this sense was reflected in the curriculum and in project activities that
young people undertook in human rights, peace, and justice.[10]

William Milliken, founder and president of Communities in
Schools, also talked of the importance of "giving back" and the sense
of caring that youngsters can achieve from community service. Local
and national organizations have arisen to guide schools and their
students into service activities. The Corporation for National Service
in Washington is among the most prominent, but there are also such
local programs as Kids in Action in Baltimore.

An example of students as caregivers could be found at Baltimore's
Canton Middle School. Some of its more troubled sixth and seventh
graders served as volunteers in a nursing home, a soup kitchen, and
the public library. They also helped with neighborhood cleanups, and
some performed community service in the school itself, aiding in
classrooms, the library, and the cafeteria. Some of the girls were
invited—without being told why they were chosen—to form a Girl
Scout troop, a vehicle not only for community service but also a way
to organize their social life. The troop was so successful that other girls
in the school who were not part of the target group joined. The school
hoped that by showing more care for others, the students would
summon within themselves the resources to allow them to find their
way out of their own difficulties.

Community service was also a vehicle for teaching care and
responsibility to some of the students at Miami Beach's Fienberg-

Fisher Elementary School who were most at-risk of verging into problematic behavior. The students were paired with a contingent from a private school—peer role models, presumably—and, together, youngsters from the two schools conducted such activities as a park cleanup or a collection of donations to aid poor children in Haiti or a play session with a group of children with Down's Syndrome. The service activities were reinforced by weekly curriculum units that dealt with the importance of helping others.

Two police officers regularly accompanied the students on their community service outings, providing an implicit lesson on the role that police can play as friendly and supportive figures. They gave the children T-shirts to wear during the activities, shirts emblazoned with the acronym GREAT, standing for Gang Resistance Education and Training. All of this was done in full recognition of the fact that as sixth graders, preparing to go on to junior high school, they would become candidates for recruitment by gangs. "We talk extremely openly about gangs, drugs, and sex," said Allison Tomchin, a staff member at Fienberg-Fisher. "We tell them: Join a gang and you will end up in jail or dead. We take them to hear talks by prisoners in prisons, and we bring in ex-gang members to speak to them."

On a day when the students had returned from painting out graffiti on the walls at Miami Beach High School, they were eating pizza in the shaded courtyard of their school, joined by the two policemen who had accompanied them. "This is a chance to interact with the kids in a nonauthoritive way," said Sergeant Richard Weissman, who, as coincidence would have it, was the son of one of Fienberg-Fisher's assistant principals. "This is also why we dress casually." Weissman and his partner, Officer Rigoberto Olivera, each wore shorts, sneakers, a T-shirt, and a baseball cap.

Students at Expo Middle School in St. Paul, Minnesota, engaged in a stunning array of community service activities. Expo did not have a service requirement per se but strived to make service integral to education. "Kids need experience in the larger community to know the resources," said the then principal, Joan Sorensen. "They also need to know the opportunities that are out there and to know about careers." Thus it was during a typical semester that 9 students were trained as puppeteers to perform for children in elementary schools, 4 students read books to the blind, and 34 students participated in a neighborhood gardening project. Several dozen other students created hands-on activities to celebrate Black History Month at the Children's Museum. Numbers of students at Expo helped throughout the year on food, clothing, and toy drives for people who were poor or homeless. Still others made gifts and decorations for the dining room of a senior citizens' center, and another group, who had learned to knit and crochet in the school's after-school program, made lap rugs and slippers that they donated to the American Red Cross. They had been taught to knit by senior citizens they worked with as volunteers. After building a rapport with the seniors, the students joined them on a trip to an elementary school, where the seniors and the middle school students taught the younger children to knit.

Expo students who were not yet ready to go into the larger community prepared to do so by performing tasks in the school. Thus students swept floors, wiped down tables in the cafeteria, chipped ice on the playground during freezing weather, set up chairs for assemblies, cleaned graffiti, picked up litter, and cleaned the glass of the trophy cases—all to bolster their sense of responsibility before sending them to perform service outside the school. "I don't want kids going out until they are ready," said Josie Ahartz, who supervised the service program. "I don't want them to fail on the outside."

Ultimately, in most of the service projects involving enhancement programs, the aim is to find ways to let students discover the caring side of themselves by helping others. And evidence shows that this can happen. In their study of Beacon schools in New York City, Michele Cahill and Karen Pittmann found that youth programs often conveyed caring very effectively to participants. According to the authors, these programs (1) created an atmosphere in which young people felt welcome, respected, and comfortable; (2) structured opportunities for the development of caring relationships with adults and peers; (3) provided information, counseling, and expectations that enabled young people to determine what it meant to care for themselves and to care for a definable group; and (4) provided opportunities, training, and expectations that encouraged young people to contribute to the greater good through service, advocacy, and active problem solving on important issues.[11]

The Civic Imperative

Young people who care about their school and about society generally would seem less likely to engage in oppositional behavior.
Furthermore, in the long run, youth participation in activities that
engender their civic identity may well lead to their assuming social
responsibility for the community's well-being as adults.[12] Time after
time, enhancement programs have tried to strengthen students' sense
of well-being in ways that would affect their value systems. Those
who shed feelings of alienation tend to behave in socially acceptable
ways that promote their own sense of well-being and that of the
community. "When there is an atmosphere of trust and honesty," said
Nitopia Walker, a student at El Puente Academy, "you are willing to
open yourself up because you know you won't get hurt. This is not
heaven on earth, but it is a place where you can be yourself."

In the CARE program (Creating a Responsible Environment) at
Clay Middle School in Clay County, West Virginia, the first period each
Monday was devoted to teaching a specific lesson related to the
youngsters' development as future citizens. Teachers in all courses
were supposed to reinforce the lesson through the remainder of the
week. Among the topics covered during a period of two months in the
middle of the 1996-97 school year were the meaning of stereotypes
and the problems that can arise from stereotyping people, the characteristics associated with dependability, the effects of fads on society, the
events of Martin Luther King, Jr.'s childhood that helped shape his
life's work, the difficulty of judging the behavior of other people, and
the importance of minority and majority opinions.

In the lesson about judging the behavior of others, for example,
the students were presented with six cases involving infractions by
teens of their age, cases revolving mostly around thefts of various
kinds—from stores, from a student's locker, from a break-in at a
house. One case involved a student who wrote term papers for his
friends. Students were asked for their ideas about the sorts of
punishments appropriate in each instance. "We are committed to
developing civic virtue and moral character in our students for a
more responsible and caring society," Clay Middle School said in a
booklet describing CARE.

One of the 12 ways in which diploma candidates at the Unidale Learning Center in St. Paul could validate their knowledge to get credit toward graduation was by demonstrating the ability to be an informed and responsible citizen. This alternative school offered few actual classes, so it was up to the student to assemble a portfolio consisting of papers, projects, and assignments. The ten-step process in citizenship, which could take as little or as much time as the student deemed necessary to do the work, started with a requirement to read a newspaper or watch the television news each day for a month, keeping a journal of up to a page a day of the news and recording reactions to it. After this step, the student had to demonstrate knowledge of the process of voter registration and elections. This called for finding out where to register to vote, defining and discussing the absentee ballot, learning the name of one's state senator, and learning about political action committees, lobbyists, and caucuses.

Third, the student investigated a current sociological issue by finding articles about it, recording television coverage, interviewing people, and attending events and meetings on the issue. Ultimately the information was used to write a paper or make an oral presentation or produce an audio- or videotape on the issue. Further steps to gain validation in the citizenship sequence involved analyzing at least three world events or issues, participating in discussions of current events, writing a letter to the editor of a local newspaper, showing an understanding of the Constitution and the laws and rights affecting citizens, carrying out a project on world geography, and demonstrating an understanding of basic economic principles.

A stress on values also underpinned the Neighborhood Academic Initiative. Cheating of any kind was condemned. As an extension of this philosophy, each student was expected to complete his or her own homework with no excuses and no borrowing from classmates. The teaching of values was embedded in classroom activities. This could be seen one morning in one of the Academic Initiative's courses for high school students on the campus of the University of Southern California. Laura Williams, a young English teacher, began her class by having students, in turn, read aloud the tenets of the academy's code of ethics:

Since I am no better than any other human being, I will treat everyone, regardless of age, race, or gender, with dignity and respect.

Since I need love, kindness, consideration, and encouragement, I will strive to be loving in my relations with my fellow scholars, to be kind and considerate when they do not perform or behave in ways I expect, to offer encouragement when things go badly for them.

Since I am not perfect, I will forgive my peers and others when they behave imperfectly.

Since I am dedicated to being the most productive scholar I can be, I will conduct all of my affairs—those at the USC Pre-College Enrichment Academy, at my home school, at home, and in my community—with honesty, maturity, sincerity, and dignity.

Since I am a scholar who has a great opportunity to better my life through the acquisition of knowledge and, because I am intelligent and motivated, I will succeed in all my academic and social endeavors.

It was in this same vein that one of the courses for students in the program explored issues related to citizenship. The 30 black and Latino high school students fit into the small classroom on the campus of the University of Southern California only by shoving the chair-desks close together. After completing the oath, they took their text from George Orwell's *Animal Farm,* a book they had been reading and discussing for several class sessions. The teacher went to the board and, without saying anything, wrote: "Power Corrupts."

"Let's take a look at the primaries," she said, trying to draw the youngsters into a discussion of the 1996 political campaign that was unfolding for the Republican nomination for president. "I asked you to follow the campaign and you're reading a book about political power and leaders." She suggested that they examine the code of ethics that they had recited a few minutes earlier against the backdrop of the political campaign and *Animal Farm.* "You're going to be leaders; some of you may go into politics. Apply the code of ethics to politics, to the Republican primary."

A student responded almost immediately: "Pat Buchanan is breaking number one in the code of ethics; he's not treating everyone with respect, homosexuals."

"Why do you say that?"

"He should respect people so that they will vote for him," the student said.

"How do you know he's not treating people with respect?"

"He said he didn't want gay people in his campaign," the student responded.

"Why is that a problem according to the code of ethics?" the teacher asked, prodding the student to reflect more deeply.

The student said nothing.

"So then it's not a problem," the teacher said.

Another student jumped in. "He's prejudiced against homosexuals."

"I didn't hear him say he didn't want their votes," the teacher challenged the student. "So I don't see the prejudice."

"The code," the male student said. "It says you will treat everyone with respect. If you told me you didn't want me in your classroom it will take away some of my dignity. He has to be an example. I don't particularly like being around gay people either, but I know that's not right."

"The code of ethics says you will treat everyone with respect," another student said in support of his classmate.

"Well, should they be role models?" the teacher asked in regard to politicians.

"No, there are other leaders who can be role models who are positive, like musical artists," another student chimed in.

"What are you telling me?" the teacher asked no one in particular. "Politicians shouldn't be role models? I'm not getting it."

Another student: "In politics, they should not be role models. They want power. That's not what people should be looking forward to. They are in politics for power."

Here was an opening to segue into *Animal Farm* and the hierarchy of power that had been established in the barnyard. "Take a look at *Animal Farm*," the teacher proposed. "Old Major dies and who comes to power?"

The students responded as one: "Snowball and Napoleon."

And so the discussion continued as the students used *Animal Farm* as an entry point to an exploration of civic virtue. It seemed to amount to the kind of conversation that Richard W. Paul, an authority on the teaching of thinking, had in mind in writing that "what students need in civic education . . . is precisely what they need in moral education: not indoctrination into abstracted ideals, not slogans and empty moralizing, but assignments that challenge their ability to use civic ideals to assess actual political behavior."[13]

A Sense of Academic Initiative

THREE

TEN

A Foundation for Achievement

James Fleming structured the Neighborhood Academic Initiative in Los Angeles so that students would grow convinced that they could succeed. The program had an almost cultlike aura to it, with regular recitations of pledges by students—formally called "scholars"—and their parents. The word became the deed as hardworking students discovered, lo and behold, that they were making it. Starting the school day in classes every morning on the campus of the University of Southern California was an uplifting experience for these secondary school students, however inconvenient it may have been. Their spirits soared, they felt better about themselves, and they began to speak of prospects for the future, a dead-end subject in the minds of many kids in south-central Los Angeles.

Self-discipline and the work ethic threaded their way through the lives of these students six days a week. From Monday through Friday their classes began at 7:30 in the morning at USC, in the very same buildings in which the university students reported for their courses. Later in the morning they were bused to their home schools, where they took the remainder of their classes. High school–level students had to return to the university campus at least two afternoons a week for tutoring if they received less than a B in any course. All of the junior high school students were tutored three days a week at their home schools. On Saturdays the students spent mornings in tutoring sessions, again at USC. And these attendance requirements were but one small part of the strict regimen to which students had to adhere.

"What makes them different from the other kids," said Kate McFadden, a teacher at one of the junior high schools the students attended, "is their attitude. They believe that they will succeed if they do the work. They are more self-confident than the others because they are trained by the program to be that way. This is not phony self-esteem. These kids know they can make it because they have done the work. I've never worked so hard on designing curriculum, but it's worth it. I've never been so rewarded as a teacher as I have in working with the kids in this program. You assign homework to 34 students and you get 34 papers back. All of them hand in work. With the rest of the students in the school, you get about 60 percent turning in homework." This enhancement program helped create the circumstances by which several hundred inner-city students were able to readjust their sights and aim higher than most of their classmates in their home schools.

It took one of the most ambitious and intensive enhancement programs described in this book to enable these students to combat the negative influences that pressed against them from almost every direction. The students' attainment resulted from carefully controlling the academic temperature—erecting a kind of hothouse. The students started out with few of the advantages that confer an abundance of social capital on advantaged youngsters. Unlike those advantaged youngsters, they did not know from an early age what was expected of them and where they were headed. The program illustrated the extent to which a school culture friendly to achievement determines how hard students will work on behalf of academic success. Other enhancements also tried to create this kind of climate. At I.S. 218 in New York City, for example, the effort was underscored by the words on a bulletin board that had been decorated for career day to carry the following message:

C communication

A aspiration

R responsibility

E excellence

E education

R role model

D duties

A attention

Y youth

Near this bulletin board was a student-made poster saying: "If you believe it, you can be it." And, farther down the corridor, still another poster: "How to Study—Read Your Class Notes, Work with a Friend, Turn Off the Television, Memorize Facts, Test Yourself, Find a Quiet Place, Sit in a Chair." The school's regularly changing bulletin boards, like wall posters in China, were meant to rally students to the cause of better education. Each class took responsibility for the bulletin board outside its room and tried to outdo other classes. In a section of the building devoted to a program with a business theme, a class posted the following:

> Creative 218 team is very proud of its team effort. The holiday cards taught us a very good lesson. The printing group did a sloppy job and we lost business because of it. People did not want to buy the cards. We also worked too slow and did not meet our deadline. Valentine's Day cards were carefully printed and we used better paper. Those cards sold fast and we had customers that were not able to buy because we did not make enough to keep up with the demand. Next Christmas we are not going to package the cards by 20. We decided to sell them as single cards. Working as a business has helped us believe in ourselves. We are determined to succeed.

Another sort of influence, the negativity of the culture of the streets, casts a pall over efforts to get students to devote themselves to serious schoolwork. Rosemary Allen, a teacher whose classroom in Newark was allied with the Communities in Schools program, spoke of a clash of cultures between what the school asks of inner-city children when they are inside the building and what the neighborhood and the streets demand of them on the outside. "I tell them to decide who and what they want to be and then to hold their ground," she said. "I grew up in Newark and I had to go through this, but not to the extent that they do."

Yet this is not to say that school culture necessarily favors scholastic achievement. Even suburban students sometimes face derision for taking their studies too seriously. The attacks on school achievement have grown so unremitting in certain sectors that students do not want to go to the stage to accept awards at assemblies lest they face ridicule by peers. The fact is that high school—for students in all socioeconomic groups—revolves around peer approval. Taking schoolwork seriously is not a route to popularity for many American teenagers. "High achievers are 'swimming against the developmental tide' of adolescence, in which one is expected to replace dependence upon adults with an autonomous sense of identity and a capacity to make one's own decisions and chart one's own course in life," said the University of Wisconsin's B. Bradford Brown.[1] Students who resist working hard in school usually see no reason for altering their approach. The vast majority of colleges accept almost all applicants, and potential employers seldom ask about grades and test scores in high school or college.

This dismissal of scholastic striving has deep roots in American soil. "Again and again, it has been noticed that intellect in America is resented as a kind of excellence, as a claim to distinction, as a challenge to egalitarianism, as a quality which almost certainly deprives a man or woman of the common touch," historian Richard Hofstadter wrote more than a generation ago.[2] In this connection, Harvard University, in the decade after World War I, was anything but friendly to Jewish applicants; they were thought to study too hard.[3]

America's youth often sneer at exhortations to put off enjoyment and strive in school. They see too many examples of behavior that refutes this approach. The pursuit of instant gratification in the 1980s, after all, produced both the crack epidemic that gripped street corners uptown in Harlem and the plague of avarice that held sway downtown on Wall Street. The legacy of that decade continues, and the lessons are not lost on the young. Teachers at all levels face classrooms full of students who eschew hard work. Resistance to long hours of study and unwillingness to struggle with difficult assignments are de rigueur among many students of all socioeconomic stripes. The National Assessment of Educational Progress has found in its various examinations that many students do not push themselves to delve into the deeper thinking that would enable them to go beyond the basics in reading, writing, and mathematics and reach the highest levels of proficiency.

Building a sense of academic aspiration was difficult, for example, among some Flambeau High School students whose families eked out a living by subsistence farming in northwestern Wisconsin. These students, on the brink of adulthood, thought they saw all they needed to survive. And education was not in the calculus. They saw trees to harvest, cows to milk, and vegetables waiting to be pulled from the ground; they could not imagine a life other than one that might include a little farming and a job in one of the factories or at the local mine. "We still battle with families that tell students that they don't need to go beyond high school and, probably, don't even need that much education, that they can make a living from the land," said Doug Spielman, the sole guidance counselor at the high school. A student in a group that Spielman took to visit the local technical college told him that he did not need any further education, that he already had access to "all that I need in life—the prettiest women, the best beer, and the most land." The student added: "I feel sorry for those who feel driven to get more education. They're suckers."

The problem may reach its nadir among poor minority students, particularly black males. Jim Brown, the retired football star, who carried out a personal crusade in prisons and high schools through his Amer-I-can program to arouse black America to the need for change, stated: "The basic way to succeed in America is through education, hard work, and dedication, but what we have happening today with young African-Americans is they're shooting each other or filling up the prisons."[4]

A seminal study by Signithia Fordham and John U. Ogbu found that black students experience "inordinate ambivalence" in regard to academic effort and success, "partly because white Americans traditionally refused to acknowledge that black Americans are capable of intellectual achievement, and partly because black Americans subsequently began to doubt their own intellectual ability, began to define academic success as white people's prerogative, and began to discourage their peers, perhaps unconsciously, from emulating white people in academic striving. . . ."[5] Trying to do well in school, in other words, became "acting white." Anyone who wonders about the pressures that this identity crisis, this living in two worlds, puts on black youths—and on black teachers too for that matter—would do well to read Fordham's latest book, *Blacked Out*.[6]

Thus in neighborhoods in which scholastic attainment seems most irrelevant to the rest of life, students may receive the least support for putting forth effort in the classroom. Some black students have told researchers that their attempts at scholastic diligence place them in physical jeopardy. One such student spoke of "being beaten up in high school by classmates who disapproved of his interest in ideas and his attention to schoolwork." When he finally made it to a university, he said that one of the features that was special to him was that "you can read in the hall or in the steps, and nobody will throw a brick at you."[7]

Psychologist Claude M. Steele discovered that even those black students who work hard and succeed in school internalize their own pressure because of fear of faltering and thereby confirming stereotypes. What he and his fellow researchers at Stanford University labeled "stereotype threat" hinders the progress of blacks—and perhaps, in the same way, the progress of female students of all races. According to Steele, who laid out his theory in a speech at the Educational Testing Service, the anxiety caused by this fear can make those so afflicted perform below the level of which they are capable. "Stereotype threat can have lifelong consequences," he said in a discussion of his work. "You don't have to believe the stereotype to be threatened by it."

Efforts to Counter Negativity

The Children's Aid Society in New York City tried to encourage achievement by using volunteers and mentors who showed children that it was okay to be smart and do well in school, that a student could care about his or her studies and still be cool. Martha Cameron of Children's Aid said that she was pleasantly surprised when she asked young people at one of the organization's centers to tell her about themselves and one started out by saying "I'm smart." Cameron expected the students to withhold such statements out of concern of eliciting resentment and disdain. Enhancement programs try to build a structure of support around participants to make them favorably disposed toward their studies and then to reinforce this attitude. "We think the program affects their value system," said Mindee Barham, a project director in I Have a Dream. "We try to keep them focused on where they are going and on what they have to do to get there. What we are trying to do is find a way—whether through counseling, through tutoring, through sports—to touch each kid and help form a personal relationship."

At the Neighborhood Academic Initiative, it was a matter of creating a culture in which learning was honored and those who strived to learn were respected. The program never let students forget about the high goals that they had pledged to achieve. Youngsters in the program fed off each other, reinforcing each other's desire for success. They outfitted themselves in ways that physically identified them as learners, wearing prescribed clothes and carrying their books in backpacks, a surefire symbol of nerdism in the inner city. Most of the students ended up getting better grades than counterparts who were not in the program.

Mike Laska, who taught mathematics to seventh and eighth graders at Foshay Learning Center, one of the schools from which the Academic Initiative drew students, said that almost all of those in the program earned As and Bs and that only a trickle got Cs. By contrast, anywhere from a third to a half of other seventh and eighth graders—those not in the program—failed math, Laska said. A problem, though, was that the Neighborhood Academic Initiative, like some other enhancement programs, did not accept students until they reached secondary school. "By this time, behaviors are entrenched and second nature," warned Antoine Gayles, the Cities in Schools project director at Bobby Brooks Academy in Newark.

The Neighborhood Academic Initiative recruited new students as they completed the sixth grade. Much of this recruitment consisted of visiting the participating feeder schools to speak to groups of sixth graders. James Fleming, a burly, almost intimidating man, disabused the youngsters of any misconceptions they may have had about the exacting program. At one such recruiting session, he cut to the quick, making it clear as soon as he strode to the front of the room, where several sixth-grade classes had assembled to hear the presentation, that the program was about more than academic achievement. The chairs were filled and more sixth graders kept streaming into the room. "I expect the young men to get up and give the seats to the young ladies," he said in a tone that left no doubt that his expectations were not open to debate. Some boys, afraid to do otherwise, immediately surrendered their seats to girls who were standing and went to sit on the floor in the open area in front of Fleming.

Fleming was a walking, talking role model—by design. He made it a point each day to groom himself fastidiously in suit and tie, a handkerchief poking out of the breast pocket and his moustache meticulously trimmed. His shoes were always freshly shined. He was all marine drill sergeant as he told the group of 11-year-olds that he was offering them the opportunity of a lifetime. Then, he paused. "I hear a murmur and it's going to stop," he said sharply. "In the academy, we stop inappropriate activity on the spot so it doesn't recur. I'm talking about the rest of your life here." He told the children that "before you know it, you'll be in the 12th grade. You must prepare and get ready for the rest of your life."

He explained that the program was different from anything they had known until that point—harder, more rigorous, more demanding, more in-your-face. "We are trying to prepare you to be excellent scholars," he elaborated. "You'll have the skills, character, knowledge, and wisdom not only to come into USC but to do extremely well, to flourish. There's no problem you'll bring to us that we will not work with you to solve. When I look at you, I see doctors and lawyers and senators and schoolteachers—successful young men and women. I see more than Michael Jordan. We're not talking about basketball; we're talking about your *life*."

Fleming described some of the classes that students would take on the campus of the University of Southern California as junior high students. He spoke of courses in language arts and in study skills, which he said included instruction in time management, note-taking, decision making, research, and critical thinking. From this point, he said the students would go on to take high school courses in English and mathematics on the university campus. Tutoring was mandatory during the junior high school years, Fleming said, and was required in high school for those whose marks in any subject fell to a C. This stark picture of high expectations was constructed on a foundation of work, work, work. The Neighborhood Academic Initiative sought to use achievement as the paving material for the road that would carry these black and Latino youngsters out of the ghetto, if only their young eyes could see that far into the distance. Fleming talked about the places that students would go as participants in the program—the Museum of Tolerance, concerts of the Los Angeles Symphony in the Hollywood Bowl, cookouts on the beach, picnics in the park. These field trips, he told them, were meant to enrich them academically and develop them socially. "All of the pieces fit together," he said, "to make a whole educational experience."

Fleming turned over speaking duties to Exhibit A and Exhibit B, two students in the program who could attest to its redeeming qualities. First, Karina, an eleventh grader spoke with assurance despite the shyness that she said had ruled her just a few years earlier: "You have to say to yourself that 'I want to be in this because I want to improve my life,' not because your best friend is joining or someone told you to join. This is like your second family, the people you see everyday from 7:30 till 5:30. You form your friendships here. We encourage each other; we don't put each other down. I'm going to have to be prepared to compete in college with students who had computers in their homes since they were born. They have had opportunities that we haven't had. My parents couldn't afford to buy books. I missed a lot. The academy gives you the chance to catch up."

Then came Alex, a tenth grader, polished and brimming with confidence: "You have a problem at home, you go to the academy and say 'I need help.'" He likened academy students to newly planted seeds. "The academy provides the soil, the water, the minerals. You are the future. You will shape the world. Should you think about football or basketball or about your own future?" The answer was tacitly implied. He told the youngsters, who were just four years younger than he, that they would end up working at McDonald's if they did not banish thoughts of sports from their minds and focus on what was going to become of them. "Take a step now. Think about it. Think about what you want to become . . . a cash register operator or the president of the United States."

The effort to inculcate a work ethic—part of a sense of academic initiative—dominated the Neighborhood Academic Initiative and figured, to varying degrees, in most enhancement programs around the country. Youngsters struggling to overcome modest circumstances were urged to place their hopes in diligence, a not inconsiderable leap of faith for those who had seen precious few examples in their short lives of people whose industriousness enabled them to escape the clutches of poverty. Furthermore, allegiance to this credo had to withstand the scoffing of peers who portrayed such attention to schoolwork as a betrayal of group values.

Self-discipline in the form of good study habits plays a fundamental role in cultivating academic initiative. The acquisition of good study habits equips young people to build structure in their lives instead of submitting to unpredictability. When the troubled school system in the District of Columbia sought to halt the academic disintegration in 18 of its high schools, a six-week academic preparedness project was instituted for incoming ninth and tenth graders in the fall of 1995. The aim—in this instance perhaps too little, too late—was to help them erect a foundation on which to attain success in high school. Thus the emphasis was on assisting students to communicate better, solve problems, think critically, make decisions, and learn independently. Similarly, much of the academic emphasis in the summer REACH program for young black males in suburban Cleveland dealt with learning how to learn, moving students away from the idea that education consists merely of memorizing facts. Clarence Lewis, a Cleveland Public Schools science teacher who worked in REACH found satisfaction in teaching students the scientific method so that they could become better observers and pose questions to direct their inquiries.

Inculcating such skills in students is a widespread goal in enhancement programs. The MegaSkills that are the subject of Dorothy Rich's writings got the attention of students, teachers, and parents at the Expo Middle School in St. Paul, Minnesota. Rich is an author who specializes in writing about how the school and the home can work together on behalf of students. The skills were listed on posters hanging in classrooms and contained on flyers sent home with children. Teachers were expected to figure out ways to incorporate the skills into their lessons. The 10 MegaSkills are confidence, motivation, effort, responsibility, initiative, perseverance, caring, teamwork, common sense, and problem solving. "They are the values that undergird our work ethic, our national character, and our personal behavior," Rich wrote.[8]

AVID's program to build a foundation for learning involved an ambitious effort to get underachieving, disadvantaged students to concentrate more intensely on lessons imparted in the classroom. The program, which began in 1980 in San Diego, spread across the United States in the 1990s. The essence of the program was the requirement that participants learn to be assiduous note-takers who used notes in all of their courses to probe the deeper meaning of what was taught. Students had to systematically record the notes and their daily assignments in loose-leaf binders.

The contents of the binders were marked weekly; grades depended on the notes' quality and on the elaborations students recorded as they reflected on the meaning and significance of what they noted. Students in AVID said that the program forced them to be more organized and gave them a way to focus more directly on the lessons. "What's important about AVID is the discipline it gives you," said Luz Vargas, a first-year student in the program. "It makes it easier to follow a routine and that carries over to the rest of your life. You get organized. You learn to be responsible."

The AVID course was an elective; students in middle school or high school enrolled voluntarily, often on the recommendations of teachers. The scholastic records of applicants were reviewed and often they were interviewed. The program strived to find students in need who were committed to improving their academic performance. Middle schoolers usually took AVID courses in the seventh and eighth grades; high school students started in the ninth or tenth grade and remained in AVID until they graduated.

AVID provided an underpinning for all of a student's subjects throughout his or her secondary schooling. The AVID class met daily;

two days covered such topics as note-taking, test-taking skills, and time management, and two days were devoted to tutoring sessions that helped participants with subject-area courses. On Fridays, students' notes and binders were checked and guest speakers made presentations. Students were encouraged to write extensively and to collaborate in their studies.

Part of the AVID process—aside from anything the subject-area teacher did—required students to formulate questions as a way of thinking about their lessons. The questions arose on three increasingly complex levels. First, on level 1, came questions having to do with such tasks as defining, describing, or listing the elements of the lesson. On level 2, the student posed questions that involved such work as analyzing, contrasting, or inferring. On level 3, the questions required the student, for instance, to apply a principle, develop a hypothesis, or speculate on outcomes.

A program like AVID points students in the right direction. Studies by researchers at the University of Wisconsin have shown that students who commit themselves to the goals of schooling and to getting ahead in the system consequently invest the effort required for success.[9] On the other hand, a considerable number of students are not imbued with a work ethic. Jerome H. Bruns, who spent more than 20 years as a teacher, counselor, and school psychologist, estimated that as many as 20 percent of American public school students are "work inhibited." He said: "They do not stay on task, do not complete class assignments, do not finish their homework on their own."[10]

A college student who was an instructor in REACH saw the goal in terms of three habits that he wanted to instill in the middle-school students with whom he worked: to take good notes in class, to pay close attention to the lesson, and to do their homework consistently, objectives not unlike those of AVID. Such goals may sound obvious, but many students lack them. Yet those who have these habits enjoy a distinct advantage in attaining scholastic success. From its inception, REACH—again, not unlike AVID—saw itself having an impact in terms of affecting *how* students go about doing their schoolwork.

"Focus" is a word that arises repeatedly in attempts to identify what makes a difference when students succeed in enhancement programs. The work of being a student requires concentration. Serious students in enhancement programs come to realize that they must resist distractions. Often it seems that the universe surrounding young people, especially those on whom poverty impinges, conspires to break their focus on academic matters. Schools and families battle to equip young people with the wherewithal to maintain focus. Learning can be hard work. The journey, like the odyssey of Ulysses, is replete with temptations to go astray for children with few models and scant reinforcement for their academic efforts. "African American males face tremendous pressure when they choose an academic path." said Eric Dina, a student at the University of Cincinnati who was a teacher in the REACH program in suburban Cleveland. "A focused student will be successful in whatever environment he is in."

Focus alone, however, may not be enough. Successful students—and, for that matter, people who achieve success in life generally—have the ability to bounce back. They do not let setbacks discourage them. Resilience is "the set of attributes that provides people with the strength and fortitude to confront the overwhelming obstacles they are bound to face in life."[11] Students must gain a sense of resilience in order to maintain their focus on demanding academic tasks, especially in disadvantaged settings when even persistence may not appear to pay dividends. Students have to learn to tolerate frustration and even failure.

Young people who are unaccustomed to high expectations may not recognize that failure to reach a goal on the first try does not constitute reason to give up. Those on whom demands have not been made may not be aware that success can require repeated attempts. "We have to let them know that even if they fail we still expect them to do it," said Ron Lewis of the national office of Communities in Schools. When educational researchers identified the most important elements for improving urban schools and pulled them together under six thematic areas, one of them had to do with the need for school environments that foster resilience.[12] Advocates of the higher standards espoused by President Clinton in his 1997 State of the Union Message must prepare themselves to ensure that students are taught the lessons of resilience along with the more demanding courses they will have to take.

Researchers at the National Center on Education in the Inner Cities at Temple University embarked on an ongoing study in 1996 to determine the characteristics of schools and communities that tend to promote resilience in children—and that continue to do so even as the cast of principals and teachers changes. In other words, how may a school institutionalize resilience in its culture in ways that outlast professional staff turnover? Margaret C. Wang, director of the center, said that such schools mobilize community resources to provide an additional network of support of their most needy students.[13] An important basis for such studies is the research of Emily C. Werner and Ruth S. Smith, who studied children from troubled and impoverished families in Hawaii over 30 years, beginning in 1955. They found that resilience figured most prominently in the success of those who prevailed. Three factors that loomed prominently in children's resilience were their positive temperaments, strong relationships with parents or parent substitutes, and a community support network.[14]

In other research, Patricia Gandara found in a study of 50 Chicanos who rose from low-income circumstances to earn medical and law degrees and Ph.D.s that a key factor in their success was someone who set an example by continually striving despite poverty. This positive attitude of their parents or caregivers caused the children to believe in future possibilities.[15] Thus resilience arises partially from within a person but also owes something to social capital, a fact underscored by the list of developmental assets identified by Peter Benson, president of Search Institute.[16] A system of support that includes parents and other adults proves crucial in building these assets that underpin resilience.

Industrious attitudes stoke the fires of resilience, and perhaps the most industrious attitudes in modern America are those that are imported. High school honor rolls around the country disproportionately contain the names of young people from China, India, the countries of southeast Asia, and the former Soviet republics, most of whom entered schools in the United States not even speaking English. Thomas Sowell of Stanford University's Hoover Institution said that the habits and beliefs that these immigrants carry with them to this country along with their meager belongings constitute the "cultural capital" that earns them success.[17]

Psychology professor Laurence Steinberg and his colleagues asserted that students of Asian background were more apt than others in schools in the United States to believe that *not* doing well in school would have negative consequences for their future.[18] When Thuy Dinh got a diploma from the University of Virginia in 1996, for instance, he was the sixth of six siblings to graduate from that institution. Their parents fled Vietnam in 1975 with little more than a dream, a dedication to higher education, and a belief in the ennobling quality of hard work. "A lot of people have lost faith about being able to succeed, like the old American dream no longer exists," said Thuy Dinh. "But if we can come over here with virtually nothing, if we were able to do it, I think other people can, too. You have to have a lot of faith and respect for one another, and then just go out and do what you have to."[19]

ELEVEN

The Promise of a Better Future

Enhancement programs never stop looking for ways to raise the aspirations of students. They try to get students to set goals, short and long term, so that they will work to achieve them. But steering by the stars can be difficult when the skies are filled with clouds. At one high school with an enhancement program, for instance, teachers complained about the inability of students to establish goals for themselves. These youngsters could not imagine what they wanted to achieve in the short or the long run. "They float aimlessly," a teacher said. "This is one of the reasons that school makes no sense to them." One way the school tried to get students to focus on educational objectives was by requiring them to sign a learning contract. Such pacts, however, were undermined by an apathetic atmosphere.

Observers are of two minds when it comes to aspirations. Harboring no aspirations can get one labeled as lazy, but aspiring to unattainable goals can be unrealistic. The challenge for educators is to help young people cultivate goals that they can realize, aspirations high enough so that they will push themselves but not so lofty that they frustrate themselves. Children in advantaged settings take on aspirations by osmosis, assuming—almost as their birthright—that they will emulate the patterns of life to which they have grown accustomed. They are surrounded by role models and informal mentors, all elements of the social capital that tends to ensure their success.

What kind of hope, though, springs within a child in an environment littered with broken dreams? What happens to youngsters who live amid adults who have stopped imagining larger possibilities?

These are children whose lack of social capital deprives them of a support structure and limits the contacts they have with those who might plant the seeds of success within them. Other than sports figures and entertainers, they cannot cite exemplars whom they regard as role models. At one high school, for example, students were asked to identify someone they admired, even a historical figure, and write a 500-word essay about the person. The essay was to deal with the student's reasons for admiring the person and include a discussion of the values that appeared to guide the person. Many students could think of no one they so admired.

Author Mark Freedman pointed out in his book *The Kindness of Strangers* that the mentoring movement has been fueled by societal and family changes that have left many youngsters without the role models they need to show them how to grow into responsible, productive adulthood and without the mooring they need to become stabilized in the mainstream.[1] "White students have legacies rich with tradition, support, and expectations that propel them through college and into careers," said Anthony Williams, a 1993 graduate of the University of Michigan. "To not go to college is unheard of in the family line. Those expectations have been ingrained since birth. . . . For the black college student there are no traditions to fall back on when the going gets rough."[2] So few men had roles in the lives of some children at Christopher Columbus Elementary School in New Haven, Connecticut, that staff member Onell Calderas said that when he first arrived at the school some of the students called him "Mrs." Calderas because they were unaware of the separate honorific for men.

Mentoring figured prominently in the summer REACH program offered at University School for young black males of middle school age. The staff was drawn from three distinct levels, each of which contributed to the mentoring process in a different way. The main instructors were regular faculty members at University School and other schools around Cleveland. Joining them in the classrooms as associate teachers were college students, mostly black, who provided a second level of mentoring. And, finally, the program employed high school students, about half of them products of REACH. The participants were surrounded by a sea of older individuals who could model behaviors and give them good counsel. "I talk to them specifically about what it means to be a college student and how it differs from being a student in a middle school or a high school," said Ouimet Smith, a middle school teacher and graduate of the University of Michigan.

Jessica Darcy, a college student, put it this way: "I want them to see the benefits and results of education. I want them to see where taking education seriously can lead them. They can get this, for instance, through exposure to people with good vocabularies, exposure to role models." Another college student working in the program, Eric Dina, said: "I take my role in REACH very seriously. I don't know what they have at home. I may be their only black male role model so I have to be the best I can be."

In poor rural areas, geographic isolation cuts some students off from the information and experiences that could help them imagine better futures for themselves. Clay High School in rural West Virginia faced a challenge in trying to get students to yearn for larger possibilities. The teachers were among their few potential college-educated role models in a county with few opportunities. The best graduates of Clay invariably left the county in search of employment. At the beginning of the 1990s, the high school decided to provide students with role models by forming an alumni organization that included graduates who had left the area. Clay is a close-knit community imbued with traditional values, and educators at the high school discovered that alumni who had moved elsewhere were more than glad to travel back for events at which they could speak to students.

At Flambeau High School in rural Wisconsin, the impact of isolation was such that a leading member of the senior class who wanted to study liberal arts in college was not even told about the PSAT examination. No one informed him that by taking the test and getting a high score he might qualify for the scholarship that he so desperately needed. And no one ever thought to tell him that with his record and ability and the geographic diversity he represented, he probably could win admission to one of the nation's leading private colleges. Williams College? Kenyon College? Reed College? He had never heard of any of them. He said so specifically when those names were put before him by this writer.

Similarly, few of the 760 students at inner-city Baltimore's Canton Middle School had ever heard of Philips Exeter Academy, the elite boarding school that prepares secondary students for the country's most selective colleges. Exeter receives 1,900 applications annually for its 300 openings. In an effort to get the most able candidates and to diversify its enrollment, Exeter sends representatives to schools like Canton to ferret out applicants from less advantaged backgrounds.

Such a recruitment visit was under way one morning in the school library at Canton, in a neighborhood filled with working-class and poor people. Rachael Beare of the Exeter admissions office was telling some two dozen of the school's highest-achieving eighth graders about the school in far-off New Hampshire. The students had been hand-picked by their teachers and were excused from their classes to attend the meeting. "You're here because you're some of the brightest, most motivated students at Canton," Beare told the youngsters. "You have a sense that there is a whole other world out there."

The existence of that "whole other world" was something that Canton's teachers wanted desperately to convey to the students, although whether the youngsters had a sense of it in their isolated corner of Baltimore was questionable. The teachers sent them to the meeting knowing full well that their chances of attending the boarding school were remote. Yet this was one more way of impressing on them that there was a world beyond the tough streets of Highlandtown. Teachers who try hardest to change outcomes for students in need strive constantly to expand their horizons, to get them to lift their eyes so they might grab a glimpse of the possibilities. "We have a $20,000 tuition," Beare said. "Some students pay it; some pay nothing. We even fly them back and forth." Finally she invited questions, telling the students: "I know this is the other end of the world for you."

Just how distant becomes evident quickly to a visitor to Canton Middle School, which sits high on a hilly street amid the row houses in southeast Baltimore. The attractive four-story brick building, completed in 1925, looms over the surrounding blocks, just a few minutes' walk from the shore of the Outer Harbor. The school's clean, well-lit corridors have a cheerful air, and brightly painted lockers line the hallways. Once this school was filled with the children of families of blue-collar wage earners, many of them Polish and Greek immigrants. Such industrial giants as Western Electric, General Motors, Bethlehem Steel, and Continental Can provided employment in plants situated along the railroad tracks at the edge of the residential neighborhood. By the mid-1990s, the sprawling factories had downsized their workforces drastically or closed altogether, leaving rats to scurry in and out of the abandoned buildings. The adjacent railroad tracks were overgrown with weeds, and the carloads of raw materials that were turned into finished products no longer rolled through Highlandtown.

Employment with decent wages became difficult to find in southeast Baltimore, and the dependency of welfare checks replaced the respectability of paychecks. The department stores that dominated commerce on Eastern Avenue, the area's main thoroughfare, disappeared along with the factory jobs. The streets around Canton Middle School remained overwhelmingly white, as they had been, and the white portion of the school's enrollment stood at 58 percent, sustained by a gerrymandered attendance zone that reached north, past Patterson Park, to claim additional whites who actually lived closer to a mostly black middle school that they were allowed to bypass.

Schools sometimes employ a system of sticks and carrots to motivate students, using the stick to punish them and the carrot to reward them. The Giants Academy of Communities in Schools in Newark, for example, used its corporate sponsorship to garner goodies for kids—field trips, tickets to games and events, banquets—enough certificates so that everyone got one for something. The idea, more or less Pavlovian, was that rewards would motivate students to behave and achieve.

At Public School 194 in Manhattan, the Rheedlen program emphasized the leadership training offered to students from 6:00 to 7:00 P.M. It was followed by the games that students played in the school gymnasium in the Rheedlen-sponsored basketball league. Students had to show up for the leadership training or else they could not play basketball. Canton Middle School tried to motivate students through incentives and prizes. Thus they had pizza parties, went on school trips, attended Orioles' games, and received pens and pencils and other school supplies for meeting various goals. Each of the school's instructional teams got $10 per student annually to pay for this program, giving the team a total of about $1,500 for incentives.

The stick has been employed around the country in the form of sanctions, as when students are told that they cannot join varsity athletic teams unless they maintain their grades at a certain minimum level. No pass, no play, the policy says. A preferable approach, the one usually attempted by enhancement programs, calls for changing the circumstances of teaching and learning so that students find reasons to achieve. As mentioned, the Neighborhood Academic Initiative promised youngsters free tuition to the University of Southern California if they completed the program's Pre-College Enrichment Academy and met the criteria for admission to the university. In addition, students were promised two years of financial assistance as graduate students at USC if they completed an undergraduate degree at another institution.

Aspirations help fuel student achievement. Young people lay a foundation for the future when they dream of making something of themselves. One of the most serious participants in a Communities in Schools project was a sixth grader in Newark who knew exactly what he wanted and seemed ready to make any sacrifice to realize his goals. Even as classmates goofed off around him, he concentrated on his homework during a late-afternoon session, after the end of the regular school day. "I want to get a good life," he proclaimed. "I don't want to do drugs. I want to follow behind good people and I want to become a leader." And you had to believe that if anyone had a chance, he did.

In the spring of 1997, Evelia Tapia was a senior at Southwest High School, just months away from entering the University of San Diego as a sociology major. She said that if not for the AVID program, she probably would not have been headed for college. "I come from a family in which college is not heard of, and I will be the first to go," Tapia said. It took several months for her to persuade her parents to let her attend college and live in a dormitory on the campus. "Miss Matthews has given me the connections and shown me how to go about doing things so that I can go to college," Tapia said of Helene Matthews, the teacher who coordinated AVID at Southwest, a school just two miles from the border with Mexico, the birthplace of Tapia's father, a sometime–delivery truck driver.

AVID concentrated on equipping students with the note-taking and organizational skills they need to cope with their studies. In many ways, however, AVID also changed attitudes and aspirations so that youngsters like Evelia Tapia—at a school where one of every four students was in a family on welfare—began thinking about goals that they might not otherwise have considered. Another student at Southwest, freshman Tiffany Logan, said that the skills and attitudes she acquired in AVID allowed her to concentrate better in class "so that my mind's not someplace else." The result: She was dreaming big dreams. "I want to go to Yale or Harvard and be a pediatrician or a lawyer," said Logan, who carried a load of seven courses and went home each day to the responsibility of cooking and cleaning for her family.

AVID, which included a tutoring component, hired as tutors only those who were enrolled in or graduates of four-year colleges. Community college students normally were not eligible for jobs as tutors because AVID wanted to provide role models whose very presence encouraged students to aspire to four-year degrees. Helene Matthews sought tutors who were graduates of Southwest High, figuring that they would serve as ideal living proof to the students that they too could make it into a four-year college. One of the school's AVID students, Ana Munoz, went off to college, went back to Southwest as a tutor during her college years, and returned to the school as a faculty member to teach in the program. An evaluation study of AVID found that tutors from colleges were "role models, coaches, academic tutors, and friends to AVID students." A problem that arose in most AVID schools was not the quality of the tutors' work but simply finding appropriate college students for the program.[3]

A faculty member like Matthews coordinated AVID at each school and served as the lead teacher—in addition to his or her regular teaching assignment. The best of these coordinators were combination den mothers/mentors who did everything possible to motivate their students, showing them how to achieve in a college-preparatory curriculum and helping them cope with lives in which disadvantage never let them take anything about the future for granted. For example, at Palm Middle School in Lemon Grove, a working class town just east of San Diego that was farmland less than a generation ago, Paula Harcos built AVID into a program that changed the tenor of an entire school even though fewer than one out of five students were in AVID. "Mrs. Harcos makes me feel like I can do anything," said Latosha Hampton, an eighth grader at Palm. "She's like a mother. She encourages us and tells us that the color of our skin doesn't matter."

Enhancement programs frequently show students what the results of hard work might be as a way of motivating them to strive. Schools search for ways to demonstrate to impoverished students that effort has a payoff. The results must be made concrete because many students simply do not seem to understand the link between cause and effect, between the level of effort they put forward and its relationship to success or failure. Some attribute their low achievement to not being smart enough when, in fact, they simply do not try hard enough. "They have to learn to take responsibility," said Martha Cameron of the Children's Aid Society. "We try to instill the idea that there is sometimes no substitute for hard work. This takes constant talking and reinforcement."

One way to illustrate rewards is to let students see what becomes of those who take school seriously. Thus a group of students from a school in Newark went on a bus tour of several black colleges in the South. "What we have here," said a representative of Communities in Schools, which sponsored the trip, "is a substitute for the families who pile into the car during the junior year and go on the grand tour, maybe doing this two or three times and going to more than a half-dozen colleges. There's no such thing for these children. We have to make up the difference and take them on the college tour. We also have to be available to answer questions about college for them because they have no one they can turn to who has been to college." Upon their return, the students could not stop talking about the experience, during which most set foot on a college campus for the first time. Moreover, the fact that they encountered college students who looked like them proved inspiring, making them feel that they too could go to college.

Similarly, when a group of students from El Puente Academy in Brooklyn departed on a bus in the spring of 1996 for a trip to the State University of New York campus at Purchase, it was like an intergalactic journey. Despite the presence of more than a dozen colleges just a short subway ride from their homes, few youngsters had ever visited a campus. Also, few had parents or other relatives who had attended college, and they had no older high school students or alumni of the high school to tell them about college because the eleventh graders were El Puente's first class. The students were awed and asked questions that sprung from their naïveté. "Are you allowed to go home on weekends?" several inquired.

They returned from Purchase floating on air, having for the first time something tangible to which to attach their aspirations. Efforts of this kind recently have helped to raise aspirations to the point that the percentage of high school sophomores in the United States aspiring to higher education increased from 73 percent in 1980 to 90 percent in 1990.[4] Of course, the dreams of high school sophomores do not necessarily translate into reality. But at least more students harbor hopes than in former years; hopes can be a starting point for changing outcomes.

The Dreams of Dreamers

Can the promise of a better future motivate students and keep them engaged in their education? The I Have a Dream program operated across the country on the assumption that the prospect of a tuition-free college education will cause youngsters to work more diligently in school. Whether program participants appreciated the full significance of the promise was not always clear, but some children left no doubt about its importance to them. One fourth grader in New York City, John, when asked why he liked the program, proclaimed: "After high school, they're going to pay for me in college," punctuating the sentence with a smile bright enough to light the darkest night. The dreamer project at Chelsea-Elliott Houses in which he was enrolled involved students even before they had reached the end of the sixth grade, when the scholarship promise was to become official.

The program, according to a parent at Chelsea-Elliott, gave the participating children an alternative source of role models. The parent said that without the program, the children would tend to find their role models among older youngsters in the neighborhood, many of whom were involved in antisocial behavior. But the dreamers, instead, had among the many project volunteers and paid staff members a ready source of people whom they could admire, including many who were black and Latino, like them. "It's important for them," said Nikki Brown, a worker from AmeriCorps who was assigned to the project, "to see young people who look like them, young people who don't have children and are seeking a higher education. Education is the only way out of public housing."

Little did Eugene Lang know when he agreed to give a speech at an elementary school in East Harlem that he would start a national movement. Lang's offer to pay for the college costs of the sixth graders he addressed was meant to motivate and reward them for the hard work it would take to complete high school. That example spurred dozens upon dozens of other offers to provide economic sustenance to fulfill the dreams of disadvantaged youngsters around the country. Built into I Have a Dream were components to support students' academic initiative as they struggled to make better futures for themselves.

It may take more than a promise, however, to get students in need through school and into college, as Sandra Persichetti Rothe discovered when she chose to sponsor one such group of students. Her group lived in Trenton, New Jersey, a small depressed city that owes its fortunes today almost solely to the fact that it serves as the seat of state government. A sign on the bridge that spans the Delaware connecting New Jersey to Pennsylvania hints at the city's lost prosperity. It says: "Trenton Makes, the World Takes." Trenton does not make much of anything anymore except for laws that the Legislature enacts over at the State House.

Persichetti Rothe, a middle-age architect with no children of her own, decided that in one fell swoop she could contribute to the lives of a few dozen children through the I Have a Dream Program. After a telephone conversation with Lang, she enlisted some 25 people from the upscale Princeton area as contributors to a program for which she would serve as the lead sponsor, the only one of the donors involved in the day-to-day workings of the project. Over coffee and doughnuts at her office, the others promised to provide $2,500 or $5,000 a year for six years. The benefactors created a nonprofit corporation to handle the funds, which would be accumulated to pay the future tuitions. The chosen children were all 59 of the pupils in the two 1988 sixth-grade classes at Trenton's Joseph Stokes Elementary School.

Students' parents were invited to a meeting at the local office of the Urban League to learn about the program. Three separate meetings were held over several days so that those who could not attend at one time could at a different, presumably more convenient, time. Nonetheless, the mothers of fewer than a dozen of the students showed up for any of the meetings. (Only eight of the 59 children had fathers at home.) None of the mothers had been to college and most had not finished high school. They were told that the benefactors were prepared to pay for the college education of their children and that the children would be provided with various support services during the next six years. The parents were asked, in turn, to do their part by providing a clean, quiet place for the children to do their homework.

To jump-start the project, the students were offered the chance to attend a weeklong summer program on the campus of Trenton State College before they entered the seventh grade. Twenty-five students accepted this opportunity and went off to classes taught by college faculty members. It was not an auspicious beginning. In their presentations, the professors seemed to forget that these were 12-year-olds, not 20-year-olds, and the children were anything but enthralled by the lessons. Once the school year began, the program provided tutors who were recruited from among the students at nearby Princeton University and Lawrenceville Academy, a top college preparatory school. The tutors helped the youngsters two afternoons a week with their homework—after Persichetti Rothe battled officials to keep the junior high school open for tutoring during the extra hours.

It turned out that this group of seventh graders needed much more than the modest homework help that was envisioned. After testing them and finding that most were reading on the elementary level, the project recruited professional teachers as volunteers to replace the earlier tutors. Eventually, four teachers showed up regularly for the one-on-one sessions to aid the students. This routine lasted for the length of the program.

A key person in every local I Have a Dream venture is the program coordinator, who involves him- or herself in almost every aspect of the dreamers' lives. Persichetti Rothe had hired an impressive young man, a recent college graduate who had been a political science major and a football player. By the end of the first year, Persichetti Rothe said that she discovered that he had gotten romantically involved with the mother of one of the students. Persichetti Rothe fired him, charging that he could no longer be a role model. Then she had to contend with the protests of the mother and her friends. Persichetti Rothe held firm in her decision and she filled in as program coordinator until she hired a replacement, who remained in the position for the next five years, as the dreamers made their way toward high school graduation.

The program gradually came to revolve around the same 15 to 20 children who showed up regularly for the after-school tutoring, which was supplemented by courses each summer on the campus of Trenton State, now called the College of New Jersey. During the summers the students lived on campus and took 90-minute classes daily in English, math, science, and public speaking. As the students went through junior high and on to high school, Persichetti Rothe and the program coordinator performed many unexpected tasks to help the dreamers cope with the problems that usually derail youngsters who lack the kind of contacts that middle-class parents can provide. This effort to manufacture social capital on demand took the two adults, for instance, to jails, maternity wards, emergency rooms, and small claims court. One such intervention occurred when a student who could not eat or speak properly needed complicated dental work; Persichetti Rothe took him to her personal dentist, who referred the youngster for oral surgery.

Finally, after six years of access to surrogate social capital, more than 40 of the 59 students who entered seventh grade from the two sixth-grade classes finished high school. Twenty-one of them entered one form or another of postsecondary education. Along the way, at least 15 of the 59 dreamers parented children, including some female students who had more than one baby before they were 18. How many children the males fathered was unknown. Over the years the program lost contact with more than a dozen students. Seventeen of the 21 who matriculated in postsecondary education remained enrolled beyond the freshman year.

For the girls in a classroom at Intermediate School 218 in Manhattan, the effort to put a focus on the future took the form of a lesson. The students, boys and girls, were reading and discussing an article entitled "Girls Speak Out" in the issue of *Scholastic News* that lay open on each of their desks. Students took turns reading sentences from the article aloud. The article appeared on the occasion of Women's History Month and dealt with female students and their career aspirations. It was illustrated with photographs of Ruth Bader Ginsburg, an associate justice of the United States Supreme Court; Marian Wright Edelman, president of the Children's Defense League; and Eileen Collins, an astronaut. The teacher imperceptibly moved the conversation toward a discussion of values and female roles. "Do you think you're treated differently at home and at school?" she asked of no one in particular.

"Girls get away with everything," a boy readily piped up.

"Any response from the girls?" the teacher prodded the female students. No answer. "So, the girls agree with this comment?" she asked again. None of the girls said anything, but they shook their heads from side to side, signifying disagreement, almost in unison. "And the guys never get away with anything?" the teacher asked, still trying to provoke the girls to respond. She launched into a discussion about whether boys and girls are treated equally, finally touching a button that seemed to get everyone in the room talking at once.

"Shhh, shhh," she said, trying to restore order. The teacher was shouting to be heard, asking the students to talk about the differences of the punishments inflicted on boys and girls for misconduct. Students, mostly boys, blurted out opinions, taking the position that they, not the girls, suffered punishments at the hands of their parents and that, therefore, treatment of the genders was not equal. "Sometimes you don't know the consequences for the girls," the teacher told the boys. "Sometimes I call their homes," she said, implying that she told the parents when their daughters misbehaved in class.

The girls were still reluctant to participate. This was a class of students mostly of Dominican background, and the girls appeared inclined to defer to the boys. The teacher continued to try to engage the girls, referring to a poem that the class had studied recently. It dealt with a schoolgirl who was tired and did not want to wash and dry the dishes every night, as she was expected to do at home. She asked the girls to tell what they thought of the poem; still no one volunteered. She called on one girl, then another, by name. Still, silence. The teacher changed her tack, calling on another girl, Tanya, but this time asking what chores she performed at home rather than soliciting an opinion.

"Doing the dishes, cleaning the rooms and the windows, mopping," Tanya said matter-of-factly. Some boys interrupted, deriding her. Then Tanya continued. "At home, I have to do all the dishes and my brothers sit there doing nothing."

Another girl jumped in. "I have to clean and my mother sits there doing nothing."

"Do you have brothers?" the teacher asked of the second girl.

"Two."

"What do they do?"

"Nothing."

Gradually, the original question—whether boys and girls are treated differently—took on new colorations for the students, laying ground for a discussion that seemed almost certain to be resumed another day.

When a motivational approach works and the values of academic initiative are instilled, students act as did the eleventh graders in the Neighborhood Academic Initiative at USC who were attending their mathematics class on the university's campus. They took turns going to the chalkboard to solve problems involving geometric sequences. The course dealt with trigonometry and advanced mathematics to get the students ready for calculus. They had already completed Algebra II. These were all Latino and black youngsters, the kinds who some critics say cannot be successful in school because they are not willing to defer gratification and work hard. Probably nine out of ten American adults of all socioeconomic backgrounds could not have solved the problems that these students were handling that day.

"Who said negative nine over two?" the teacher asked the class of 11 males and 5 females. "Come to the board and do it. Show the class how you got it."

A wiry young man named Johnnie went to the front of the room and executed his solution with confidence. Alfredo challenged the solution, and the teacher invited Alfredo to the board to demonstrate his solution. This pattern of challenging each other continued as the class confronted several problems involving geometric sequences. "Now spend a little time working independently or in small groups," said the teacher, a balding man in a hooded sweat shirt with the inscription "Manual Arts," one of the high schools from which the program drew its students. "We will move at the same pace so we don't leave anyone behind. Let's do the problems we haven't done."

Meanwhile, in a neighboring classroom, other junior high school students were in an English class studying the poem "The Unknown

Citizen," supposedly written on the occasion of the state erecting a marble monument. It was a paean to an everyman who offended no one, carried out his duties and responsibilities, and showed little introspection. "It's like an obituary," a student said.

"Good observation," the teacher proclaimed in encouragement. "Keep that thought."

"Maybe it wasn't a real person," offered another student.

"A viable question," said the teacher.

"It refers to a marble monument," said yet another student in the class of some 30 youngsters. "In real life a person is not really that modest, honest, and good."

"But he says 'He was found by the Bureau of Statistics to be one against whom there was no official complaint,'" the teacher prodded the students. "How could he not be real? We've got to dig some more." The teacher moved the conversation around to words revealing that the monument was erected by the state and asked the students: "Why does the state think he's good? He was selfless. Everything he did, he served the community. Why does the state think he's good?"

"He was contributing. He had five children," offered one student.

"He did his job," said another. "He did good."

The teacher was trying to get them to dig deeper, to analyze why the state was so satisfied with this man who never roiled the waters, who assiduously adhered to the status quo. The students seemed unable or unwilling to probe deeper. The poem's sarcasm appeared to evade them. "The whole poem means nothing without the last two lines," the teacher said, pointing out that the ending stated: "Was he free? Was he happy? The question is absurd: Had anything been wrong, we would certainly have heard."

"This is just how the state wants people to be," said a student.

"He asked no questions," said another.

"In a democracy you should have opinions," said a third student. Now they were getting somewhere.

TWELVE

Great Expectations

The class of eighth graders at Intermediate School 218 was studying algebra, a subject that the students would not normally have taken until the ninth grade. "We sell an attitude," said teacher Al Simon, who saw his role as making connections for kids, with math as the vehicle for completing the link. "Kids should be challenged and they should be willing to struggle to succeed." And it was a challenge for most of them. These were ordinary eighth graders at an inner-city school; they were not hand-picked. Nonetheless, Simon kept expectations high as part of the attitude that he was trying to instill in the students. If they passed the statewide Regents examination at the end of the year, the acceleration would continue by having them take tenth grade mathematics in the ninth grade. Those unsuccessful on the Regents test at the conclusion of the eighth grade would repeat the course in the ninth grade. "And they'll do great the second time around," said Simon, who confided after the class that almost all of the youngsters had poor preparation in mathematical problem solving in the sixth and seventh grades.

The lesson of the day was on square roots, and Simon was trying to get the students to think about rational and irrational numbers. "Remember," he reminded the 26 members of the class, "I said that the number 25 is a perfect square. That means its square root is rational. How do you prove that the square root of 6 is irrational? How do you prove that 6 is a rational number, but that its square root is irrational?" He was stalking the room, a bearded man in blue jeans and a plaid shirt, threading his way between desks, up one aisle and down another. Simon juggled a stub of chalk from one hand to the other as he paced. The students were rapt. He was prepared to give them square roots until the cows came home, however long it took for them to get it. "Starting today," he promised, "square roots of whole numbers, square roots of fractions, square roots of decimals. We'll study them all."

Back to the question about the square root of 25. Simon wanted a number other than 5. "Why is negative 5 also a good number?" he asked no one in particular. "If I take negative 5 and square it, I also get 25. Both are right answers. So the real answer is both positive 5 and negative 5. Most people would be happy with positive 5, so that's called the principal root." As they reviewed one square root problem after another, Simon pressed for meanings. The words flew: rational, inside number, radican. "Picture it in your head; put it in your mind's eye," he urged the students.

Before the class ended, he returned a test that the youngsters had taken just days earlier. "The problem on interest kept a lot of you from getting 100," he said. "Many got everything else right. This tells me a lot—that there is either a language problem or the concept of business confuses you." Later, after the students had left the room, Simon hypothesized that for these youngsters of Spanish-speaking background, the difficulty lay in the language, not the numbers. During class, the fateful test question was reviewed: A merchant sold a stereo speaker for $150, an amount 25 percent above his cost. The students were to find how much the speaker cost the dealer. Simon digressed to tell the youngsters, few of whom had business experience, about how a merchant makes a living by marking up merchandise. He explained the term "markup." "That marked-up price," he said, "represents 125 percent of the original price. Now you find the original price. Add that to tonight's homework."

The exam had been taken as part of a homework assignment. Simon was unhappy. "I found out that five or six of you did the homework exam together. Coming in with the right answer is meaningless if you don't know how you got it." Simon wanted the moon and the stars for his students. He believed that no matter how much I.S. 218 showed the youngsters that it cared about their egos, looked after their well-being, and encouraged them to attend school regularly, they ultimately would have to make their way in the world based on what they knew and what they could do.

More typically, schools serving disadvantaged students are notorious for low expectations, which, in turn, inevitably lead to low achievement. The problem is not new. While attendance requirements make it clear that students are expected to attend school, history shows that schools have no similar expectation in regard to academic achievement.[1] Sharon P. Robinson, a former assistant U.S. secretary of education, criticized what she called a "tyranny of low expectations" in American schools that serve minority students.[2] In a report based on extensive field visits to schools in six major cities, the Carnegie Foundation for the Advancement of Teaching found, often by the teachers' own admissions, that seriously low expectations prevailed for inner-city minority students in many areas.[3]

One of the more thorough recent studies of the issue, an analysis of data on more than 11,000 students in 820 secondary schools across the country, confirmed that youngsters from low-income and minority backgrounds, with records of low achievement, were more likely to find themselves in classrooms that emphasized low-order skills, repetitive drills, and basic knowledge.[4] Schools institutionalize low expectations by giving students watered-down courses.

In a classic inquiry into the effects of teacher expectations, researchers Robert Rosenthal and Lenore Jacobson determined that student outcomes may well be the result of self-fulfilling prophecies. In other words, students may do well when teachers expect them to do well and fare poorly when that is what teachers expect. Teachers may communicate their expectations to students by what they say and how and when they say it as well as through facial expressions, postures, and even touch.[5] Other researchers have confirmed that teachers' expectations have implications for student achievement, but they caution that the processes by which this happens may be more complicated than originally believed. In some instances, "teachers' expectations for student behavior are not necessarily inappropriate."[6]

Enhancement programs also have had to struggle within a milieu of low expectations. "These children are expected to fail," said the sponsor of an I Have a Dream project. "The people they spend most of their time with—their teachers and their parents—have low expectations for them. No one respects them so it's tough for these kids to have any aspirations. The only ones who get anywhere are the drug dealers and the athletes. One of the students approached me early in the program and said not to bother putting aside any money for him to go to college. 'I'm going to be a professional baseball player,' he said to me. 'So spend the money on someone else.' I said, 'What about just in case you decide to go to college?' Needless to say, we did put aside the money for him and he did, in fact, go to college."

Disadvantaged students, growing up in poverty and deprivation, may voice no opposition to policies of low academic expectations. One black student who had transferred as a tenth grader into an elite private school—University School in suburban Cleveland—from a public school, where the majority of the students were black, said: "In a lot of public schools that are predominantly black, it's cool to be stupid. Kids get used to being stupid and lazy. It's the whole environment. When teachers notice them slacking, the teachers start teaching them differently because they think the kids don't want to learn it anyway. Because now I go to this school [the private school], where it's cool to be smart, I have different expectations for myself. I was a good student in public school, but I think that if I had stayed there I wouldn't have been able to remain focused and I would have ended up a knucklehead. I'm easily influenced."

A college student preparing to be teacher spoke with amazement about her experience as a student teacher in the high school of an inner-ring suburb of Cleveland, where the black enrollment had grown to be a majority. She observed the proceedings in an English classroom for an entire semester, from September to January, watching as the students were asked to write just a single paper—one writing assignment in five months—and it was to be only five paragraphs in length. Furthermore, the regular teacher told the students what each of the five paragraphs was to contain. "It broke my heart," the college student said. "One girl wanted to write something more original and she was told that was not acceptable. The teacher didn't think they could handle anything more challenging."

The next term, the novice, who was black, got to teach a class on her own with supervision, a lower-track class that was virtually all black in this integrated high school, and she made demanding assignments and challenged her students. The supervising teacher was surprised by what the students were able to do, but the students—accustomed to facing few academic demands—reacted negatively, resentful that the future teacher was asking so much of them. "They were used to everything being easy, and the low expectations had had a negative effect on them," she said.

Schools around the country frequently have lowered standards deliberately to accommodate students whom policymakers thought otherwise would not succeed. This happened early in the century as child labor was ending and greater numbers of the children of immigrants and minority members were knocking on schoolhouse doors. Robert L. Hampel, a professor at the University of Delaware, said: "The proliferation of easier, practical courses reflected a widespread assumption that many of the newcomers could not take on serious academic work."[7] Whatever one may think of vocational education today, it is clear that much of its growth was attributable to this kind of thinking. In 1914 Congress enacted the first major federal assistance program for elementary and secondary schools, the Smith-Hughes Act, as a way to promote vocational education in high schools. Underlying the legislation was an emerging view of schools as a source of an endless supply of labor for the factories and sweatshops of industrial America.[8]

Do students recognize when serious academic demands are not being made on them? Yes and no. Some students in inner-city high schools, immersed in a culture of modest demands and low achievement, appear not to realize that their level of work amounts to no more than what students in the middle grades of a suburban elementary school might do. On the other hand, researchers and educators have found evidence that students may recognize a difference. Antoine Garibaldi, formerly an administrator at predominantly black Xavier University in New Orleans and more recently the provost at Howard University, surveyed high school students on this question. Forty percent said that they thought teachers did not set high enough academic expectations for them. Garibaldi observed:

> All of the burden for academic failure cannot be blamed exclusively on students. Those responsible for selecting curricula and delivering

instruction must also recognize that they can play a major role in reversing negative academic trends. Schools which are more concerned about graduation rates rather than student performance after high school are patronizing students. . . . If school reform is to succeed, curriculum and teachers' expectations of students' abilities must be addressed first.[9]

In support of Garibaldi's observation, research shows that teachers with a high sense of their own efficacy—that is confidence in their ability to influence student learning—are more apt to view low-achieving students as reachable, teachable, and worthy of their attention.[10] Teachers with a lower sense of their own efficacy do otherwise. Schools do youngsters no favor by giving up on them. They should challenge students and encourage them to strive. The National Association of Secondary Schools had this in mind in recommending an end to the exclusivity associated with honors and Advanced Placement courses. The group called for a policy under which high schools open the most demanding courses to all students, describing the expectations and letting students try to meet them, all the while giving youngsters the requisite support.[11]

The New York Times editorial page, objecting to proposals to create separate schools for black males, stated: "If public school officials are serious about helping young black men, they will adopt approaches . . . in which expectations are so high that students are willed to succeed. . . ."[12] Whether all students can meet raised expectations is unclear, but it is certain that the cycle of poverty will persist as long as students believe that no one expects them to learn enough to break free.

Nevertheless, to expect better results suddenly, without any extra assistance, may be to invite frustration and failure. The national standards movement, however well-intentioned, can hardly succeed unless the students get the added support that they require. Extra courses, tutoring, enrichment, professional development for teachers, and programs reaching into the home may all be needed. "We don't ask them to aspire to anything we're not prepared to support," said El Puente's Frances Lucerna. Thus, along with inserting the expectation that students will take the Regents examinations at the completion of their courses, the school provides tutorials. Some see this kind of support for success as crucial to efforts to raise expectations. Coaching, counseling, parental support, and academic support are all needed to make "the difference between hopes dashed and dreams realized."[13]

Schools have to match higher expectations with the full structure of support that will make the expectations viable. "Expectations alone don't yield learning," said Chester E. Finn, Jr., an Assistant Secretary of Education during the Reagan Administration. "Successful education also demands well-conceived standards, a proper curriculum, high-quality materials, astute instruction, ample time, a conducive atmosphere (for example, a safe and watertight school) and having the rest of one's life in decent enough shape that one can concentrate on the three R's."[14] The focus of most of the enhancements written about on these pages has been on the last part of Finn's equation—getting lives in order as a prelude to learning.

As this book has emphasized repeatedly, while the American public condemns the failures of schools populated by poor children, it overlooks a host of complicated and interlocking social pathologies— yes, pathologies—that pose monumental obstacles to these schools. Add debilitating conditions that suburbanites would not tolerate for even a day and it is readily obvious why small gains sometimes become reasons for cheer. Thus in the absence of quantifiable gains, reformers may settle for and celebrate the progress that they see, however slight it might be. At one inner-city middle school with an enhancement program that had extensive community connections, for instance, an atmosphere of humanness prevailed and the students seemed to truly enjoy attending school. One teacher, though, thought that the school had, in effect, lowered its expectations to make the students happy. "It's a question of whether they are being babied," she said. "Are they learning to take the kind of responsibility that they will need to succeed in high school? It's too loosy-goosy. You need more structure, more discipline."

At another program, this one operating as an alternative high school, the administrators and staff admitted privately that they followed essentially two separate standards in dealing with the students. The program had begun as an attempt to serve the needs of perfectly able students, overwhelmingly white, who simply could not cope with the regimentation of the usual school environment. They had demonstrated an ability to do the work but were unmotivated. Some got involved with drugs and others got caught up in ugly family situations. Many had dropped out of school or were on the verge of doing so. The alternative program was a chance for them to complete a diploma in a freer, more accepting setting. But they had to meet standards to earn academic credits.

Later the same alternative high school took in increasing numbers of students who, like the first group, could not deal with regular high schools. But the newer group, mostly minority, had seldom shown that they could do the work and many, in fact, lacked the fundamental skills required for high school studies. The alternative program helped both kinds of students advance toward diplomas. However, the requirements for the latter group were seriously diluted. No one actually disclosed the double standard to the students and the school privately rationalized its leniency on the basis that the diplomas would enable minority students to find opportunities that would not otherwise be open to them.

"You don't lower the expectations just because kids have problems, but they do have so much to deal with in their environment— unemployment, verbal abuse, physical abuse, drugs, alcohol, gang fights, lack of food in the house, even wearing the right shoes," said Clarence Lewis, a science teacher at a high school in Cleveland. Sometimes added to these environmental considerations are shortcomings more closely associated with the schools themselves—a lack of teaching materials or the continued employment of inept teachers or the absence of preparation for teachers who are asked to implement new, unfamiliar programs. The education of children in need also may be adversely affected by the pervasive corruption of school boards and high-ranking administrators who operate more like crooked politicians than like people with the destiny of children in their hands. School investigators in New York City, for instance, found that while fewer than one-third of the students in District 7 in the hard-pressed South Bronx could read at grade level, the district superintendent had kept members of the local community board, his bosses, satisfied by hiring their relatives, organizing parties in honor of local board members, and routinely approving their often extravagant expense vouchers.[15] This happens far less frequently in locales where more educated, more sophisticated citizens hold school boards accountable.

Even when enhancements in elementary or middle schools enjoy a degree of success, the gains can fade in the absence of continuing support at the next level of schooling, where expectations may be lower for students than they were in the elementary school. In Arizona, for instance, an elementary school that had made progress in working with parents and the community to improve youngsters' education found that the middle school had adopted none of its innovations. Parents and teachers in the elementary school were disturbed to see the students in jeopardy of losing hard-won gains once they reached middle school.

Thus reformers who seek improvements in learning must take steps to implement appropriate educational strategies all along the line. Success for All, a program carried out by Robert E. Slavin of the Johns Hopkins University and his colleagues, proceeded on the twin premises that every child can learn and that the knowledge is available to create schools in which they *will* learn. But a reorganization of teaching and careful monitoring, not slogans, underpinned the program. Reading tutors who provided students with one-on-one coaching were instrumental in the program. And a family support team strived to enlist parents' aid when problems at home seemed to be blocking the child from reaching his or her potential.[16]

The family has a clear responsibility when it comes to nurturing academic expectations in children. Parents who were volunteers at Christopher Columbus Elementary School in New Haven enthusiastically described the impact that their being at the school had on their children. And, in turn, they spoke of the effect on other students of never seeing their parents in the building, sometimes not even for mandatory conferences with teachers—although certainly their jobs were what prevented some from coming to the school. One mother said that her daughter had begun to see elementary school as part of a continuum that leads to high school, college, and a good job. She deplored the behavior of fellow parents who she said did nothing to raise their children's aspirations.

Expectations also are reflected in the content of the courses that students take and the ways in which those courses are taught. Rigor makes a diploma meaningful. The Edna McConnell Clark Foundation's middle grades initiative, which had a specific goal of raising expectations, was marked by increased writing activities; increased offerings of algebra, computer-assisted instruction, and special math programs to promote thinking; and increased questioning techniques that called on students to demonstrate understanding.[17] Some enhancement programs, the Neighborhood Academic Initiative in Los Angeles, for one, expected—to the point of mandating—students to take a full array of precollege science and math courses. Such courses are a barometer of expectations, but not all students enroll in them. Figures show that students from families of higher socio-economic status take courses in math and science at greater rates than disadvantaged students.[18] In turn, students who complete more math and science courses show higher achievement score gains during high school, regardless of gender, race-ethnicity, and socio-economic class.[19]

For this reason, statistics on graduation rates do not tell the whole story. For example, the Census Bureau disclosed in 1996 that blacks and whites were receiving high school diplomas at roughly the same rate.[20] Those who yearn for equity can hardly dismiss the significance of this achievement. Yet the high schools attended by poor children frequently expect less academically and offer fewer opportunities for advanced studies in science and math and in other courses as well. There are diplomas and there are diplomas.

When Expectations Rise

In the face of overwhelming odds, enhancement efforts persist in their attempt to build social capital for children in need so that the students will have something remotely resembling the support system that advantaged children enjoy as they pursue their education. And, hand in hand with these efforts, dedicated teachers try to get students to think, enlarge their knowledge base, and hone their creative skills. For their part, the students, ultimately, have to extend themselves and accept the idea of hard work. Expectations figure mightily in this equation. Jeremiah Thompson, a high school student, recalled that his earlier teachers made a big difference to him. "My fifth-grade teachers said they expected a lot of me and I feel that I owe them a lot," he said. "Now I have expectations of myself and others have expectations of me." One of those fifth-grade public school teachers learned of REACH, a summer enrichment program, and steered Thompson into it. Eventually Thompson left the public school system altogether and transferred to University School, where achievement was expected and honored. He told of his former best friend who had already run afoul of the law, and said that he too might have gone astray if not for REACH.

The life of W.E.B. Du Bois presents one of the most striking examples of the positive influence of high expectations. His principal at Great Barrington (Massachusetts) High School in the 1880s, Frank A. Hosmer, kept him out of the vocational courses that otherwise would have claimed him and suggested that, instead, he take the college preparatory program. It was an era when few whites went to college so certainly Du Bois, as the only black in the class, could very readily have been shunted toward courses that would not have prepared him for higher education. But Hosmer would have none of that for the young man in whom he saw glimmers of brilliance.[21] Years later, as the first black recipient of a Harvard Ph.D. and as America's most notable black intellectual, Du Bois would remember Hosmer as someone to whom he owed "more than to any single person, the fact that I got started toward the higher training in my youth."[22]

In West Virginia's Clay County, where poverty was the only growth industry, the highest expectation that the school system could have for its graduates was that they would be educated well enough to leave the county. That was about the only way that the vast majority of youngsters could go to college or get jobs. "Education is their ticket out," said Kenneth Tanner, principal of the high school. The county had no institution of postsecondary education, and the largest employer was the school board. Jobs in the coal and timber industries had been drying up for years. Because of the desirability of the natural resources, 80 percent of the county's land was owned by outside businesses. By 1997 the property-poor countywide school system was carrying a deficit forward for the eighth consecutive year, producing a situation in which some vendors would not extend credit to the Clay schools and demanded payment before delivery. "The challenge for teachers is to light a lamp and help students see there is a better way than staying around and living off the federal government," said James Reynolds, a science teacher at the high school.

Indeed, the figurative lamp of which Reynolds spoke burned brightly at Clay High School, where 33 of the 45 teachers were local people who had been raised in the county and knew full well what they had to do to provide students with passage out of poverty. "Our greatest quality is our people," said Jerry A. Linkinoggor, the district superintendent. "The teachers are very dedicated and they do whatever it takes to make a difference in the kids' lives—from getting them something to eat to getting them help in an abusive home."

Tanner, who kept a Bible on his desk in the principal's office and a statue of the school's symbol, a panther, on the table behind him, echoed Linkinoggor's sentiments: "You live in the community you work in and take a personal stake in it. Your next-door neighbors are the kids you teach. You are particular about the example you set. You are accountable 24 hours a day." And so it was that this dedication led Clay to win a "School of Excellence" designation from the U.S. Department of Education for its high school, its middle school, and the largest of its four elementary schools. One of those whom Clay educated well enough to leave in the 1990s was Carolyn Conner, who went from Clay High School on a scholarship to study mechanical engineering at the University of West Virginia, where she attained a straight-A average. Then Conner journeyed even farther, winning a Rhodes Scholarship to attend Oxford University to study physics and philosophy. She came from a family in which her father was a school bus driver and her mother was a teacher's aide.

Understandably, few students at Clay achieved at such a lofty level, but many understood that their performance had to be good enough to enable them to leave. For example, senior Amy King, who intended to go on to postsecondary education, said: "I'd like to work in Clay; I like it here a lot. But the prospects are not good. I don't think of Clay County as a poor place, but I guess there are a lot of poor people here." Principal Tanner, a graduate of the school, also appreciated the economic pressures that weighed so heavily on the families of most students. While he attended Clay High in the 1970s, his family was poor enough for him to qualify for the federally funded summer jobs program. Tanner's work ethic so impressed school officials that as a student he was kept on the district payroll after the summer and given a part-time job during the regular school year. He ended up making his life's work in the Clay County Schools. The summer program was still much the same in the late 1990s, when Tanner helped oversee it, offering minimum wage employment to more than 150 of the high school's most impoverished students. They spent their vacation cleaning and painting the district's classrooms, stripping and waxing tile floors, maintaining the grounds, and handling clerical tasks—much as Tanner had done when he was a student.

In the best of circumstances, higher expectations instituted for some students end up permeating an entire school. This happened in some instances with AVID, when it affected not only participating students but the whole student body, the vast majority of whom were not actually in the program. This phenomenon could be seen at Palm Middle School in Lemon Grove, California, where only 120 of the 650 students were actually enrolled in AVID. Yet teachers expected all students to organize their notebooks and keep assignments the way that AVID students had learned to do. All sixth graders, for example, took a nine-week minicourse in note-taking in which they were initiated into an organizational approach to school consistent with the AVID philosophy. The school also changed its policy to allow students to take two electives instead of only one, responding to the wishes of students who did not want to use up their only elective taking AVID. AVID's impact was heightened by the fact that its annual summer institutes had been attended by more than two-thirds of the Palm faculty, even though only one member taught the AVID course itself. Teachers joked that the school had been "AVIDized."

In fact, AVID's emphasis on aiming every student toward college helped underpin Palm's implementation of an annual schoolwide college day when many students and teachers wore sweatshirts with college insignias and teachers started their classes talking about college. Students would end the day having heard six or seven different teachers relate their college-going experiences. Given the school's inclination to use the AVID approach to get students to pay attention to lessons, Palm tested the students—and awarded prizes to the top scorers—a few days later based on the facts they had learned about their teachers' college experiences. Adhering to AVID's emphasis on collaborative learning, success on the test required students to talk to other youngsters to obtain information about teachers who taught classes in which they were not enrolled.

One such teacher, Nina Drammissi, revealed herself to her seventh-grade science class on college day in a way that teachers seldom do. "My college background is a little strange," she said by way of a beginning. She went on to tell of being accepted in 1979 as a high school class valedictorian into the University of California but being unable to go because she could not afford it. Ultimately Drammissi attended San Diego State University, working her way through as a waitress. She began as a premed major but strived so hard for an A average that she suffered what sounded curiously like a nervous breakdown, though in relating the story to the students she said only "I was freaking out." Drammissi, a small, slim woman with straight dark hair, changed her major five times before she finally decided she wanted to teach science. "The lesson," she told her students, "is to do your best in school but don't get so out of touch that you get sick."

AVID's ever-widening impact on an entire school also could be seen in the biology course that Steve Wavra taught at San Diego's Southwest High School. Speaking of his expectations for all students, Wavra said: "I treat them all like AVID students." Wavra had attended an AVID summer institute even though he did not actually teach an AVID course. "I like AVID's strategies and the idea of applying them throughout the curriculum," he said. "It means that students can get As and Bs and prepare for college. You see the difference in AVID students in the quality of their work."

The students in Wavra's class had to clip an article about science each week from a newspaper or magazine, write a report on it, and make an oral presentation to the class. The writing component, unusual for high school biology, was directly related to AVID's emphasis on having students do a great deal of writing. The four-part assignment called for describing the article in terms of purpose, scientific facts, proposed solutions, and implications for biology generally. Of the 23 students in Wavra's class one Thursday morning, 21 had prepared the assignment and were ready to deliver their oral reports.

He sent the two boys who were not ready to the back of the room with a clipping about the cloning of a sheep, which had occurred just a few days earlier, and told them to work on the assignment. The rest of the students broke into small groups to read each other's papers in preparation for the class presentations. Students wrote comments to each other, not only about the scientific content but also about spelling, grammar, and clarity.

Wavra, a fastidious man, ran the class with precision. He kept expectations high and the students gradually responded. When he first instituted the assignment, they clipped very short articles to write about, but eventually more and more students selected longer pieces. Also, at first he had to provide copies of newspapers and magazines for the students to peruse. Then they began finding articles on their own; some even worked with librarians to download articles, which he encouraged as way of enhancing their technological skills. The students tended to give their oral reports in barely audible voices, truncating the information and responding to questions with one-word answers. Whether they would gain confidence and turn into better speakers after gaining some experience as speakers remained to be seen. For their part, the students in AVID said that the public speaking aspect of their program had, in fact, emboldened them as speakers.

More Examples from the Classroom

The effort to raise expectations could be seen at El Puente Academy, where a reading assignment for tenth graders was drawn from a book of short stories by Jack Agueros, an author who sought to convey a taste of the particularities of the Puerto Rican experience in New York City. When some students were slow in filing into the room for the 12:33 start of the class—El Puente used no bells—Alpha Anderson, the teacher, looked out into the hall and said simply to the students who were milling about: "It's time." As the stragglers took their seats, she asked for a volunteer who was ready to read an essay about the title story in the book, *Dominoes*. First, though, she reminded the class that she wanted them to concentrate in their essays on one of the story's four dramatic elements—character, setting, plot, or theme.

The assignment was especially salient because in two days Agueros was due to visit El Puente under a PEN program that sent authors into the schools. The students knew that they would have the chance to discuss the stories with the man who had written them. Elizabeth volunteered to read her essay and promptly launched into a comparison between Wilson, a character in "Dominoes," the title story, and her brother Raymond, whom she believed had a similar personality. The rest of the class was asked for reactions as soon as Elizabeth finished reading her two-page essay.

"Short and to the point," a classmate said, by way of praise. Two teacher aides from AmeriCorps were assisting Anderson in the class, and one asked for a word that summed up the appraisal that the student had just offered.

"Terse" came the response from another student. Repeatedly this technique was used, asking students to demonstrate the results of their vocabulary-building by having them offer a synonym for what someone else had said. The other aide—both were college students—congratulated Elizabeth for enriching her essay by drawing comparisons between her brother and a character in the short story.

Next Franklin, one of four students wearing baseball caps, read his essay. He defined the story by what he liked about it and what he disliked. He endorsed the descriptive style but disapproved of what he regarded as a portrayal of Latinos as "loudmouths." Like most of the other essays that students read that afternoon, Franklin's took a firm position and offered some supportive evidence but was decidedly lacking in the quality of its analysis. Yet it was clear that the students who presented their essays had read the story and were engaged by it. At one point, an aide admonished no one in particular: "Give reasons why you believe what you believe. Take it to another level if you really are writing a literary analysis."

In another tenth-grade class at El Puente, this one in social studies, the students were in their last day of conducting a trial of Christopher Columbus and his associates. The historical figures stood accused of kidnaping, invasion, disrespect toward the inhabitants of the lands they invaded, taking advantage of Native Americans, acting with cruelty, rape and abuse, destruction of Native culture, torture and murder, and terrorism. The purpose of the exercise was to teach the students how history is shaped and interpreted, the role of power in transforming historical episodes, and the importance of gaining a wide understanding of the events and people whose experiences become part of history. The lesson also had the advantage of letting students learn about the legal process.

Various members of the class had assumed the guises of prosecuting and defending attorneys, jury members, witnesses, and other principals in the case. All of the students, whatever their roles, had to read required materials, including the International Declaration of Human Rights, discuss what they had learned, and work together to write a script for bringing history alive in a trial. In the process, the students learned about such legal procedures as summonses and complaints, discovery, motions, pretrial conference, selection of jury, the conduct of the prosecution and defense cases, closing statements, the jury verdict, and sentencing. This particular class session was the time for summations at the trial. The teacher, Hector Caldero, wearing a judicial robe, sat on an improvised bench as the judge of this human rights tribunal.

Luis, who had attired himself in white shirt, tie, and blue blazer for the occasion, rose as a defense attorney to sum up the case. Glancing at notes he had prepared, he reviewed the testimony of one of the witnesses against Columbus: "The person who was in jail with Columbus said he was Columbus's best friend. Another time he said that he never saw Columbus. I don't believe his testimony is credible." He then read from the testimony of other witnesses against Columbus whose veracity he said that he distrusted, pointing out contradictions and irrelevancies. Luis concluded: "Columbus is being framed. He was not involved. How can you blame one person for the vanishing of a whole culture? Only one of three witnesses was credible and his testimony isn't relevant." Two other students serving on the defense team elaborated on Luis's statement and, finally, the defense rested.

One of the prosecuting attorneys rose to speak: "A captain has to go down with his ship. If you are a captain, you are in charge of the men or women you bring with you. Columbus claimed to have no knowledge about what his men were doing. The fact is that he could have put his foot down. His men were under his command and going by what he said. He was just as guilty as they were. I don't believe he was not knowledgeable about what was going on." The prosecution rested.

The jurors, each carrying a fistful of notes recorded during the proceedings, gathered around a table in the middle of the room and began weighing the evidence. The remainder of the class, students who had played the various roles during the trial, sat at desks surrounding the jury, observing the deliberations. Teacher Caldero urged the members of the jury "to have reasons for what you decide." It was quickly clear that the jury, not fully persuaded by the arguments of either side, would have difficulty rendering a verdict by the end of the class, its assigned limit for deliberating Columbus's fate. Caldero suggested that the process might be made easier by considering the charges one by one rather than lumping them all together.

Higher expectations at the secondary level are not enough. Expectations must be raised for the youngest students, too. This effort could be seen in Public School 5 in New York's Washington Heights, where many of the third graders in one class were crowded together on a rug in a corner of the room. Their classmates sat at desks adjoining the rug. An expanse of windows above the children faced a park, where chunks of rugged granite poked out of the rocky cliffs of northern Manhattan. About half of the 30 youngsters in this room participated in the various after-school programs run by the Children's Aid Society.

A series of charts was pinned to the wall in front of the students. One chart, titled "Groups of 2," listed such examples as hands, feet, eyes, and nostrils—all of which had been proposed by the students to illustrate items that come in twos. The "Groups of 3" chart included such examples as a tripod, a tricycle, and triplets. "Groups of 4" included the sides of a square and the legs on a chair, and "Groups of 5" included a handful of fingers. High on the wall, above the charts, was one of the school's ubiquitous reminders of the primacy of reading at P.S. 5. It proclaimed: "When you read, good things happen. Your life becomes more interesting and so do you. So grab a book." The words were attributed to Beverly Cleary, a popular author of children's books.

The teacher, Lud Capps, a big, easygoing man in jeans and a flannel shirt with a turtleneck underneath, drew three parallelograms and began talking about the figures. "Who can make a statement about parallelograms?" he asked. "A cow has four legs," he prodded the class by way of example. "What can you say about a parallelogram?" Three hands shot up, but Capps ignored the eager respondents so that he could call on someone who did not volunteer, a technique he used several times to engage more students in the discussion. None of the non-volunteers upon whom he called had the answer. Finally Capps got the response he was seeking: "A parallelogram has four sides."

Students were fidgeting all around him, but Capps ostensibly paid no attention to them. He was trying to get the youngsters to frame statements about the properties of the geometric figure. "Who can make up a question?" he asked, still referring to the parallelogram. Mostly the same hands rose again and once more he bypassed them, this time announcing: "I'm calling on the person who is most calm. We have three parallelograms," he continued. "Each has four sides. What questions can you make up about them?"

A student said: "I have three parallelograms. Each has four sides. How many sides are there in all?"

Now Capps was making progress. "How can I write that in a sentence?" he asked, trying to move the youngsters in the direction of formulating an arithmetical expression. The restlessness had spread to the extent that the class was on the brink of disruption. "Should we go back to our desks?" asked Capps. "Some people don't know how to sit still."

"Three times four," volunteered a student, putting the multiplication in a line sentence. Then the discussion diverged in a geometric direction as some students talked about similarities and differences of parallelograms, squares, and rectangles. Capps tantalized the students by offering to reveal the name of a figure that he told them they were not supposed to know until they were in the sixth grade: rhombus. He once more had to stop talking to quiet the boisterousness. "I'm waiting," Capps said softly. "I really need your attention. José, Alice, Isabella, Jonathan, Kelly, Nina." He called out some names, trying to quiet some of the least attentive youngsters. No one was bad, simply unruly.

Capps talked about 12s, using the idea of a dozen eggs to prod the students. "We have 36 eggs in all. They are in packs of a dozen. What's the question?" Again, he tried to avoid the youngsters who volunteered to answer the question. He moved the discussion around to number sentences, getting the students to think in terms of 3 times 12 = , drawing a square on the side of the equals sign where the x would appear to represent the unknown number in an algebraic formula. Then he turned it around, 36 = 12 times x . "There's a number missing," a student observed.

"What's the number?" asked Capps.

How much of the progress of the students in school could be attributed to the extra enrichment provided through the Children's Aid Society? How much was simply the result of Capps's work? The questions, virtually impossible to answer, were further complicated by the fact that half the children in the class chose not to participate in the after-school program. This writer could only observe with relative assurance that P.S. 5 would not have been the school it was if not for the involvement of Children's Aid. Could the New York City Board of Education have filled the gap if the society were not in the school? Theoretically, yes; practically, no. Schools without the Children's Aid Society clearly did not offer the same enhanced program. The enhancement helped support a higher level of expectations in the regular classes.

THIRTEEN

Engaging Students

When University School near Cleveland taught history and literature to black males just entering their teens in its summer REACH program, the emphasis was on the Underground Railroad and its role in helping to liberate slaves. The students took field trips to Oberlin and other "stations" along the Railroad, and they read accounts of passages to freedom. They even created a "Jeopardy" game with questions based on their newly acquired knowledge. One day, for instance, a group of seven sixth graders took turns thinking up questions for the game.

"The Underground Railroad wasn't *really* underground. Why did they call it that?" one student asked. Then the others chimed in.

"Why did the slaves not try to take over where there were more blacks than whites?"

"How many slave states were there?"

"Since Quakers didn't lie, what did they say if they had a slave hidden in their house and someone came looking for him?"

In another class in the REACH program, a different group of students—eighth graders—was preparing for a mock trial in which each would take a role, complete with costumes, as the court tried to decide whether an escaped slave had to be returned from Indiana to servitude in the South. The students received packets of factual material about the roles that people played in actual trials involving attempts to return fugitive slaves. They used the information to create a story and to write the parts for roles that would be the basis for the trial they were about to conduct. An objective of the exercise was to get the students to hone their writing skills.

The teacher quizzed each student to see what he knew about the responses his character might be expected to give. Students took the roles of escaped slave, owner, slave-catcher, opposing lawyers, witnesses, judge, and members of the jury. "Make sure you don't contradict the source material in the affidavit," the teacher reminded them, subtly underscoring the fact that these students were also using the exercise to learn about judicial procedure. The teacher drew a circle on the board and lines radiating out of the circle, each line representing a different character in the trial and the vantage from which that character viewed the unfolding events.

"We're talking about perspective here," said the other teacher in the room. "Perspective, do you know what that is?" The lesson continued in this manner as the two teachers seized on every opportunity to inject a vocabulary word and unwrap its definition.

"Point of view," one student volunteered hesitantly.

The two teachers talked for a while about the workings of a trial. Then it was time to practice their roles, and André, playing the part of one of the lawyers, rose to his feet. Suddenly it was 1857 and the youngsters projected themselves into a courtroom. "What do you think of Alex as a person?" the mock lawyer asked the mock slave owner.

"Alex, to me, is only three-fifths of a person because he is a slave." If the poignancy of a black playing the role of a slave owner struck anyone in the room, they did not show it.

"Why are you on the witness stand? What are you trying to show?" one of the teachers asked the "slave owner," trying to get him to reflect deeper on the meaning of his testimony. The teacher did not wait for an answer. "You're trying to prove he couldn't survive without you. You're contributing to the idea that he's not fully human."

Amid the national concern about academic standards, some critics forget that standards mean little if schools cannot engage students in the first place. Schools can hardly expect students to strive to their utmost when they feel no connection to school and see no reason for devoting themselves to academics. Some teachers, such as those in the

REACH program at University school, have sought to whet students' appetites for knowledge by asking them to learn material that they are apt to value. Doing so heightens the chance of engaging them.

In this same vein, El Puente Academy in Brooklyn operated from the premise that students must like being in school before learning is apt to occur. Unlike so many of the tens of thousands of youngsters enrolled in New York City's neighborhood high schools, many at El Puente seemed enthusiastic about school. They felt at one with their school, and many liked it enough to remain for an after-school program that lasted until eight or nine, five nights a week. They were learning to examine issues critically and to assess their own roles in society. Students talked of the experience at El Puente as making them more confident to speak their own minds.

Yet this was happening in a setting that did not conform with traditional notions of what a high school ought to be. The science program, for example, struggled to make do in a building totally lacking laboratories; the space was so inadequate for teaching science that a water faucet was all that distinguished the science room from other classrooms. Thus biology, chemistry, and physics were taught without laboratories. When students wanted to analyze air samples, they went to York College to use the equipment. And when the time came for dissections, they used a computer program that allowed them to conduct the procedures bloodlessly on the screens of computer monitors by manipulating a mouse instead of slicing into one. El Puente had an air of academic permissiveness, but the school believed in the merit of what it was doing. "These kids are on the way to becoming lifelong learners and active participants in the life of their community," said Frances Lucerna. "I see no contradiction here with academic rigor. Yet it is presented as a dichotomy. You don't open minds if you don't open souls." By 1997 the board of education had approved the conversion of a factory building into a new home for El Puente, and it was only a matter of time before the school would have improved facilities.

Wherever they are located, however, schools can try to make academic content more appealing by altering the curriculum or varying teaching styles. Such approaches are deemed "soft" by some observers, but why do adults who castigate schools for trying to appeal to students' interests expect that students will respond favorably to content and teaching that do not engage them? These same adults do not read books that they find uninteresting; they do not watch movies that bore them. Why do they think young people should exhibit diligence and devotion when they are not drawn into the content? Critics of education must waken to the reality that teachers have to do more to engage their students. *Breaking Ranks*, the report on high schools by the National Association of Secondary Schools, urged teachers to design work for students "that is of high enough quality to engage them, cause them to persist, and, when successfully completed, will result in their satisfaction and their acquisition of learning, skills, and abilities valued by society."[1]

College professors Lillian G. Katz and Sylvia C. Chard referred to "the need to cultivate the life of the young child's mind" in their book entitled *Engaging Children's Minds: The Project Approach*.[2] Claudia Geocaris, a science teacher in Illinois, told of changing the way she designed her lessons to heighten students' interest in the subject matter. She used the example of a lesson on DNA and its connection to the diversity of life to describe how she infused a lesson with rigor, thought, self-expression, and authenticity.[3] Vito Perrone, director of teacher education at the Harvard Graduate School of Education, gave future teachers a nudge toward engagement by asking them about their deepest interests or passions—things they felt particularly articulate about, were in control of, and adept at doing. Then he encouraged them to point their students toward similar levels of understanding, learning that lasts beyond the next test and beyond school itself.[4]

A kind of engagement sometimes called "teaching for meaning" or "teaching for understanding" relies on three sources, according to Michael Knapp, a professor at the College of Education at the University of Washington, and his associates. First, students are encouraged to find meaning in their academic work; second, they derive meaning from seeing the relationship of the parts of knowledge to the whole rather than dealing with isolated bits of information; and, third, they connect new learning to what they already know.[5]

Fienberg-Fisher Elementary School used an academic theme to engage its students. Taking advantage of its Miami Beach location, the school decided to link its science curriculum in the fourth, fifth, and sixth grades to the nearby ocean. The result was Seascope: Young Mariners' Program, which became a focus for studying marine and aquatic ecosystems. In part, Seascope was integrated into math, reading, and other subjects as well as into some of the students' computer work. This approach resembles what is used in magnet schools which seek to promote an instructional motif that captures student and parent interest.

Fienberg-Fisher became replete with aquariums after a dozen of its teachers took a graduate-level course in marine biology to prepare for Seascope and learned how to set up saltwater aquariums in their classrooms. The money for the aquariums came from Citibank, and the tuition-free course was made available by Barry University. "The teachers understand they have to bring learning to life and relate it to the real world," said Judy Lazar, a teacher who played a major role in writing the new curriculum units for the program.

Normally, the attitude of adolescents toward going to history class is more or less the same as they feel about getting acne. As teens put it, in their inimitable language, they both suck. It was therefore a startling testimony to Bruce Cunningham that his class, entitled U.S. and World History 1900 to Present, was arguably the most popular among students at Clay High School in West Virginia. The 46-year-old teacher won praise the old-fashioned way: by lecturing. At a point in the school reform movement when lecturing was dismissed as a deadening, passive, outmoded instructional technique, Cunningham used the lecture to engage students with great success. His combination of corny humor, arcane tidbits, and animated presentation kept students thinking about the lesson even if the names, places, and events were totally new to them.

Students also seemed to like Cunningham because they believed that he cared about them—even if he was demanding. One day when Pam showed up after missing class the previous day, Cunningham asked her in front of the entire class why she had been absent. Told by the girl that she had overslept, Cunningham offered to call her each morning. Although it was a bit of sarcasm, no one doubted that he would be on the phone if she truly wanted him to do it. "So, what's happening in the world today?" he said by way of shifting the students into a social studies frame of mind. "What about OJ?" Cunningham used this approach in racing through a litany of current events to grab onto his class before he put them into a time capsule for a trip back to the beginning of the century.

A tall, rangy man with dark thinning hair, Cunningham fit the profile of the average American teacher—middle-aged, a quarter-of-a-century on the job, and pay of about $40,000 a year after beginning his career at $313 a month. And, perhaps not so typically, he conveyed a devotion for what he did that helped maintain his students' interest in the subject. This particular class session came during the week that President Clinton had spoken to Congress, and Cunningham used the occasion to give the students some history of the annual speech, which none of them could identify by name as the State of the Union Message. Soon Cunningham had segued into Theodore Roosevelt's era and the class was in full swing. He was walking up one aisle and down the next, past the desks of the students as each was required to recite a fact that he or she had learned about TR. No one could use a fact that someone else had mentioned earlier and so, as he reached the last of the 27 students, they were straining to dredge up something new. This class knew its Teddy Roosevelt.

Suddenly Cunningham made it clear where the term "pop quiz" got its name as he announced that each student should take out a single sheet of paper. The ten questions further tested the students' knowledge of Roosevelt's turn-of-the-century administration. After reviewing the answers—no one got all ten and only two students got nine right—Cunningham was lecturing on material that he assured the students they would not find in their textbook. He painted a fascinating picture of the United States as it was in 1910, even describing the incidence of heart disease at that time. On that pretext, Cunningham returned to modern times, mentioning the AIDS epidemic that people did not have to worry about in 1910. "I can't preach enough to you about self-preservation," he said, changing the subject in a way that hardly seemed a digression to the attentive class. "Don't trust anyone when it comes to your personal life."

Cunningham quickly reverted to his portrait of life in the century's first decade, telling the class that toothpaste did not exist and people had to use tooth-powder. "If you're not true to your teeth, they'll be false to you," he said, not able to resist dispensing a little of his cornball humor. Cunningham delved into some additional facets of early twentieth-century life and, imperceptibly, made his way to the 1940s, which allowed him to mention a poker-playing incident involving Truman and Churchill. Quick as a flash, he was back at the start of the century and the dawn of aviation— "Orville and Wilbur Wrong," as Cunningham would have it. A silent moan ran through the class. Then it was on to Henry Ford and his contributions to industrial development. In a melange of interesting tidbits, Cunningham was talking about the production of early motorcycles, the San Francisco earthquake, Annie Oakley, and Isadora Duncan. In fact, Cunningham did almost all the talking, but—like a storyteller spinning tales around a campfire—he seemed to have an uncanny ability to keep the students engaged.

Reforming Schools to Make Them More Engaging

Much of the educational reform movement has been about changing governance, organization, and structure to make schools more flexible. Flexibility to what ends? Although it is often not explicitly spelled out, a main reason for breaking the rigidity is to make it easier to engage students. A notable effort in this direction was undertaken at Baltimore's Canton Middle School, where reform meant, more than anything else, reorganizing instruction in ways designed to make the students more active learners. Under the inspired leadership of a new principal, Craig Spilman, the school, starting in 1991, literally rebuilt its faculty and administration, educator by educator, to assemble a group that subscribed to the reformulated approach.

Spilman, a slim, energetic man driven by a vision, left no doubt at the outset about who was in charge. But as the school improvement team gained experience and the fledgling faculty started to stretch its wings, Spilman found it within himself to yield authority to others. By 1996 only 5 of the school's 45 classroom teachers were holdovers from the time before Spilman's arrival. "My whole life has changed," said Nina Parish, head of the English department and one of the five survivors. "I have been empowered beyond what I ever thought was possible."

Teachers were encouraged to leave the school for positions elsewhere if they were uncomfortable with the changes. Spilman recruited new teachers from among former Peace Corps volunteers, members of Teach for America, the Military Placement Program for exiting veterans, and the city's alternative program for those who had not studied education, injecting a steady flow of enthusiastic newcomers into the faculty. Given the growing number of younger teachers, the school even converted a girls' locker room near the gymnasium into a day care center for the preschool-age children of faculty and staff members.

Concurrent with Spilman's arrival, Canton was chosen as a Maryland site for the Carnegie Corporation's middle grade school state policy initiative. Following many of the tenets set out for reform in the report *Turning Points*, Canton Middle School organized its faculty into interdisciplinary teams with about 150 students, sixth graders through eighth graders, assigned to each team. Each class of every course had an equal mix of students—of the full range of abilities—from all three grades. After 1993 the regular classes also contained disabled students under the school's policy of full inclusion of those with disabilities. Almost 20 percent of the school's students—about 30 of the 150 youngsters assigned to each teaching team—were classified as disabled. Canton used ability grouping in its regular curriculum only for mathematics. Cooperative learning, an instructional approach that involves students working in small groups in which they help each other, played an important part in the program. The teachers themselves wrote much of the revised curriculum. Funds to pay them to do so during the summer came from a state challenge grant and from private donors, such as Baltimore's Abell Foundation.

The school essentially was broken into two separate schools, or "houses," within a single building, and each had its own head, who reported to Spilman. Each house had two separate instructional teams, each having its own group of about 150 students. A fifth team, assigned to neither house, was formed simply because the school's enrollment of 770 was too large to fit all of the students into one of the two houses. Each instructional team—working with the same 150 students—included two language arts teachers, a special educator for the language arts, a science teacher, a social studies teacher, a special educator who moved between science and social studies, an intern from the University of Maryland Baltimore County, and special area teachers who moved from team to team every trimester to provide instruction in Spanish, physical education, art, music, and home economics. The special education teachers, while focusing mostly on disabled students, also sometimes taught groups that included nondisabled students. A separate mathematics department taught the subject to all students. One innovation at Canton enabled each student to have a double period of English each day, one period for reading novel-based literature and the other, for writing.

The responsibility for preparing a new curriculum and learning new pedagogical approaches placed a considerable burden on teachers, making it necessary for them to update their skills and knowledge. Ordinarily teachers in most schools pursue professional development, or what is sometimes called inservice training, in a perfunctory manner. But Canton Middle School could not afford to take a haphazard approach if it wanted the reforms to succeed. The school's schedule evolved to allow for a 70-minute daily planning period for each team of teachers. Also, students attended classes only in the mornings every other Wednesday; the afternoons were free for teachers to pursue professional development activities. Additionally, Canton ran professional development classes after school for new teachers and interns assigned by the University of Maryland Baltimore County. All of this extra time without class responsibilities was especially important in the effort to figure out how to include disabled students in the regular program, which the school had to modify to accommodate their special needs.

Canton showed it was serious about raising the position of teachers by installing a telephone in each classroom so that they would have at least the same basic amenity that every clerk has in the business world. Teachers were even given money to paint their own classrooms each summer so that they could keep the surroundings bright and cheerful. Educators at Canton felt so positive about their experience that they proposed that the school become a training site for the professional development of other teachers in Baltimore, who would rotate through Canton and work temporarily side by side with the Canton faculty. Canton also sought to influence the practices of the elementary schools from which it received students and the high school to which it sent most of its students. This desire arose from the simple fact that policies of the other schools that they attend can restrict the impact of school reform on the learning lives of students.

Most sixth graders arrived at Canton, for example, with poor test scores in every subject. So many had low scores, in fact, that when the school pulled together its top-achieving students for special enrichment activities, it was difficult to find enough youngsters functioning at the 50 percent level to fill the classes. Thus, the head of Canton's math department helped two of the three feeder elementary schools implement the same math program that the middle school used. Finding little receptivity to its reform overtures at the neighborhood high school, however, Canton took to coaching its students on the test that could win them admission to the more selective citywide high schools.

Learning and Earning as Engagement

The relationship between learning and earning can serve as a needed hook to catch the interest of young people and pull them from the sidelines and into the heart of education. Students in the welding course at Flambeau High School in Wisconsin, for instance, worked in small groups, designing and building products that they hoped to sell, ideally by getting local stores to carry them. Two of the most successful products had been the lantern holders that found 13 buyers and a four-wheel ramp for the back of a pickup truck, which 10 people bought. The vocational program also started a course in aquaculture. The school converted a milk bulk storage tank—Wisconsin has many of those—into a fish tank for raising rainbow trout so that students might explore new ways of earning a living in a part of the country more accustomed to raising cows. Such ventures were part of an attempt at Flambeau to engage students in their education by showing them a link between the working world and what they did in school. For all too many students, especially those in dire economic circumstances, education frequently lacks meaning because they cannot see how it is connected to the realities of their lives.

Entrepreneurship figured prominently in many aspects of the educational program at Flambeau, a high school serving a series of small towns, some of which are hardly more than a crossroads with a gas station, a farm supply outlet, and two or three stores. Students were taught that in such settings with relatively few salaried jobs available, their ability to eke out a livelihood might depend on creating their own sources of income. Furthermore, the school hoped that such students, once they harbored ideas for commercialism, could inject vitality into the stagnant local economy. "We tell them that they need to determine their own future and not be exploited," said the administrator of career programs.

The emphasis on entrepreneurship at Flambeau High School exemplified the sort of engagement that some enhancement programs deem essential for keeping students from dropping out. The school found that jobs at McDonald's provided an incentive for about a half-dozen of its students who were at greatest risk of not completing high school. The school was delighted to have a role in placing these youngsters. "Our challenge is to create opportunities for them by helping them learn skills," said a school administrator. Flambeau officials believed that their students, the ones working at McDonald's and others as well, were ideal candidates for entrepreneurship programs because of the region's strong work ethic. These were young people, they said, who got to work on time, respected the boss, and were willing to work hard.

For some of its other students, in 1995 Flambeau began offering REAL, a national program based at the University of Georgia. The acronym stands for Rural Entrepreneurship Through Action Learning, and, as its name indicates, REAL focuses on young people who live in isolated locales where they must invent their own economic opportunities. Each student in the course, which met at Flambeau for two hours each school day, drew up a business plan for a company that he or she hoped to start. The course work was built around the individual business plan.

As a result, one day the students were working at computers in the ground-floor classroom, going over the details of their spreadsheets. A 20-foot-long poster stretched across one side of the classroom saying: "You are not finished when you lose. You are finished when you quit." This interdisciplinary course gave students the chance to learn research skills and the fundamentals of finance. They did much of their work on computers. They practiced their writing by keeping daily journals and preparing résumés. They also went through mock job interviews. Most of the business plans probably would never be realized, but one graduate actually launched a home health care business based on the plan that he had developed. Another, using his plan from the course, was trying to start an after-school child care business that would use mostly high school students to oversee toddlers in the community.

This sense of entrepreneurship permeated the school system even down to the district's two elementary schools. A portion of the funds from its Annenberg Rural Challenge Grant paid one day a week for the time of a young art teacher, Mike Fretchel, who was trying to engage fifth and sixth graders, particularly the students at greatest risk, in projects with money-making potential. They would design pins to sell and paint a mural that they would then photograph. They would take photos of the mural to local merchants to try to interest them in hiring the students to paint murals for them.

Fretchel stressed the importance of teaching the students early that skills acquired in school eventually could earn them money. He also was going to lead the students through the steps of preparing a book that they would illustrate with drawings of plants and animals taken from a pond. Fretchel said that he wanted the students to see that their work could lead to a product and that the product could have commercial potential. This, he hoped, would make schoolwork more relevant and keep them more interested in it.

Schools around the country increasingly use the world of work, including so-called school-to-work programs, as a tool for engaging young people in their education. It is an approach that may not please academic purists, but students like those in northwest Wisconsin know full well that, sooner or later, they must make their own way in a world in which they have seen their parents consistently thwarted by economic realities. Occupational links, therefore, engage students in ways that learning for the sake of learning almost never seems to do.

Baltimore's Canton Middle School, the urban antipode of rural Wisconsin and half the country away from Flambeau, shared this interest in engaging students—at least certain ones—through work. The three dozen or so eighth graders at greatest risk of becoming school dropouts were eligible for the Canton Project, a program that the school used to try to arouse their interest in learning. Students became candidates for the program as a consequence of behavioral problems and excessive absenteeism. All of them had been retained in grade at some point, making them at least 14 years old, and, therefore, eligible for working papers. Part-time jobs for the students were the main feature of the Canton Project, which evolved from a partnership with the Sheraton Inner Harbor Hotel. Ten employers provided jobs by 1996. During the fall term, the youngsters received preparation for conducting themselves properly at the job site. A curriculum entitled "Our Future Workforce" was prepared to help them learn what to expect on the job. In one series of exercises, for instance, students had to figure out how to react in situations such as these:

- You're enjoying lunch with a friend when you realize that it's time to get back to the office. Your friend says, "Don't worry about being a few minutes late. The boss is at a meeting and won't even miss us." What do you say? Do?
- You overslept and know that you will be at least a half-hour late. What do you do?
- Your supervisor gave you an assignment to be completed by the end of the day. He will be at a meeting for the rest of the afternoon and you have a question about the job. What do you do?[6]

At the start of the second term, the students began going to the job site once a week, attending school the other four days. Regular attendance during the four days was essential for them to remain in the project. Employers paid students $5 an hour, and the project coordinator was remunerated through a state grant. In 1991, the first year it offered the program, Canton Middle School was criticized for authorizing the students to skip a day of classes each week to go to work. The criticism rang hollow in light of the fact that previously most participants were absent much of the time.

Enhancement programs use the link between school and workplace in other ways as well. The Children's Aid Society in New York City, for instance, formed a corporate advisory committee to help expose students in middle school and junior high to career opportunities and to teach them about job preparation. The activities included job shadowing, workshops, summer jobs, and internships. It was readily apparent that the youngsters knew little about career paths and had no idea of the existence of certain kinds of jobs. A series of eight workshops that ran every other week for 16 weeks made it possible for about two dozen students to go to a corporate work site for two hours at the end of the school day. During the visits, they were taught, among other skills, how to write a résumé and how to conduct themselves during a job interview. Booz Allen & Hamilton, the consulting firm, voluntarily developed a curriculum that was adapted for use by the various participating corporations.

Employees of companies and firms were asked to commit themselves to the program by spending time with the students in their schools and acting as hosts when students visited the corporate offices. These employees, ranging from clerical workers to executives, agreed to mentor individual students for a year at a time. Children's Aid provided training for the mentoring role and the companies gave employees release time. The single-minded, underlying goal of the program was to motivate the students to remain enrolled in school and not drop out as soon as they reached age 16. The mentors tried to build personal relationships with the youngsters, tutoring them, assisting them with homework, teaching them social skills, and helping them gain confidence in their abilities. Each mentor even coached his or her student for New York City's annual examinations in reading and mathematics. In an attempt to deepen the students' cultural awareness, the visits to corporate sites alternated with outings to such places as the Dance Theater of Harlem, Sullivan Street Players, the New York Film Forum, and the New York Stock Exchange. A questionnaire distributed to the students at the end of the program revealed that they felt more informed about the world of work, but they did not like the cultural trips.

In Minnesota, the world of work loomed large at the St. Paul Area Learning Center's Unidale branch, one of a network of alternative high schools. The state required alternative high schools that served students who had been unsuccessful in traditional settings to provide a program of career exploration. Students also got academic credits for work experience. A credit was awarded for every 60 hours of work on a job, and students could earn as many as one-third of the credits they needed for a diploma through work experience. About two-thirds of the students were employed, many on a full-time basis. They showed their pay stubs to receive the academic credits. The credits were also contingent on the student either passing a test that validated knowledge required in the workplace or completing a textbook assignment that covered such topics as communicating on the job or writing a résumé or a business letter.

The idea of engaging students by linking school to the real world also figured in the programs of Communities in Schools, a notable example being the Fish and Roses Project at Cleveland High School in Seattle. The plan called for students to work with an array of outside benefactors—including the Boeing Corporation and Price-Costco—and with teachers to create a business that sold seafood and flowers. A prototype tank was built at the school in 1994 for raising fish through aquaculture, and in 1995 the school's greenhouse was renovated so that students could start growing the flowers. Eventually facilities were built to grow flowers and vegetables by hydroponics, using waste water from the fishtanks to fertilize the gardens. "What school ordinarily teaches these kids doesn't interest them," said Jerry Tobalski, executive director of Communities in Schools in Washington State. "This is a way to keep them in school."

Students' interest in growing and selling fish and flowers was connected to the curriculum in math, science, social studies, and merchandising courses. They learned about sales, purchasing, and marketing. Ted Howard, the principal of Cleveland High School, agreed with the idea of adopting bold measures to engage students' interest. He even used the addition of the Fish and Roses Project as an occasion to add marine biology to the curriculum. The school of 650 students served a low-income enrollment in which 82 percent of the students were members of minority groups, the largest representation being youngsters of Chinese and Filipino extraction. "This kind of program works with kids who would otherwise be losers," Howard said. "It saves them."

A Sense of Knowing

FOURTEEN

Providing a Knowledge Base

The teacher had written four statements on the chalkboard at the front of the classroom:

a. A right angle has 90 degrees.

b. All angles in an equilateral triangle have the same measure.

c. An angle with a measure of more than 90 degrees is called acute.

d. An angle with a measure of more than 90 degrees is called obtuse.

"Which statement is not true?" she asked the class. "The reason I'm putting a question like this up here, even though it is not difficult, is because you will be asked questions like this on the CAT exam."

The CAT exam, officially the California Achievement Test, would be administered in about six weeks. The drilling was part of a concerted effort to help the students, almost all of Latino background, do well on the test—not only by teaching them about the expected content but also by getting them to know the best way to take the test. The youthful-appearing math teacher with her black pants and baggy sweatshirt looked not much older than the students in her class of eighth graders. She tore through the material with occasional admonitions to "listen up" when the students started talking among themselves.

"You have to be careful about questions like this," she explained. "Read each possible answer carefully. Don't rush. Usually the first one *is* true. You can do most questions on this test in 20 to 25 seconds." It turned out that 'c' was the only incorrect statement in the question that she had written on the board.

A sense of knowing undergirds academic achievement. Previous experience provides students with a foundation upon which to place new knowledge. Those who know have a firmer basis for knowing more. Every child needs such a structure upon which to build intellectual attainment. Parents use their resources to begin the process when infants are still in cribs and playpens, and it continues for the length of childhood. James Atlas, a staff writer describing the all-consuming approach of parents of private school children in Manhattan, wrote in *The New Yorker:* "In our child-rearing, this 'perfectibility of man' aspiration manifests itself in a whole array of goods and services: private coaching sessions to boost SAT scores, camps for the overweight, manners tutoring for the Park Avenue set."[1] The development of language, above all, depends on careful nurturing so that knowing how to speak, read, write, and listen with precision becomes second nature. Parents speak to children, read to them, converse with them, and ask them questions. Virtually every program described in this book, in one way or another, tried to erect at least a part of this foundation. At the same time, the programs attempted to compensate for omissions in the sense of knowing, struggling to make up for what did not happen earlier in building a network for the child's support and development.

Sociologist James S. Coleman recognized this reality when he wrote:

> The elements provided to the child's education by a strong family can be described as 'social capital' . . . not human capital as defined by economists, but the knowledge and skills of parents and of the adult community outside the family . . . resources that reside in the social structure—norms, social networks, relationships . . . Beyond the family, social capital in the community exists in the interest, and even the intrusiveness, of one adult in the activities of someone else's child.[2]

Human capital, by comparison, refers to the internal capacity that social capital helps the child to develop within him- or herself to perform functions of value—strength, knowledge, and skills to earn a living as well as the skills and wisdom to create a home and family life and to participate in the community.[3] And one cannot help but expect that social capital enhances the development of the human capital that allows an individual and a nation to prosper.

Imagine the impact on a country of a policy of neglect under which a substantial segment of the population is left with unfulfilled potential, contributing little to the collective human capital. Inevitably this will weaken the nation and diminish its greatness. Yet this problem exists and is ignored in the United States, as if inattention might cause the difficulties to disappear. Even rude reminders of the neglect are treated obliquely when they intrude into the public consciousness. Think, for instance, of the uproar in early 1997 over the proposal by the school district in Oakland, California, to recognize ebonics in the education of black students. A mighty crescendo of indignation rose throughout the country, denouncing the proposal as a threat to American unity. But where was this outrage during all the many years in which black students languished, being prepared for little more than humanity's scrap heap? Is ebonics any more a threat to the nation's future than the neglect that turns children in need into social castoffs who are abandoned to the alternatives of indigence or predation? Why had those who condemned the idea of ebonics not displayed similar concern for the generalized failure of education in the big cities, where youngsters lag, bereft of social capital?

For a teacher in Tucson, the differences in the social capital available to children were driven home when her class paired off for reciprocal visits with a class in a distant, more affluent part of town. "Our children don't have much chance to go outside the neighborhood, and they are used to seeing children who only look like them," she said of the Mexican American students in her combined kindergarten - first grade - second grade class. "Those other kids are way ahead of them. I have children who arrive at school not even knowing how to hold a pencil. Sometimes I worry that I don't expect enough of them, especially when they turn around and do more than I think they are capable of."

Programs that concern themselves with building social capital put much of their emphasis on creating synapses to bridge gaps so that students will cultivate the sense of knowing so essential to academic progress. What the programs attempt to accomplish happens with regularity in affluent families that ensure that their children have every possible experience to bolster their sense of knowing. Why else would these parents devote so much time and money to preschools; to summer camps; to books, software, and computers; and to expensive lessons in everything from ice skating to piano? Advantaged children, after all, enjoy access to the social capital that provides them with a steady, rich array of intellectual enrichment and recreational opportunities during the nonschool hours. Besides getting tutored and taking lessons of all kinds, they go on family outings, play Little League games on manicured fields, and generally have so many productive ways to spend their out-of-school time that the issue becomes one of setting priorities.

Efforts to build a more elaborate sense of knowing for poor kids rely on an extended school day, a longer school week to include Saturdays, and—for those in such programs as REACH—even time carved out of what other children consider summer vacation. This extension of school into leisure time is an added burden, not necessarily welcomed by children who would rather pursue other activities during the hours that they are not legally required to attend school. The challenge represented by such programs could be seen one afternoon in Newark as Antoine Gayles, head of the Bobby Brooks Academy for Communities in Schools, confronted a youngster whose absence from the after-school program had come to his notice.

"Have you been going to the after-school program?" Gayles asked the lad, fully knowing what the answer would be.

"Ain't got no time," said the boy. "I have to take care of things for my mother."

"You're missing a lot of the after-school activities," Gayle said.

"Yesterday I had to do something."

"Did you tell the teacher?"

"Yes."

"So I have to talk with your mother then."

"For what?"

"So you'll come."

"I'll talk to her," the boy said, trying to keep Gayles out of it.

"Sounds like you're not telling me the real reason why you're not going. I'll call your mother right now," Gayles said, reaching toward a telephone.

"No," the student objected. "The reason is sometimes it gets too boring and stuffy and I just want to go home and cool out."

While respecting the knowledge that each child possesses upon his or her arrival in the classroom, schools with enhancement programs nonetheless take a responsible course when they recognize the inadequacies of some students' backgrounds. Educators owe children no less than this sort of added attention. Enhancement programs usually proceed on the premise that extra time devoted to learning is essential to making up for gaps. No less an authority than Rudolph F. Crew, chancellor of the New York City Schools, acknowledged that some children enter school lacking the vocabulary they need to become proficient readers. He called on schools "to build a 'scaffolding' by offering an extended school day and year," extra time for learning that he called "value added."[4]

Extending the Time for Knowing

Schools around the country that serve students in need are starting to acknowledge that, as Chancellor Crew pointed out, even under the best of circumstances the normal school day may not be enough for children who need closer academic attention. This added time for learning—more concern with a sense of knowing—impels the activities of many enhancement programs as they try to squeeze more hours onto the clock dial, more days onto the calendar. As a result, tutoring and extra work at the end of the school day and on Saturdays is becoming de rigueur in some places. At one urban elementary school, for instance, a remedial teacher of mathematics said that the after-school program provided extra tutoring to reinforce the skills that she tried to give children during the regular day. The remedial reading teacher at that same school said that the existence of the after-school program also meant that the children who were lagging had a wholesome setting in which to spend the hours between the end of the school day and dinner. By staying in school for tutoring and other activities, they avoided what many of them almost certainly would otherwise do: Sit alone in a darkened home for hours doing nothing but staring at a glowing television screen. She said that the after-school program, in effect, reinforced what she called "positive academic behaviors." On the other hand, extending the school day, especially at inner-city elementary schools, poses problems in regard to getting the youngsters home. It means having to run extra buses or asking parents and older siblings to pick up the students or providing escorts to walk them home.

Summer, as well, is becoming a time for enhancement. As it is, the long summer layoff interrupts even the ablest students' learning momentum.[5] For those already lagging, the impact of three months away from schooling can be devastating. In 1996 I Have a Dream offered its first nationally coordinated summer camp for dreamers who were entering fifth grade. This was a way to begin addressing academic and social development just as the children were about to start the program. The site in Riverhead, New York, near the eastern tip of Long Island, had a working farm and facilities for studying science.

Similarly, University School operated its REACH program each summer for youngsters entering the sixth, seventh, and eighth grades. The goal was to bolster the academic skills of participating students for the high school years that lay ahead of them. Classes in English, history, science, and mathematics met each morning; in the afternoon the youngsters participated in sports activities and in such electives as photography, music, and dramatics. The program tried not only to counter the learning loss that threatens so many students over the summer but also sought to give them a boost that would carry over when they returned to school in the fall and encountered some of the material with which they had familiarized themselves over the summer. REACH aimed to ensure the participants' academic success in college preparatory courses.

This could be seen in a science class at REACH where students were learning about the interdependency of the parts of an ecosystem. "We give off carbon dioxide," the teacher said. "Is that waste?"

"To us," answered a student, "but not to the plants."

"What kind of waste does a plant give off?" the teacher fired back.

"Oxygen," a student said.

"That's not waste to us," the teacher responded, underscoring the idea of interdependency. The students, all seventh graders, were seated on stools around lab benches, preparing to go outside and carry their inquiry into the 200-acre wooded campus. The teacher distributed a lab sheet to them, detailing the information they were to record on ten different kinds of populations in the ecosystem that they were about to encounter. He talked about such populations as plants, bacteria, and fungi, saying that humans were relatively unimportant in these ecosystems. Words flew from his chalk onto the board, and he pressed the students to join him in defining them—ecosystem, community, population, habitat, niche, biotic, abiotic, competition, predation, ecology, detritus, heterotroph, autotroph, feed web, food chain, symbiosis, parasitism. The students had mixed success, and it was soon time to go outside in groups of three or four to find pieces of decaying logs to bring back into the room.

Once they and returned to the classroom, the teacher circulated from group to group at the lab benches, helping students find beetles, potato bugs, termites, ants, and other organisms that they removed with tweezers and stored in plastic containers. For some students, it was an experience unlike anything they had done in their regular schools. "We just talk about science out of textbooks," said one youngster. "We don't even mix chemicals. We just read about what happens if you mix them. Here we do it."

One of the more ambitious attempts to slow down the clock and stretch the calendar was undertaken by the Rogers Elementary School in Stamford, Connecticut. The school's entrepreneurial spirit knew no bounds as programs proliferated as quickly as donors could be found. Science for Girls, for instance, was launched in the afternoons, after the regular school day, with a grant from Bristol-Myers Squibb. Twenty-two girls in the fourth and fifth grades studied the ecology of the nearby Long Island Sound. Their work led to a trip to the maritime center in Norwalk, only a few miles up the coast but a place almost none of them had visited. They also got involved in the Jason project, studying information from a space satellite, an activity usually restricted to high school students.

Another after-school activity at Rogers was the Lego club in which children used Lego building blocks to study concepts in math and technology. The club offered its program to different grade levels at different times throughout the year and accepted the first 25 or 30 kids who signed up, whatever their academic backgrounds. Some parents reported that the club became the highlight of the day for their children. Yet another after-school program, called ACE (for Academics Challenges Enrichment), was a collaboration with the Urban League to reach students who were struggling academically. The goal was to involve ten students—particularly those identified for remedial assistance—from each grade level, giving them tutoring and homework help three afternoons a week. Parent training was also included in the program. Vignettes from other programs around the country also reflect efforts to lengthen the school day:

- Children's Aid Society at I.S. 218 in Manhattan paid the school librarian to keep the library open for an extra hour and a half after the regular school day ended. I.S. 218 is situated between two public libraries, each about seven blocks away. But many families preferred that their children remain in the building and use the school library, considering it safer than having their children walk through the city streets. Students flocked to the school library, working on projects that they could not find time to do during the day and that they tacitly acknowledged would not get done if they waited until they got home. The librarian found that she had to shoo the children out each day.

- Students who participated in the extended school day at the Expo Middle School in St. Paul, Minnesota, gathered in the small basement cafeteria at 2:45 P.M. for a snack of cookies and drinks as soon as regular classes were dismissed. Loud, noisy, and seemingly disorganized, the milling youngsters signed up each day for the activities they wanted, choosing from a smorgasbord that ranged from the vigorous jumping and running of basketball to a sedate session at which they could sprawl on the floor and play the board games of their choice. Each youngster selected two activities—one for the first hour and one for the second hour, and then they dispersed to the assigned rooms.

- At its Giants Academy in Newark, Communities in

Schools ran a program that began at 7:30 A.M. and concluded at 3:45 P.M. several days a week, while other students in the same building were arriving an hour later each morning and leaving an hour earlier each afternoon. Students got an extra hour of basic skills and an extra hour of homework help.

- Almost three dozen teenagers in New Brunswick, New Jersey, who were on the brink of entering high school, spent six weeks during the summer of 1996 in a program that aimed to motivate them and raise their aspirations while providing some grounding to promote their academic success. The most immediate, most tangible reward was the $4 an hour they each got from the federal government's Job Training Partnership Act. Perhaps most important of all, they were removed from the negative influence of the streets and put among peers with whom it was all right to take a favorable attitude toward school.[6]

- The Beacon program at P.S. 194 in Harlem included what was called an academic continuum for 40 students whose records indicated they were in danger of failing if they did not get special attention. For three years the youngsters received one-on-one tutoring after school. In addition, the program put eight people from AmeriCorps into classrooms to work closely with teachers, including those of the borderline students, during the day.

- In Miami Beach, at the Fienberg-Fisher Elementary School, students stayed after dismissal for the homework club that was established at the urging of parents who recognized that many children lived in apartments so small that there was no place for them to find the solitude that homework required.

The extended day program at Intermediate School 218 in New York City created extra hours during which the school tried to shore up students' academic underpinnings. When Betty Rosa arrived as principal in 1995, she acted quickly to obtain printouts of the reading and mathematics scores on standardized tests for all of the school's students. She was concerned by the many low scores that she saw and persuaded the school's partner, the Children's Aid Society, to set up small, intensive classes from 3:00 to 5:00 P.M. to immerse students in the basics. Educators generally have no legal way of compelling youngsters to attend school after the 3:00 P.M. dismissal, but officials at I.S. 218 reached into their trick bag to secure the attendance of those who were not already attending the extended day courses. Invitations were sent to students' homes informing parents that their children had been chosen to attend special reading courses after school. Some parents were told more directly that their children had better attend to avert failure.

The upshot was that at 4 o'clock a few months later, five students and a teacher were studying parts of speech in a classroom while a custodian swept the floor around them. They ignored him and he, in turn, paid no heed to them. All of the desks except the ones at which the students were sitting had the chairs set on top of them for the night. The teacher used no desk, pacing across the front of the room, intent on drilling home his message. The students had been studying nouns and pronouns earlier, and now the session concerned itself with adjectives. The teacher, wearing a necktie and a crisp shirt, wrote a sentence on the board: A house stood on a hill. "If this were an art class," he said, "and I asked you to draw this sentence, you would draw a house on a hill. But this is a simple sentence, a boring sentence. What kind of house? What kind of hill? What if I stuck 'haunted' in front of house and 'steep' in front of hill? The picture would be clearer." That, he told them, is what adjectives do for nouns. "What an adjective does is give you a better picture. It makes it more interesting. It clarifies." The session was all business, and although the students were not always particularly attentive after having been in school for eight hours or so already—one boy kept putting his head down on the desk as if to fall asleep—they did not misbehave. The teacher called them "Mr." or "Miss" and they responded respectfully. He was soon resurrecting the discussion of nouns and asking them to distinguish proper nouns from common nouns. When a student struggled, the teacher got right up close and put his face in the youngster's, as if to try in one mighty effort to pry out the answer.

In another classroom a teacher was leading the students down a different road in an attempt to strengthen their reading. This room was filled with computer terminals. Each of the 15 or so students sat in front of his or her own monitor, fingers dancing across the keyboard. Some students were peering at scrambled letters in order to form a word. Another program presented three words at a time, requiring students to pick the one that was misspelled. Yet another program offered a short paragraph with a word missing from one sentence. Only the first letter of the missing word was provided, and the student had to determine the rest of the word from the context.

These add-on efforts contained many crucial elements: hardworking students who were giving up their after-school hours, dedicated teachers who meant to assist the youngsters, and a school clearly committed to helping its students move ahead. It remained to be seen, though, whether young teens reading poorly were getting sufficient opportunity to grapple with meaning. The ability to discern common nouns from proper nouns or to unscramble words does not necessarily create comprehending readers. People have to read to become readers, working with teachers who prod them to define words and urge them to search for meaning in sentences and in paragraphs—leading them through the steps of thinking and reasoning that produce proficient reading. In any event, the quest for more hours drives many enhancement programs in the hope that impoverished students can make up for lost time. For youngsters whose time is spent more productively in the first place, such as those from advantaged households, the extended day is not considered essential. They already reap the benefits of one or another kind of private lesson after school and of living in homes chock full of books, gadgets, and other objects of mental stimulation.

The children in the I Have a Dream Program at the Chelsea-Elliott Houses in New York City came from the various schools that they attended during the day and gathered at 3:00 P.M. in the auditorium of P.S. 33, adjacent to the housing project. From there, in groups, they went with adult leaders to the second floor for tutoring, homework help, and games. The gym also was available to them. It was up to the children to tell the staff people about their homework, and because contact between the program and the teachers in the home school was limited, some children omitted mention of assignments and thereby avoided doing their work. By contrast, a fourth grader named John, who lived with his mother, father, sister, and two brothers, said that he liked doing his homework during these after-school hours better than doing it at home. "This way when I get home," he said, "I have more time to play because I've finished my homework." He observed, however, that "some of the kids take advantage of this and lie. They say they don't have any homework and so they just play here."

Even for some students who spent the time doing homework, however, the assignments from their schools sometimes were simply busy work that did little to promote a sense of knowing. The extra hours could be nothing more than child care. One Thursday after-noon, for instance, two of the students most busily occupied with homework were dreamers who attended St. Columba, a Roman Catholic school. They were doing their homework for religious studies, dealing with an assignment that was hardly likely to spur higher-order thinking skills: They had to copy—word for word—a page out the textbook.

In the Neighborhood Academic Initiative, the enhancement program of the University of Southern California, tutoring was done by undergraduates and graduate students—some volunteers, some paid at a rate of $8 an hour—who were trained for the work. The college students formed a sort of tutoring club, following the lines of other campus organizations, specifically to work with the students in the program. Club members hoped eventually to receive academic credit for their tutoring work. Some 60 university students belonged to the club and more than a dozen worked at the tutoring sessions on any given afternoon. The tutoring organization tried to ensure that university students represented strengths in a variety of disciplines so that assistance was available regardless of the subject. "This is a great program," Jean Schneider, a university freshman, said of the initiative in which she served as a tutor. "These kids are very motivated and they are making progress."

A bus set out each afternoon from the campus to the two high schools to pick up the students. Even this personalized service did not always ensure a smooth transition from one venue to the other. One day, for example, the bus arrived at Manual Arts High School to find only four students waiting, although many more were supposed to attend the tutorials. It happened that the high school had dismissed students early that day, and the dismissal was not coordinated with the tutoring schedule. Most of the students who were scheduled to go to USC just left rather than wait for the bus.

On this particular afternoon, the college tutors outnumbered the high school students. Furthermore, even though the tutoring always centered around daily homework assignments, several students had neglected to bring their books. In one room, where two students were doing their English homework, a youngster was reviewing Richard Wright's *Native Son* with a tutor and the other was getting help from a tutor in writing a short paper on Voltaire that was due the next day. She had read *Candide* and was trying to relate it to the satire in a specific political cartoon. The tutor happened to be an English major who wanted to become a schoolteacher.

In another room a tutor was helping a high school student write a paper based on *Candide*. In this case, the paper was to deal with cause and effect. "Put yourself in the situation," the tutor urged the student, who was having difficulty with the assignment. "Describe a real or imagined personal characteristic. Ask yourself why you're in the situation or why you have chosen the characteristic." Eventually the student chose to write on the potential effects of deciding not to write the assigned paper. The student and the tutor considered some of the possible causes of this inaction: lethargy, listening to music, taking a long shower. In yet another room, several tutors were helping a group of tenth graders who were working collaboratively on a homework assignment in which they were to adapt and videotape a scene inspired by Alice Walker's novel *The Color Purple*. The overhead lights in the room were off and the only illumination came from the light for the camera. One student was lying on a table at the front of the room, moaning as if giving birth. Another student read a narration aloud. The students had spent two weeks writing the half-hour script and had memorized their parts in anticipation of wrapping up the filming.

The extended day program that became part of El Puente Academy was established in the early 1980s by the El Puente organization to serve neighborhood children, whatever schools they attended. With the advent of El Puente Academy, the program had been refocused to serve mainly the students who attended that school plus a few other youngsters. Sessions were offered in such activities as dance, karate, video making, mural painting, creative writing, English as a second language, and tutoring. Also, the extended day was a time for what amounted to group therapy; one group, for instance, delved into youth issues and another, into women's issues. In many cases, El Puente staff workers taught the same subjects during the extended day, further strengthening the bonds between students and adults.

El Puente called the extended day program its leadership center, in part to make the participants feel important but also as an indication of the effort's underlying goal. The program was a vehicle for the organization to propagate its view of Puerto Rican culture, community development, and human rights. El Puente's philosophy set the tone for the leadership center. In keeping with this philosophy, one aspect of the program, holistic individualized process, was a systematic approach to allowing a young person to set goals, make plans for fulfilling them, and assess his or her progress. The holistic individualized process was meant to help bolster body, mind, spirit, and community, according to Rossy Matos, director of the extended day program.

El Puente tried to weave the parts of the student's day—the regular school day and the extended day—into a seamless fabric, tying some after-school activities to the regular curriculum. Youngsters who might very well have fallen prey to a host of dangers and evil temptations on the streets had the protection of a familiar setting that occupied them through most of their waking hours. But El Puente did more than keep kids busy. It provided a milieu for social and intellectual growth, a place where youngsters grew comfortable trying on the mantle of cultural heritage—as defined by El Puente—and learned that the hours outside school could be put to productive and fulfilling advantage. At one point, when the students wanted to do something for the many homeless people in their neighborhood, they organized and ran a soup kitchen out of the school building. The extended day was also a venue from which they could head off in other directions, going together to a Yankees game or a cultural event in Manhattan. Usually free tickets to attend such events were proffered as rewards for the kind of behavior that El Puente wanted to encourage during the school day, as, for instance, perfect attendance or no tardiness during a given month.

* * *

For students who have been deprived of the kind of stimulation that contributes to success in school, the parameters of the normal school day are anachronistic. The reconceptualized school day should take cognizance of the full needs of students and use time accordingly. This means, for instance, that one part of the school day should not be the "regular" day and another part—early in the morning or late in the afternoon—the extra part. If the entire time that students spend under the aegis of the school, including even Saturdays and summers, is viewed holistically, then new possibilities will be available for building the knowledge base that all students ought to possess.

FIFTEEN

Enhancing What Students Know

Unlike the many other enhancement programs that provided a base for a student's sense of knowing during the hours and days added to the school year, AVID reached students during the regularly scheduled portion of the school day. But AVID was different from other classes in that it provided students with the wherewithal to succeed in the rest of their courses. AVID strengthened their ability to cope with the college-preparatory curriculum in which all AVID students enrolled.

True, students gave up the possibility of taking some other elective in order to participate in AVID, but that was a small price to pay for having to struggle less in the rest of their courses. The acronym AVID came from Advancement Via Individual Determination, a name taken when the program began in 1980. Mary Catherine Swanson conceived of AVID and implemented it when the San Diego high school at which she was teaching became integrated and had to accommodate many students with less adequate academic preparation than the school's previous enrollment. The students in AVID today resemble those for whom it was founded—underachieving, disadvantaged youngsters.

AVID teachers were people like Helene Matthews of Southwest High School in San Diego, who taught the same number of courses as her colleagues but included AVID courses in her regular instructional load. Matthews, normally an English teacher, was joined in her AVID classroom by college students who got $7 to $8 an hour to tutor the high school students in their subject area courses. At Southwest, 145 of the school's 2,247 students took AVID as an elective. An AVID classroom on a tutoring day was usually a place where students worked in small clusters, sometimes only with each other and sometimes with one of the several tutors. One group might be solving algebraic equations, another group discussing a social studies assignment, and yet another group reading aloud to each other from papers they are writing for English. "Without AVID, a lot of students don't think the work is worth the effort," said Hugo Vera, who spent two years participating in the program as a high school student and then returned to Southwest as a tutor while he attended college. The son of parents who remained in Mexico, Vera lived with a family in a trailer so that he could attend high school in the United States.

In effect, AVID changed the culture of the school for its participants. The requirement that they take elaborate notes in all of their courses forced students to be more attentive. As a result, they could not help but know more about the content of their courses than they would have if they were not in the program. Gathering each day with like-minded students in the AVID course provided them with an atmosphere that centered around encouraging and rewarding academic effort. The orientation toward preparing for college added a strong, unifying goal that all AVID students held in common. "AVID, in a very real way, takes students who might not achieve these goals without the program and moves them to a higher level," said Christine Aranda Smith, the principal of Southwest High School, where 45 percent of the students were poor enough to qualify for federally subsidized lunches in 1995-96.

AVID, like a spreading vine, reached beyond the classrooms in which its study skills were taught and the tutoring took place. Anyone on the faculty of an AVID school could participate in the program's annual summer institute, where sessions instructed teachers in how to apply AVID principles in the various subject areas. This staff development was crucial in equipping teachers in AVID schools to reinforce the program in their courses by, for example, requiring all students—whether they enroll in AVID or not—to use the program's approach to note-taking. AVID required each school to form a team from among the educators who had attended its summer institutes to oversee the program; the team's mission was to institutionalize AVID principles throughout the school.

AVID demonstrated that with conviction and a determined approach, a school could do much within the normal school day to enhance outcomes for students in need. Poverty should not be confused with ignorance. Youngsters can attain high achievement in spite of their modest economic circumstances. Their schools must ensure that they receive work that requires them to perform at a level befitting lofty goals. Building a base for a sense of knowing depends on a school's ability to transform the entire school day in ways that programs have tried to do in the after school hours. The enhancement of knowledge cannot be limited to an add-on; the philosophy inherent in the programs described in this book must come to permeate the school during all of the hours that it serves students.

The commitment to its very best students by tiny Flambeau High School, for example, included a physics course that was offered even though only 6 students enrolled, far fewer than, say, the enrollment of 21 in the school's sole chemistry course. The topic of the day in physics during one particular session was friction. Joe Groothousen, the teacher, was telling the students, "Friction is kind of like a woman, you can't live with it and you can't live without it." Then he turned to the only female in the class, as if he had not noticed her, and added: "Oh, hi, Karen." Everyone laughed. The students, seated on stools at lab benches, assiduously took notes as Groothousen told them that friction depends on the nature of the material. "How do you increase friction?" he asked.

"Increase the weight," a student fired back.

"How do you increase the weight on a farm tractor?" Groothousen asked, using an example that almost assuredly would not have resonated with urban students. Without giving the class time to respond, the teacher suggested that more weight could be loaded on the tractor or that its tires could be filled with fluid instead of air. "How else can you increase the tractor weight?" he asked. A student suggested that the tractor could be fitted with wider tires, which would increase the surface contact. Not until later in the session did the student discover that this response was wrong because of the principle that greater surface area does not affect friction.

"Sliding friction is less than starting friction," Groothousen said. "What does that mean?" To show the class, he set a board aslant and pulled a block with a gauge attached to it along the board. He had the students gather around him and read the dial on the gauge. He demonstrated that it took less force, according to the gauge, to pull the block along the board than to stop it and then start pulling again. Groothousen showed the difference between the friction on one side of the board, which was rough, and on the other side, which was smooth. The class digressed to the real world to discuss the change in friction on a nearby county road after it was resurfaced with fresh gravel. "The amount of friction can vary a lot, depending on how smooth the surface," the teacher explained. Then he turned to the chalkboard behind him and wrote a formula for the coefficient of friction, expounding on the fact that sliding friction is less than starting friction. As Groothousen worked the formula, he solicited help from the students, all of whom had already taken a course in advanced math. They talked about the differences in sliding and starting friction for various surfaces, including glass and steel.

These seniors, unlike many of their classmates, were headed for college—all of them, that is, except for the one student who said that he would rather fish and hunt after he got his high school diploma. The teacher understood the attraction that the area, with its farms and wilderness, had to a physics student who wanted to enjoy the outdoors instead of continuing on to higher education. Groothousen himself had attended Flambeau High and had studied physics in that very room. "I left the area for a while, but I came back," he said. "You have to experience it out there. I didn't like the concrete jungle."

Due to Flambeau's remoteness, small size, and shortage of fiscal resources, some courses simply did not get onto the schedule. The high school, for example, did not offer the College Board's Advanced Placement courses. It did, however, participate in a statewide instructional television network through which students individually could take courses that augmented the regular schedule. Sitting at desks in a small, glass-enclosed area in a corner of the school library, a handful of students at any time during the school day pursued academic credits in one or another of the televised courses. Through this method, the school was able to offer psychology to three students, advanced English and precalculus to two students, and nursing to one student. Although not formal Advanced Placement courses, the offerings—in addition to leading to high school credits—enabled students to earn credits at participating Wisconsin colleges.

An effect of poverty, whether rural or urban, is that children may miss some of the learning experiences that better prepare them for schoolwork. They can end up starting school at a disadvantage and never reach the level of those half-dozen at Flambeau who pursued physics. The effort to fill in gaps in the students' backgrounds at such a place as Public School 5 in Manhattan began in the Head Start program that preceded kindergarten. In part, this meant trying to draw parents into the program, because experiences in the home are so crucial to setting the stage for a child's success in school.

The program at P.S. 5 conducted a needs assessment not just of the child but of the entire family as the youngster entered the Head Start program. "We're trying to build a partnership with the family," said Rosa Rivera, the director. "We look at the family's needs in terms of language, education, and job training." Parents were invited to participate in the program as volunteers on the condition that each adult submit to a complete physical examination, which the school could offer because it had its own health clinic. The goal was to promote the physical, social, and emotional health of the entire family. The child was viewed as part of a unit in which the well-being of each member affected him or her.

Head Start provided workshops for parents and also asked them to join some of the outings, an invitation that was extended not merely so that the children would have chaperones. Parents went—sometimes accompanying the children, sometimes in adult-only groups—to such places as the library and the Bronx Zoo. They attended Broadway plays and traveled to a farm outside the city to pick apples. The theory was that once parents went to such locales, they could return with their children on their own. In addition, parents were encouraged to recognize how they could promote their children's development simply by taking the youngsters places in the neighborhood and discussing the experiences with them. "We want to expose the parents to their community," Rivera said. "We take them to the library and other places and give them the tools that more affluent parents have. We're working with parents from another culture [of

Dominican background] and we are not asking them to give up that culture, but to absorb the culture here." As a result of the attention, some families that might otherwise have sought to move out of the neighborhood remained, wanting their children to attend the Head Start program and the elementary school program at P.S. 5.

Head Start, a national program that began in 1965, received $3.9 billion a year from Washington by 1997. Congress has been favorably disposed to Head Start over the years because of a feeling that it helps compensate for gaps that the conditions of poverty create in the lives of children. At P.S. 5, Head Start even tried to align its effort to build reading readiness with the reading instruction that the youngsters would encounter once in kindergarten and first grade. Skeptics across the country, however, have long wondered about whether the gains of the program endure once students enter regular school. Many local Head Start offerings, unlike the one at P.S. 5, are run not by schools but by churches and other nonprofit groups with questionable credentials in the field of education.

Plainly put, some Head Start programs are better than others, and probably the inferior offerings are the ones whose effects fade most readily. New insights into the lasting impact of Head Start has come from research that found that elementary schools themselves contribute toward wiping out the earlier gains made in Head Start, however good the program may have been. Children who go on from Head Start to the worst schools seem to be the ones who most readily lose whatever advantages the program provided them.[1] Thus for children who require outside intervention to assist them in acquiring knowledge, the attempt to form a foundation for a sense of knowing can be derailed at many points.

A measure of the effectiveness of enhancement programs revolves around the extent to which students in need end up attaining academic success approximating that of advantaged students. Many of the ventures try to demonstrate their impact in terms of higher scores on schoolwide, districtwide, statewide, and national tests. Enhancement programs usually want to find some way to represent a sense of knowing. This reliance on traditional tests as a yardstick may displease critics of such examinations, but program officials maintain that until assessment methods change for all students, those in need must demonstrate success according to the same measures as are applied to others.

Thus some enhancement programs placed great emphasis on test-taking skills. If savviness when it comes to tests is part of one's social capital, then surely students in need must gain such knowledge to compete on equal footing. For years only the affluent got special coaching that helped them reach a sharp edge for such examinations as the Scholastic Assessment Test (SAT), but the underlying idea of coaching for success on examinations is growing more widespread. Kevin Guyton, the teacher of a Communities in Schools class in Newark, even worried about whether his seventh graders ate breakfast before taking New Jersey's Early Warning Test.

Proper nourishment is but one of a host of factors that may contribute to higher test scores. At one school with an enhancement program, an early childhood teacher, who had previously taught in the preschool programs of elementary schools in both the inner city and in a highly affluent suburb, compared the children she encountered in the two settings. A difference, she noted, was that the suburban three-year-olds came into the program possessing a good deal more knowledge relevant to success in school than the urban children did. By contrast, she found that the urban children had strengths that did not get tested on the typical standardized examination. Inner-city youngsters were more self-reliant and more resourceful than the suburban children. They had to be this way to survive, she explained.

She recalled the different reactions when she first set cartons of cereal, milk, bowls, and utensils on the tables in the morning. As a result of their independence, the inner-city children unhesitantly poured the cereal and the milk into the bowls and commenced to eat. The suburban youngsters sat waiting for someone to do it for them, as if they did not have the ability to act on their own—or were accustomed to being served. The suburban children, she found, were also more attached to their mothers and more apt to suffer separation anxiety when they were dropped off at preschool.

Yet mainstream measures of success recognize the value of some kinds of knowledge and ignore other kinds. For older students who have not had earlier preparation, attempts to raise performance levels on tests may very well include coaching, especially if they are preparing to take the SAT. This examination, according to its designer, the Educational Testing Service, predicts performance during the freshman year in college. For better or for worse, scores on the SAT are used to compare students as well as to compare the high schools they attend. Historically, black and Latino students have not fared as well on the SAT as whites and Asian Americans. Exacerbating attempts to narrow the gap has been the inclination of more advantaged students to pay for special courses outside school to prepare them for taking college admissions tests. These courses are offered principally by such commercial organizations as the Princeton Review and the Stanley Kaplan organization.

Poor kids cannot afford to pay fees exceeding $700 for commercial test-preparation courses. Thus some enhancement programs try to assist them by providing free SAT coaching. El Puente Academy in Brooklyn, for one, ran such a course that met from 11:00 A.M. to 4:00 P.M. on Saturdays for four months, starting in the winter and running into the spring. Half of the school's eleventh graders participated in the program, which relied extensively on volunteer tutors, some of whom had taught such classes for Princeton Review. "We try to compensate for the fact that our students are from disadvantaged families," said Gino Maldonado, director of vocational and educational support services for El Puente. "We try to bridge what's missing. If the family is aware of the student's educational needs, we try to work with the family to support the student. Where the family doesn't exist or is difficult to work with, we provide a mentor and tutors, and resources for the student." Some students came into the SAT preparation class at El Puente not even sure of how to add, subtract, multiply, and divide decimals, computations that should have been second nature to them by that point.

Josh Thomases, the coordinator of El Puente's SAT coaching program, described the serious challenges facing such an endeavor when poverty and inferior education have left students languishing. "The fundamental difference here and in an affluent community is that in the affluent community the conversation about college begins much earlier for the students. That conversation does not begin here until we begin it. When I started the conversation about college with the eleventh graders in the fall, they looked at me like I was from the planet Pluto." El Puente's SAT coaching program differed from that offered by a commercial company in that it also contained a good deal of remediation along with the coaching in test-taking skills. In addition, Maldonado spent time with students individually, trying to get each to understand what he or she would need to do to get ready for college. When a youngster said that college was not important to him or her, Maldonado tried to probe the youth's other interests, asking the student to imagine what sort of life he or she was apt to be living in five or ten years. That provided the groundwork for further discussion, and Maldonado talked about the kind of education that would advance the young person in the imagined direction. "I build on their interests and relate those interests to college," he said.

El Puente did not wait until students were preparing for the SAT before trying to address academic gaps. The students' poor mathematical skills, according to teachers, were a legacy of years of earlier schooling in which they advanced from grade to grade with hardly anyone evincing concern over their lack of achievement. Such situations are endemic in schools attended by children in need. Students often have no idea of how far they lag behind more advantaged students of their age who are enrolled in schools elsewhere. Surrounded by impoverished classmates like themselves, very often in a milieu in which academic achievement is held in disrepute, the students may not realize that though they have reached high school, they function academically at the level of a much younger suburban youngster.

This phenomenon was verified during visits to schools in big cities: "Frequently they do not possess a realistic understanding of just how badly they are lagging. They have no basis for drawing such academic comparisons, because they hardly ever come in contact with anyone other than similarly low-achieving students. 'I don't think I'm having too much trouble with reading,' said a young woman at a high school in New Orleans. She was in the tenth grade and had a reading test score that placed her on the third-grade level."[2] El Puente responded to this sort of problem by reconfiguring math classes so that students could get more attention individually and in small groups. Eleventh graders who had been in math classes of 20 students were reassigned, depending on their needs, to much smaller classes.

Efforts to enhance the sense of knowing in impoverished settings must start early and receive continuous reinforcement. These efforts must be incorporated into the regular school day as well as appearing in after-school programs. If the race is to the swiftest, then these youngsters require more of the kind of training that will enable them to run the full distance at speeds that their potential allows. Inside and outside the school, they need the kind of academic nurturing that leads to success not just in school but in life itself.

SIXTEEN

Attaining Social Competence

It is easy to overlook the provinciality and isolation of children living in the center of a major city. Poverty and crime restrict their mobility. They cannot readily afford to leave their neighborhood, and, even if they could, they fear that harm will befall them once they stray from their own blocks—even on the way to and from school. However objectionable their immediate environment, at least it is familiar, and that breeds a degree of comfort. They sharpen their survival skills—street smarts, if you will—to suit their needs in a circumscribed area. Larger life experiences are few.

Numbers of students at Canton Middle School had never even been to Washington D.C., less than an hour away. Many seldom left their inner-city Highlandtown neighborhood in southeast Baltimore. So, when a busload of students from Canton Middle School rode to the Friends School on the leafy northern outskirts of Baltimore, the Canton youngsters were awed by what they saw. They asked whether they were still in the State of Maryland, which they did not equate with the block after block of gracious and elegant buildings they were passing on St. Paul and North Charles streets.

Disadvantaged children tend to know little of the larger world—except for televised distortions of reality. The only intellectual stimulation for most of them comes from school, from activities associated with it, and from programs of the sort described on these pages. It is no wonder that these young people have a dearth of social capital available to them. They do not get to the library or the circus. They participate in little conversation of substance outside school. They are not taken on vacations, and they may not have met anyone who ever attended a play or a concert of classical music. In some instances, they may not know adults who get up every morning of the week, day in and day out, to go to work at full-time, salaried jobs with benefits. They do not have computer games to amuse them in their bedrooms, and their homes have few books or magazines. A trip to a restaurant means going to McDonald's or Burger King, and they may have never eaten off a table covered with a cloth. Meals with family members may be unusual occurrences.

A sponsor from I Have a Dream told of taking children in her program to dinner almost every week, selecting a small group of four or five each time. She always took them to a proper restaurant, where they could sit down at a table with a tablecloth and a setting of tableware. She insisted on acceptable grammar during the dinner conversation and corrected their mistakes.

A teacher in another program described children who did not know that there was a proper response when he said "good morning" to them. And some of the same youngsters thought there was something wrong when he smiled at them. "The reality of poverty is that they lack acceptable social skills," said Rosa Agosto, a program director for the Children's Aid Society. These children may never have the chance to hear the steady drum beat of socialization that pounds its way into the unconscious of more advantaged youngsters so that they grow familiar with social dictates even if they opt not to follow them. Less advantaged children often have had no such lessons and do not know better. "The match between socialization practices implicitly learned at home and the culture of the classroom appears to give middle-income students advantages over their working-class counterparts," wrote Hugh Mehan, a professor of sociology at the University of California, and his colleagues.[1] One inner-city high school student who was working with younger children as part of a service program was disappointed that he did not receive the deference and respect that he expected from his juniors. On the advice of program personnel, he took to wearing a pressed shirt and a necktie and discovered that not only children but adults as well acted differently toward him.

Social knowledge is an essential but often overlooked component of the requisites that smooth the way to the mainstream for youngsters who have been raised with few amenities. The various enhancement programs operate on the assumption that they must provide such a grounding for the young people they serve. "Often their families are dysfunctional," said Rosa Agosto. Someone who worked in another enhancement program said: "Not only do we have to educate the children, but we have to educate the parents as well. They are entrenched in behaviors." There was disappointment in the office of the Neighborhood Academic Initiative, for instance, because some parents of the children that the program served did not seem to know when saying "thank you" was appropriate. Although the program distributed 80 holiday baskets to these families, only 8 sent notes of appreciation.

Sharon Robinson, former head of the U.S. Department of Education's Office of Educational Research and Improvement, included the need for programs that provide a cultural and social base for intellectual development among the nine conditions that she listed as necessary for urban students to achieve at high levels. Her report urged that opportunities for social development be "equivalent to those enjoyed by those in suburban settings," saying that "such experiences are common in suburbia and practically non-existent in hard-core poverty urban schools."[2]

Isolation, whether in an urban or rural setting, spins its confining spell over poor people, robbing children of some experiences vital to their acquisition of social knowledge. They lack options and outlets for building the social capital so crucial to breaking free of the limitations isolation imposes on them. The rural remoteness of impoverished northwestern Wisconsin, for instance, restricts youngsters in many of the same ways as urban poverty—although without the overriding fear of crime and violence. In fact, the highest concentrations of American poverty exist in rural regions, not in inner cities, and two-thirds of these rural poor are white non-Hispanics.[3] The Flambeau School District, the third largest in Wisconsin, spreads over 282 square miles to encompass the 722 students in its two elementary schools and one secondary school. For some families, an annual shopping trip to Eau Claire, a town of 56,000, is the most cosmopolitan event of the year.

A student at Flambeau High School said: "It's very closed off here. You can't really do anything because there's nothing to do. You can go to the one movie theater or walk around town, and, I guess, go bowling. It's just boring around here." Ladysmith, the largest town in Rusk County, had a small youth center but it closed in 1994 because some youngsters sold drugs there. On school field trips, some teachers stopped at restaurants where youngsters could sit at a table and order meals, a first-time experience for some. A high school student, one of 13 children in his family, said that he tasted shrimp for the first time on such a trip.

A scholarship that she won in a competition sponsored by the Junior Statesman Program enabled one Flambeau student, Erin Spooner, to spend the summer after her junior year in high school away from Rusk County, far away: at Yale University. Spooner said that attending classes and living in a dormitory at Yale in a special program for 200 high school students introduced her to people of backgrounds she had never before encountered. "I met black people and Jewish people and many kids who weren't even born in the United States," she said with some amazement. "Knowing them makes me more confident about saying that they aren't bad. You hear a lot around here about these other people not being productive, but I found that they were dedicated and hardworking." At the same time, Spooner said that she gained appreciation for Wisconsin's advantages. Her teacher in a constitutional law course at Yale was a visiting professor from the University of Wisconsin-La Crosse, which underscored for her that despite its remoteness her state had something to offer. "It shows that I can stay right here and get a good education," she said.

Thus the accumulation of social capital depends on access to both people and situations that help youngsters learn the ways of the larger world. In most enhancement programs, trips to concerts, museums, and theaters figure prominently, the assumption being that such exposure will help students rise above their circumstances. While no one can say with certainty that going to see a ballet or an art exhibit will alter someone's place in the world, those who run the programs feel such experiences represent boosts toward the mainstream. As one parent said: "The program gives them a chance to see how others live."

Knowing What to Do

The irony of Robert Fulghum's *All I Really Need to Know I Learned in Kindergarten*, is the reminder that some of the most important lessons of socialization—fair play, sharing, saying you're sorry, for instance—can be taught at a tender age and remain with a person for a lifetime.[4] Unfortunately, many youngsters growing up in poverty do not learn these lessons in kindergarten, in the home, on the streets, or anywhere else. Some of the enhancement programs struggle to make up for the lapses, but results have been mixed. In a social studies classroom at Flambeau High, for example, a series of cartoon characters hung on the wall encouraging the oblivious students to be mannerly, courteous, thoughtful, helpful, polite, and considerate.

"Many of these kids don't have a clue to the social skills," said the community liaison at a middle school in the Midwest. "If they don't get it at home and we don't teach it, how are they going to get it?" She and the teachers took every opportunity to instruct students in how to behave in social situations. On one occasion, the teacher took a group of kids to a banquet, carefully reviewing for them in advance the appropriate clothing and behavior. "If you talk to them beforehand and set standards, kids will rise to meet them," she said, pointing out this had not been done enough for the students. "They've just never been exposed to these experiences." Another time the students went with her to a luncheon at which bankers and brokers discussed the stock market. The students had been studying the stock market so they had rudimentary notions about investing. "Just as I did when I took the other group to the banquet," she said, "I talked about behavior down to the point that if they didn't like what was served they didn't have to eat it, but that they were not supposed to make an issue of it. I told them, as well, not to talk with their mouths full."

At this particular middle school, which drew part of its enrollment from a homeless shelter, personal hygiene—or its lack—sometimes became a serious problem. "Some live in homes where they learn nothing about personal grooming and hygiene, not even about brushing their teeth" said the community worker, whose job got her into many of the students' homes. "I see some kids who are pretty scruffy and they've been that way, not taking a bath for some time. One child who was dressing in pretty dirty clothes told me that it was because he fell on the ground on the way to school, but it is clear that these were the same dirty clothes he was putting on each morning." The school tried to cope with such situations by maintaining a supply of used clothing, soap, and shampoo. Students whose clothes got too shabby were given replacements—clean used clothes—and the community liaison made certain that those who needed shampoos and showers got them at school too. She also provided enough soap and shampoo so that those who were particularly lacking could take some home.

The Children's Aid Society, working through schools and also through its own free-standing centers to improve the circumstances and scholastic outcomes of poor youngsters in New York City, found that students' communications skills were weak. Not only were the youngsters deficient in reading and writing, but their ability to participate in the social discourse crucial to upward mobility was limited. Few adults other than teachers had engaged them in sustained, substantial discussions. They did not learn the give-and-take of conversational skills outside school. Children's Aid organized a weekly workshop in personal development to help students learn about mainstream culture, to communicate, and to present themselves better. Sessions delved into such skills as speaking correctly, arguing constructively, knowing the difference between public and private behavior, and succeeding in a multicultural environment. Even such matters as dining etiquette and grooming were taught. The idea at the beginning of the program was to organize the students into three separate groups—eighth graders, high school students, and college students. "But the older students didn't have any better social skills than the younger ones so we decided to mix them all together, and it has worked," said a Children's Aid official. The workshop used games, role playing, and skits to teach its lessons.

Critics of this kind of approach would do well to recall the Katherine Gibbs Schools of old or the dozens of private two-year colleges that used to function as finishing schools. Attire, makeup, manners, and conduct in interpersonal relations were very much a part of what was taught. A modern heir to that tradition was Double XXposure, formed in the 1980s as "a charm school for rap artists." It handled their publicity, management, and image control. Recording companies sent some of their stars to the 24-week course designed to smooth rough personal edges.[5]

On the other hand, whether they are rap singers or not, young people from the inner city who learn the social behavior of the folks downtown may find themselves straddling two worlds. Staff writer John Lahr, in an incisive article in *The New Yorker*, described the experiences of some students of the arts from Harlem who attended the prestigious Julliard School. Lahr wrote of a special class that the students took that was "not a charm school but a kind of laboratory for multicultural living—for inhabiting that liminal zone between cultures which increasingly defines the American cultural experience."[6]

In this connection, some critics might question the very premise of trying to increase the social capital of poor minority youngsters by helping them become more adept at dealing with the social conventions of middle-class whites. Ricardo D. Stanton-Salazar of the University of California, San Diego, in writing of the socialization of racial minority children, alluded to their having "to cope effectively with institutional and environmental forces that threaten to compromise their human development and their life chances." He said: "Sociocultural barriers are erected when the cultural components in one world (e.g., the home, the ethnic community) are viewed as less important than those in another, or worse yet, when they are denigrated or tacitly cast as inferior." Stanton-Salazar maintained that the accumulation of social capital for low-status children is problematic because of the differential value that society accords these children, the barriers that make participation in the mainstream uncomfortable for them, the processes by which they are recruited for such efforts, the institutionalization of distrust and detachment, and the ideological mechanisms that hinder the seeking or giving of help in the school.[7]

Nonetheless, the efforts continue, and the enhancement programs, by and large, put much importance on facilitating the route into the mainstream for all youngsters in need. When the Children's Aid Society organized its workshops on personal development, a special attempt was made at one center to draw in teenage boys, perhaps the most difficult group to attract. A group called Hoop Brothers was started for more than two dozen teen boys. Mentors from the business world attended the weekly sessions, which included, after the workshops, basketball games involving the mentors and the teenagers. In addition, each mentor was to talk by phone to an assigned student at least once a week and have the student to his office once a month. "The boys needed role models so they could see these skills we were trying to teach them in adults like themselves," said Martha Cameron, director of citywide youth developmental services for Children's Aid Society in New York. When possible, the mentors were of the same ethnic background as the boys; in some cases, the mentors even had grown up in the neighborhoods in which the boys lived. "I've seen boys who wouldn't speak before a group now able to speak to the group," Cameron said.

Related to this idea of personal development is the concept of *productive capacity* that the Wilder Foundation in Minnesota used to denote the set of attributes that it wanted to promote in its services to children and families. With productive capacity, reasoned Wilder, people could learn to use educational and community resources to their advantage. This meant assisting individuals and families to develop adaptive skills, linking individuals and families with services, and creating opportunities to address systemic problems. In sum, such a program would promote social competence, vocational success, economic stability, and the ability to function better in the community. Wilder Foundation was hopeful that the greater productive capacity of children and families would begin to reverse the poverty cycles for targeted families and neighborhoods.

While Wilder thought of productive capacity mostly in terms of adults, surely a support structure for attaining productive capacity is put in place during the years that a young person from an affluent family spends growing up. Greater productive capacity would enlarge upon the social capital available to those in need and increase their chances of gaining membership in the mainstream. Wilder said that some of the personal indicators associated with this transition would be for a young person to develop effective relationships and the know-how to access support, to participate in the community, and to cultivate academic skills appropriate to setting goals, completing tasks, managing frustration and anxiety, and accepting instruction and limits.[8]

The elements of productive capacity, as envisioned by policymakers at Wilder, would change over the course of a lifetime. At any given point, however, these elements would involve the knowledge and ability to use the resources of the system to achieve relevant goals. By way of example, Wilder developed an exercise that a person could use to ensure that he or she had assembled some of the paperwork needed to gain basic access to the system, calling these "community credentials." The crucial credentials are a social security card, a birth certificate, a state-issued identification card or driver's license, a medical identification card, an alien registration card (if appropriate), a telephone or voice mail number, a library card, a bank account, evidence of voter registration, a bus card or transportation plan, and a change of address notification for the post office in the event of a move.

Some of the most important lessons that students in enhancement programs learn about socialization have to do with how to conduct themselves in the world of work. It is clear that many young people who emerge from poverty cannot hold onto jobs—if they are fortunate enough to get them—because they do not understand what the workplace requires of them by way of attitudes and deportment. Part of their socialization therefore deals with gaining an appreciation of the importance of such virtues as punctuality, reliability, honesty, and loyalty as well as of the interpersonal skills that will allow them to get along with fellow workers and supervisors. Sometimes these skills have been bred out of them by the demands of the rough communities in which they live, places where holding back and not giving too much of one's self can be the difference between avoiding danger and not living long enough to see tomorrow's sun rise.

The Communities in Schools program, which has largely focused its efforts on keeping young people from dropping out of high school, more recently came to recognize that getting a diploma is only a milestone on a much longer journey. Increasingly, the organization has sought to ensure that the high school graduates it helps have marketable skills to accompany their diplomas. "At first, CIS saw its job ending with just getting the students to graduate high school," said Sally De Luca, a national official of Communities in Schools. "Now we are looking beyond that point."

Teachers at a high school at which significant numbers of students were being turned down for part-time jobs tried, with the aid of an enhancement program, to help the teenagers remedy the situation. "A lot of them have been out on several interviews and don't get called back and wonder why," a teacher said. The teachers led students through discussion on how to talk at a job interview, for instance. "A big thing is to get them to think about what they wear to a job interview," a teacher said. "I say 'look at how you dress for school. That's no way to dress for a job interview.'" Some teachers also put jars into their classrooms and asked students to drop in quarters each time they cursed as a way to get them to think more about their language, reminding them of the unacceptability of the F-word in the marketplace. "I m making them aware of things that no one has taught them," said a teacher.

Teachers themselves are among the most important of the role models in trying to provide living examples of how to employ social skills. Kevin Guyton at the Cities in Schools' Giants Academy in Newark walked the walk and talked the talk, dressing neatly each day in a suit and tie so that his seventh-grade class could see success personified. A mannerly young man of dignified bearing, Guyton clearly had made a considered decision to show his students in Newark's impoverished central ward the kinds of behavior that he hoped they would emulate. He was happy at least to note that attendance had improved and his students' attitudes toward school were better than they had been. A few of the students in Guyton's class had even started talking about higher education, which previously had had as much relevance to them as the Alps. Guyton's approach mirrored what apparently was happening in some inner-city schools around the country, where teachers were modeling the conduct that they were asking students to demonstrate, according to an informal survey by *Education Week*.[9]

"One of the principal functions of school is to teach children how to behave in groups," said Neil Postman, a professor at New York University whose writings frequently deal with interconnections between education and society. "The reason for this is that you cannot have a democratic, indeed, civilized, community life unless people have learned how to participate in a disciplined way as part of a group."[10]

For the Neighborhood Academic Initiative, the impact of such an approach was seen not only in students' academic attainment, but also in their attitudes and conduct. In sex education classes for seventh graders at Foshay Middle School, the home school for many of the participants, students sometimes were asked to assume parts in role-playing exercises dealing with their responses to peer pressure involving drugs and sex. Those who were not part of the Neighborhood Academic

Initiative tended to choose partners of the same gender for the role playing, clearly feeling more comfortable that way. But students in the USC program readily selected members of the opposite gender, a practice that the teacher saw as evidence of the social confidence and maturity that the youngsters had gained in the program. Also, said Stephanie Hoffman, a science teacher at Foshay, students in the USC program were better conversationalists and volunteered in class more frequently to answer questions. "Their grammar is more refined and they know how to rephrase questions," she said. "They get a lot of practice doing oral presentations in the USC program."

The Neighborhood Academic Initiative attempted to give its teenage participants a wide range of experiences designed to increase their social and intellectual knowledge. "It affects everything about you from note-taking to the way you speak," said one of the partici- pants, Alejandro Venegas, an eleventh grader. "It helps you in school and in the outside world. It has gotten me into other environments and has made it easier for me to cope. It's not only study habits, but character, how to get along with others." Students in the program were taken regularly to plays, museums, concerts, and even the beach. Parents were invited to accompany their children on some of the outings. Often the trips were used as rewards for good behavior, and the few students who had infractions of one sort or another were told they could not go on a particular trip.

"We have a cultural agenda," said a Neighborhood Academic Initiative representative. "We want them to acquire social skills. We want them to see that the world extends beyond their bounded area. Some have never been out of their neighborhoods. It's the first time that some have seen a play or even seen the ocean. We talk with them before we go about what to wear. Before we went to the Hollywood Bowl, we explained about having to keep quiet during a concert. After the trip to the Hollywood Bowl, they said they couldn't believe that 20,000 people could sit there without carrying on like what happens at a rock concert."

Attempts to give schoolchildren in need experiences comparable to those enjoyed by advantaged students challenge the school. This could be seen when two high schools in New Jersey serving very different kinds of enrollments decided to send their choirs on trips to Europe. Princeton High School, situated in one of the country's most privileged small towns, wanted its 78-member choir to travel to Moscow to participate in that historic city's 850th anniversary celebration in 1997. The school's choir had been making trips abroad regularly every three or four years since the first such journey to Berlin in 1964. Two-thirds of the $156,000 required for the trip to Moscow was pledged by parents and the remainder was readily raised from foundations and other willing donors. In addition, 10 chaperones and 22 other guests accompanied the choir, all paying their own way.

By contrast, the previous year, in Plainfield, the effort to send 30 members of the high school chorus to Europe was a touch-and-go affair. Plainfield was a town so devastated by racial unrest in the 1960s that the high school eventually lost all of its white students and three decades later half of its enrollment was poor enough to qualify for federally subsidized lunches. The trip by the chorus to Prague, Budapest, and Vienna remained in question when the fund-raising drive stalled with only $43,000 of the requisite $70,000 in hand. More donations were eked out and, finally, the last of the needed dollars were provided by a foundation and by the school system. Stefanie Minatee, a vocal teacher at Plainfield High School, said that not coming from affluent families made it far more difficult for the students to embark on such an adventure. "They miss a lot and just don't have the experiences that others have," she said of her students. "They need programs where they can develop the talent they have."

Supermarkets, Residential Schools, and Golf

Enhancement programs also try to socialize and assist parents, believing that, ultimately, the children will benefit. One inner-city program found it broadening—curious as it may seem—for indigent people who lacked transportation and lived in isolated circumstances to go on trips to a suburban shopping mall. In some ways, enhancement programs function today as surrogates for the settlement houses of old, which were founded in the late nineteenth and early twentieth centuries. The settlement house often concerned itself with a wide range of services needed by people in poor neighborhoods. It contributed to equipping immigrants and other poor people with social capital that helped them better their circumstances. Another institution with roots in the nineteenth century, the black college, similarly aided in the uplift of those in need. Founded in the wake of emancipation and functioning as scarcely more than high schools, black colleges provided academic knowledge and socialization to a people just removed from slavery.

The late Stephen J. Wright, president of two black colleges and then head of the United Negro College Fund, said to this writer in the 1970s that even the end of segregation in education did not obviate the need for black colleges. He explained that some young black men and women, because of poverty and a lack of advantages, remained reliant on institutions that would take the time to teach them the social skills that other colleges and universities would never bother imparting. He specifically cited the teaching of table manners as a small example of what he had in mind, singling out an act as mundane as "folding a napkin onto your lap." As recently as 1996, some two decades later, William H. Gray, a successor to Wright as head of the United Negro College Fund, echoed a similar sentiment when he stated: "Black colleges tend to be a nurturing and friendly atmosphere, especially for the first generation of college attendees, much the way Catholic colleges were for early immigrants."[11]

This idea of inserting youngsters into a controlled environment so as to minimize outside negative influences and carefully regulate their academic and social experiences has had some appeal to those trying to improve outcomes. For several decades A Better Chance sent inner-city youths to independent residential preparatory schools to immerse them fully in a very different sort of life. The students received not only a dose of substantial academics but also what amounted to a course in how to dress, groom, converse, and act in social situations, underscoring the role of these places as "preparatory" schools.

Samuel D. Proctor, the minister emeritus of Harlem's Abyssinian Baptist Church, proposed that a network of 50 residential campuses be established as secondary schools for inner-city teenagers. He spoke of the "population of unsocialized pupils"[12] that might be reached in new ways. The first step toward making a reality of Proctor's vision came in 1997, when the State of New Jersey in its first wave of charter schools authorized the creation of a public boarding school in New Jersey to serve students from Trenton and Ewing Township. The 48 students for the first classes of seventh and eighth graders were chosen by lottery, and the school was scheduled to open in September 1997 on the grounds of a residential school for the deaf. It was aptly named the Samuel DeWitt Proctor Academy Charter School, the progenitor of what its sponsors hoped would become a network of such schools. Proctor died just four months before the school opened.

Variations on this theme have wide appeal to those who think that students in need would benefit from new kinds of educational settings. Charles Mingo, the principal of DuSable High School on the South Side of Chicago, which served one of the most deprived populations in the country, wished that the school could build its own dormitory to help students get away from adverse and threatening influences. Officials of the Neighborhood Academic Initiative in Los Angeles and REACH in Cleveland spoke not so much of residential facilities as of establishing free-standing high schools that the students could attend so that they would not have to go back to their regular schools and environments that were less sympathetic to learning.

Part of the attempt to bolster social knowledge includes an effort to get needy youngsters to broaden their interests. This can mean, for instance, prodding them to become familiar with some of the kinds of activities usually associated with social advantage, which in sports might mean such endeavors as tennis, golf, and sailing. The idea is to encourage young minority students to think beyond basketball and football, as both spectators and participants. An attempt of this sort could be seen at the assembly that opened the REACH program for young black males each summer morning at University School. "Something historic happened yesterday in sports," said a teacher, waiting to see if any of the youngsters chimed in with what they thought had occurred. Hearing no response, he told them that MaliVai Washington had become the second African American male ever to reach the final round in the Wimbledon tennis tournament. He quickly segued into the program's own tennis program and urged more of the students to participate. He told them of a biography of Arthur Ashe, the first black man to reach the Wimbledon final, and suggested that they would enjoy reading the book.

From its inception, according to Kevin Kay, the first director of REACH, the program "wanted to work consciously to get kids away from a narrow conception of what it means to be black"—to counter the idea that their skin color meant they were supposed to like certain things and dislike others. He explained: "It's ridiculous to think that certain things aren't for black kids. We did that not only through the experiences we gave them, but through the people we exposed them to. We'd have them meet a black guy who likes to go camping or a black classical musician. We wanted them to come out of this program thinking anything is possible for them."

When Fuquan K. Brown, a student at West Side High School in the heart of Newark, played on that school's golf team, he took some verbal abuse from other blacks who told him that he was pursuing a white sport. Nonetheless, he and his teammates at the virtually all-minority high school persisted, traveling to suburban country clubs to play matches and losing by large margins. Their game inevitably improved, but they were learning lessons besides how to avoid slicing and hooking. The season always began with their coach lecturing to them on the dress code and decorum that golf expects of participants.[13] Similarly, the sailing team formed in 1995 at Virginia's Hampton University, a black institution, had to deal with the swells and winds of competing in a so-called white sport, but this was just one more way to broaden students' exposure.

Another symbol of the determination not to allow students to become ensnared by self-imposed stereotypes that cut them off from broader experiences is the game of chess. Representatives of two of the Communities in Schools programs in Newark taught children to play chess and ran after-school chess clubs. Antoine Gayles of CIS's Bobby Brooks Academy first offered chess to the students once a week after school, but they pressed him to include it more often and sometimes the chess boards came out every afternoon. He was delighted by the students' enthusiasm, pleased that they enjoyed the game enough to remain in the school building hunched over the boards until they went home for supper. In a locale like Newark, it meant that they were in a safe haven and away from the trouble that might besiege them on the streets in the dangerous, unsupervised hours between school dismissal and dinner.

Late one afternoon, for instance, four girls and four boys were occupied in chess games. The students carefully pondered their moves, looking ahead to the match scheduled the following week with a school in suburban New York. They noted each move they made on pads that Gayles collected at the end of the afternoon. He returned a critique to each youngster, making notations that would determine which of the players went to the match. Gayles gave special attention to whichever student he happened to be playing. "Gilbert, you can't win this game; it's over," he announced abruptly as a checkmate loomed. "Stop for a second. Although I said 'it's over,' why do you want to go all the way down there?" he asked, prodding the youngster to reflect on a move that he had made to shift one of his pieces away from the action. "Why don't you get your rook out? You're not playing your pieces, son."

Despite the expectations that playing chess placed on them, these inner-city students appeared devoted to the game. Each child had his or her own little tale about its personal significance. "It's a man's game, but women can play too," conceded Eric Greer, 13, adding: "It makes me feel good when I win. Chess is a lot like life—you have to set up your opponent." Twanda Burney, who gave her age as 12 ½, said that chess helped her concentrate and taught her to make decisions. Shareefah Washington, 13, was first attracted to the game because of all the rules. For Iesha Laing, another student who said she was 12 ½, it was simply "stimulating," and Levita Pickett, 11, wanted to play the game so that she could compete against her brother, who had also learned chess in the Communities in Schools program.

Gayles used another unfamiliar device besides chess to broaden the youngsters' experience and make them more conversant with the mainstream: the stock market. He went into a classroom regularly to lead the students in game in which they had $100,000 of imaginary money to invest. They made mock purchases and sales and tracked the value of their ersatz portfolio. One day, as the regular teacher stepped aside and Gayles replaced her at the front of the classroom, the students had their copies of the *Star-Ledger,* New Jersey's largest newspaper, opened to the pages with the stock market quotations. The students, not surprisingly, were particularly interested in the shares of consumer corporations whose names were familiar to them. They had $10,000 in pretend cash remaining to invest. They were thinking about buying 50 shares of Pepsi, which was then selling at $63.25 per share. Gayles used the occasion to inject a math lesson. "With a broker's commission of 2 percent, how much will this cost us?" he asked. The students had to perform the math on paper. Then Gayles encouraged them to consider whether their overall portfolio was going "in a positive or a negative direction." They were supposed to nominate stocks to weed out of the portfolio and sell.

"Should we sell Schering-Plough?" asked a student. Another student mentioned Microsoft in a noncommittal way.

"Should we decide on the basis of one day's change in price?" Gayles asked the class about Microsoft. "How long have you been looking at the stock?"

Based on the trends they observed in stock prices, the students organized their holdings into two groups. In one group were Tommy Hilfiger, Nike, Reebok, and The Gap. In the other were Exxon and Schering-Plough. "Is there any news that could give us any indication of why The Gap is not doing well?" Gayles asked, trying to get the students to look beyond the tables listing the prices of the stocks. "How would news about The Gap affect its price?"

A student suggested that maybe The Gap was lagging because the company suffered from shoplifting in its stores. Gayles told him that the issue was to determine whether theft was widespread in Gap stores. A little more conversation and the discussion turned to Reebok and Nike. "Who supports the Reebok and Nike markets?" Gayles asked.

"Me," one student responded quickly.

Gayles laughed. "But who do you represent in the population?" he continued the line of questioning.

"Teenagers," the student said.

The class agreed that the teenage market was crucial to the makers of athletic sneakers. A quick poll showed that most students were wearing shoes made by one or the other company. Gayles suggested that they continue their informal research by keeping their eyes on the feet of fellow students. Then the class returned to trying to determine why the price of stock in The Gap was weak. Gayles did almost all the talking and it was not evident that the students could evaluate the portfolio on their own. He ended his time with the class by telling them that the next day he would teach them about "return on investment." The larger return was the one at stake in the investment that Communities in Schools was making in these children and their future.

SEVENTEEN

Enlisting the Home

Advantaged and disadvantaged students and their varying experiences usually can be compared only from afar because students of different socioeconomic backgrounds attend different schools. For the most part, schools across the country reflect housing patterns, and impoverished families tend to live separate from affluent families. But a magnet school visited for this book was open to students throughout the district and contained both disadvantaged and advantaged students. Every attempt was made to mix local and bused-in students in the same classrooms, so-called heterogeneous grouping, out of a belief that this practice would benefit the students. Thus a particular mixed-age classroom accommodated first, second, and third graders in this school in a poor neighborhood, where the enrollment was divided about equally between local children and those from more expensive parts of town.

On this day, students were scattered about the classroom, working at various learning stations. They spent about 30 to 45 minutes at each table, selecting a different station at which to work each day. It was Black History Month, and the activities mostly reflected that theme in this school in which Latinos and Anglos each were more numerous than blacks. Students at a listening table wore earphones over which they heard stories about the Underground Railroad. Four or five books on Harriet Tubman and the Reverend Martin Luther King, Jr., lay on the reading table, and students came by and thumbed through them. At the writing table, a small group of students carried out an assignment about Harriet Tubman. Students at the art table were making drawings related to Tubman and the Underground Railroad. The math table was the exception to the theme; there students used manipulatives to study place value.

The teacher, who was walking from table to table, said quietly to a visitor that she saw "huge" differences among the neighborhood children and those who came from other areas. Those from the local neighborhood, she said, "don't feel as good about themselves." They tended to hang back and not try various activities rather than risk failure. In general, the students from outside the neighborhood were better readers, although there were exceptions. The previous year, for instance, one of the strongest readers in the class was a local child who, so far as the teacher could determine, received "no reinforcement whatsoever" in the home.

Some affluent parents of the bused-in students tried to help the class in various ways. One offered to buy tickets for every child in the class for a special attraction. That parent also paid for each student to receive a book on Harriet Tubman. The first week of school, when students were assigned to bring three items from home for show-and-tell, some of the advantaged children from distant neighborhoods brought items they had acquired in travels abroad. This embarrassed some neighborhood children, who felt that their items were too insignificant even to mention. Finally, after some encouragement, one little girl, who said what she brought was "not good enough," shyly agreed to show her items, all objects that she had made at home.

Throughout the year, the classroom teacher often found herself trying hard to "reinforce" the local children, making positive statements about them whenever possible and frequently asking one of them to go first at some activity. Slowly, over the course of the school year, the teacher witnessed some changes as students from the two groups worked together more; increasingly, some neighborhood children gradually gained confidence and grew more assertive academically. "To some degree," she said, "the out-of-neighborhood children serve as role models for the local youngsters. I'm not seeing as much low esteem as at the beginning of the year, but I can't say it fixes everything; that's unrealistic."

A main issue in enhancement efforts, although it is not fashionable to discuss it, is the lack of support for schooling in the home.

William Raspberry, an op-ed columnist for the *Washington Post,* wrote that the fundamental problem facing big-city education in America was "how to enlist low-income, poorly educated and (most often) single parents in the education of their children."[1] A teacher in a Communities in Schools classroom, being brutally frank, said: "You can't change a kid overnight. They spend most of their time with their parents and relatives. They are shaped by their environment. The parents are the key." Under the best of circumstances, parents influence the educational outcomes of their children in at least three main ways. They do this by modeling behaviors and attitudes that contribute to success in school; by reinforcing those behaviors and attitudes in their children with interest, attention, praise, and rewards; and by directly instructing their children in school-related learning.[2] The impact of these influences can vary in accord with such imponderables as the teacher's performance and the school's expectations.[3]

A basic tension attendant to efforts to ensure that children in need acquire the kind of knowledge base they need for success has to do with what they know when they arrive at school. Some educators stress school readiness, presuming that certain children are missing a great deal that they require to succeed. Other educators embrace a so-called developmental approach, emphasizing the desirability of organizing instruction around the store of knowledge that the children already have, however different their experiences may be from those of advantaged youngsters. "Is the experience of a child whose family piles into the car for a weekend trip down to the old hometown in Mexico any less valuable than that of the child who spends a ski vacation in the Alps?" asked one educator in Tucson, leaving no doubt that he considered the experiences equally important.

Some educators advocate in this regard that schools adopt a special teaching approach for urban students, rejecting the idea that they are in any way "culturally deprived, lacking in ability, unmotivated, and at-risk." These educators maintain that schools should develop instructional activities that take note of urban children's cultural knowledge, social experiences, and the ways they speak and behave.[4] In the Educational and Community Change Project in Tucson, teachers said that the connection between home and school grew stronger as they began to acknowledge children's knowledge, backgrounds, and their community as legitimate bases for further study. This philosophy affected the content of the curriculum and the nature of pedagogy at Ochoa Elementary School.[5]

Not every student in the suburbs receives all of the parental support that he or she needs for academic success, but usually affluent youngsters start with advantages regarding the influence of the home. They therefore enjoy an academic edge simply because they encounter fewer of the distractions that go hand in hand with the daily struggle deprivation inflicts on children and families. In addition, advantaged children benefit from the stability that comes with knowing that where they live today probably will be where they will live tomorrow, next month, and next year. Their mothers got adequate prenatal care during pregnancy so that they were not born so small that their health was imperiled, and they continue to receive sufficient medical attention during the growing-up years. Nutritious food fills the pantries and mortal danger does not lurk on every corner. Parents have the satisfaction of gainful employment, and the family generally views formal education as a source of upward mobility. In other words, school counts and expectations are high. "My children have me and my husband and that makes a lot of difference," said Lisa Fuentes, who worked for the I Have a Dream program at Chelsea-Elliott Houses and had a daughter participating. "But many of these children have single parents and it's not easy for them raising children on public assistance and without the skills to hold a job."

Educational Testing Service published a report calling the family "America's smallest school," citing the critical role of the home in preparing and motivating children to learn. After reviewing the statistics, the report stated, for example, that the more types of reading materials in the home, the greater a student's reading proficiency; the more a student reads at home, the better a reader he or she is; the more a student watches television, the lower his or her academic proficiency; and the more homework done by a student, the higher his or her achievement.[6] Thus President Clinton stood on solid ground when he noted in his State of the Union Message in 1997 "how important it is for parents to begin immediately talking, singing, even reading to their infants."

The research of Betty Hart and Todd R. Risley, two senior scientists with the Schiefelbusch Institute for Life Span Studies at the University of Kansas, underscored the differences from home to home in the language enrichment that small children receive. They found that the development of vocabulary and rich and complex language patterns from the time a child began talking until the age of about three was highly dependent on parents' education and socioeconomic background. On average, parents on welfare addressed about 620 words per hour to their children; working-class parents, about 1,250 words; and professional parents, more than 2,150 words. Further, parents who talked more to their children did more explaining, asked more questions, and provided more feedback.[7]

Statistics show that higher-achieving students generally come from households in which parents have more education and higher incomes than the parents of lower-achieving students. Researchers from RAND Corporation have affirmed that the most important family influences on student test scores are the level of parental education, family size, family income, and the age of the mother when the child was born,[8] factors that often weigh against poor pupils. One of the latest studies, which tracked 25,000 teenagers over of six years, found that family income counted more than race, ethnicity, gender, or scores on achievement tests in determining the youths' expectations and future educational attainments.[9] The link is firm between poverty and unfavorable scholastic outcomes.

The rural Flambeau School District in Wisconsin tried to offset some of these disadvantages by earmarking the children of 16 families in its two elementary schools for special attention. Visits to the homes—some of them no more than dilapidated house trailers—were a key part of the program, said Judy Bone, the director, who tried to do her work without actually letting the families know the children were singled out because they were deemed to be at highest risk of failure. She said that these were students who apparently received little support for school at home. The program, Families and Schools Together (FAST), operated with a grant of $100,000 from the state's Department of Public Instruction. One of Bone's goals was to get the parents into the school regularly in an effort to establish a link between school and home. She persisted in inviting parents to open houses and in asking them to sign up as classroom volunteers. Bone also tried to make the students feel special by taking a small group of them aside at least once a week and eating lunch with them. Bone said of the families in the FAST program, "These are parents who frequently don't know how to parent."

Reaching Students through Their Parents

Many enhancement programs proceed on the assumption that educating the parents will redound to the benefit of the children. In other words, smarter, better-informed parents presumably act in ways that make stronger students of their offspring. Children, especially young ones, who believe that their parents value education may end up caring more about their own schooling. The presence of parents in the school at the same time as the children, for instance, seems to influence students favorably. James Comer, who formulated the School Development Program, thought that reaching parents would help children, a proposition to which other programs now subscribe. Parents who bother investing their own time in the school, as many of the enhancements encourage them to do, probably are more apt to reinforce the goals of their children's schooling. Finally, some parents who get involved in self-improvement through programs at their children's schools end up pursuing formal education in a serious way. The knowledge and credentials they acquire may raise their self-esteem and increase their employment opportunities.

Myrna Teron, who began working at the Christopher Columbus School in New Haven as a volunteer and eventually received a small stipend to assist a classroom teacher, thought that her exposure to the school changed her in ways that had a major impact on her children. She found herself discussing television programs with her children to get them to think about the content of what they watched. She made books an important part of the interaction with her youngsters, prodding them to identify the shapes and colors that they saw on the pages, just as she had seen the teacher do with the students in the classroom. Pretty soon she was taking her own children to the library twice a week, often inviting neighborhood youngsters to accompany them.

Teron also attended the parenting sessions that the school offered through its parents' center. She said that she learned "how to talk to the children" instead of shouting at them when she was displeased.

She was sure that her children's improved conduct was a by-product of all that she had learned. Another parent at Christopher Columbus, Esteban Cruz, one of the few male volunteers, spoke of the need for more parents to make a greater commitment to their children's education. Speaking in Spanish through an interpreter, he said: "My kids were doing bad before I volunteered. Parents should come to school instead of spending time on the couch watching soap operas."

In many homes parents do not do enough to prepare children for school or do not reinforce the lessons learned once youngsters are enrolled. Sometimes such behavior is the result of minimal parental interest in school, but other times parents simply do not know what to do even though they would like to do something. One teacher who was skeptical of an enhancement program worried that waiting to involve parents after their children had reached school might be too late. She said: "The children have to be surrounded by books from Day 1, when they are babies. They can look at the pictures. It's the exposure to the stuff that counts. How many children in this school don't own a dictionary or a thesaurus or any book of their own? Not just library books. They have to be exposed to books at a very early age. Parents have to hear this. This has to happen in addition to parents getting more literate and having more self-esteem."

In another locale, a teacher despaired over her inability to help students whose own parents contributed little support for their schooling. The teacher said: "You do the best you can while they are here, while you have them." Teachers told of children in elementary school who were permitted to watch television until late at night, sometimes because a single working mother was at a second job and only a sibling was available to supervise the younger child. A teacher in Tucson, concerned about a seven-year-old who attended school sporadically because the family would do nothing to ensure that the youngster got to school, made it her business to stop at the child's home to pick her up each morning. Teachers saw the legacy of parental neglect in students' low achievement, which had a cumulative effect as children in need in school district after school district fell farther behind with each passing year.

A sense of knowing—helping children gain control over a body of knowledge—needs constant reinforcement, especially in the home, where children spend much of their time. Parents are less able to do this when their own education is limited, or they do not speak English, or their time is consumed by simply coping, or poverty and ill health rob them of the personal resources required to become involved in their children's development. "It is difficult for parents who need help themselves to get involved in helping their children," said Maria Nunez, who taught a combined kindergarten–first grade class at Christopher Columbus School in New Haven, Connecticut, a school serving many immigrant Latino families. "Some of these parents don't know how to read or write in English *or* Spanish. I send assignments home in Spanish, but the parents can't even read them. Most of them are on welfare, and, now, under the new law, they are going to have to go to school or get work so they will have to find baby-sitters for the children in the afternoon. There are some smart kids here, but without influence for education at home they are going to be lost."

Some parents—and generally they are mothers—defy all odds and on their own equip their youngsters with what they need for school success. One teacher of students in need said that in her class, "without exception," the children with the longer attention spans had parents who visited school and took an interest in their children's learning. Another teacher almost came to tears as she described a parent, impoverished and a single mother, who would not let hip surgery interfere with her going to the school for a conference about her child. Moving slowly with the aid of a walker, breathing heavily, and hardly recovered, the mother let it be known that she would not miss such an event. "I wanted to get down on my knees and thank her," the teacher said. This mother, according to the teacher, was one who communicated regularly with the teacher about her son's schoolwork.

Presumably, when parents grow more attuned to education they affirm the value of schooling in the lives of their children. Antoine Garibaldi observed: "Teachers alone cannot change students' desire to learn and to succeed. There is an equally important role for parents who spend more time with their children."[10] This effort to instill commitment in parents characterizes programs that aim to build social capital for students. Proceeding on the assumption that a parent who feels at one with the school will be more likely to reinforce educational goals, the various programs adopt measures to engage and inform parents, to win their allegiance, and even to educate them. The representative of an enhancement program said: "I suspect that one aspect of literacy for our children is having their parents involved in literacy activities. It would strengthen their self-concept and the bonds that they have with their children. This is all important to the kids attaining success in school. Helping the parents will help the kids. I hear the kids talk when their parents are here for computer classes. The kids are very accepting of that. And the parents say 'I'm going to learn too.' They're becoming good teachers of their kids."

When the Children's Aid Society helped plan the new Intermediate School 218 for Manhattan's Washington Heights, the organization arranged for a parent program to be embedded in the school from the start. The aim was to give parents in this poor but proud community some of the support that is more readily built into the lives of more advantaged families. "We wanted it to be a different kind of school for parents," said C. Warren (Pete) Moses, associate executive director of the society. "They were enthusiastic but wary. We let them know that we couldn't run the school without them. We were going to give them real things to do. We tried to say yes on some level to everything that they wanted." The basic tenets of this approach proclaimed that I.S. 218 was to be a place where parents also could learn. The school would minister to the health of their children and provide them with a haven that would extend beyond the normal school hours, into the weekends and throughout the summer. The family was assured that it could build its life around the school. Children would even learn the rudiments of employment through part-time jobs that they would hold in the school setting.

This was the kind of school—a genuine community center—that the neighborhood needed desperately. So many women signed up for the aerobics class that men milled around outside during the session, wondering what kind of guy could be leading a class that so many of their wives and girlfriends wanted to attend. The Children's Aid Society turned around and created a weight-lifting facility so that the men had their own activity to pursue while the women exercised. There seemed to be no end to the recreational and educational offerings—citizenship classes, family life and sex classes, preparation for the test for the General Equivalency Diploma. Showing up regularly for such programs was a new experience for many of the participants, unaccustomed as they were to finding anything rewarding in a school building. The long-range goal was to build a more positive relationship between school and home, forging ties that would benefit the children.

The attempt by the Beacon program in New York City to build social capital for poor schoolchildren was based on strengthening links between home and school so that the family could better reinforce the school's efforts. The Beacons strived to:

- Increase parent presence and involvement in the school
- Offer educational activities for parents and other adults in the community
- Offer arts programs for youth adults that relate to the culture of the families
- Offer informal educational activities that emphasize reading and writing
- Hire parents as staff in after-school and evening programs and as outreach
- Involve Beacons directors in the school
- Provide family support programs[11]

Some of the Beacon projects seemed to produce dramatic changes in the extent to which parents involved themselves in their children's education. Like so many other enhancement programs around the country, however, the Beacons could not readily determine whether greater parental involvement translated into academic improvement for students. The Beacons hoped to develop systematic strategies to produce more student learning as a result of greater parental involvement, and not just assume that this would be the result. One of the Beacon initiatives, the Rheedlen program at P.S. 194 in Harlem, had a goal to "make it possible for parents to be educators of their children," an objective usually taken for granted in middle-class homes. Yet it cannot be assumed that highly stressed families will change parenting practices if mere suggestions are made to parents and they are provided with more opportunities to interact with the school. A study by the Harvard Family Research Project emphasized that the effectiveness of such programs depended on the availability and quality of a range of such other resources as child care and recreational facilities, and services related to housing, jobs, and health care.[12]

In accord with such objectives, the Neighborhood Academic Initiative at the University of Southern California offered a family development institute in conjunction with its Pre-College Enrichment Academy for secondary students. The academy aimed to bring students to the level that they could qualify for entrance to USC; the institute tried to help parents and guardians engage in their own uplift so that they would be better able to support the youngsters in reaching their goals. A parent, guardian, or advocate of the student had to sign a contract agreeing to participate in the institute, which met most Saturday mornings on the university campus. It offered lectures and workshops on such topics as parenting, citizenship, human sexuality, nutrition, cultural awareness, intrafamily conflict resolution, employment skills, and other areas likely to help low-income families. In addition, classes were given in English as a second language at both beginning and advanced levels, Spanish as a second language, literacy, computer use, and mathematics. During the same hours, the students attended classes and tutorials elsewhere on campus.

Gathering in the auditorium of a campus building, the adults, often accompanied by the family's younger children, were asked to recommit themselves each week to support the students through the arduous program. Usually, the session included the recitation of the institute's pledge of allegiance and support:

> As a family, we pledge our allegiance and support to the USC Pre-College Enrichment Academy and Family Development Institute. We joyously commit our energies to making these programs a total success for our scholars, ourselves, and our communities. We happily contribute our talents and time to enrich all of the academy and institute's activities and programs. We incessantly encourage our children to be the most well behaved and productive scholars they can be at school, at home, and in the community. Likewise, we take advantage of every opportunity offered by the family development institute to enhance our abilities to attain and enjoy a better life for ourselves and our loved ones. We affectionately embrace and

celebrate the colors, histories, and cultures of all our family members.

Many parents of children who participate in enhancement programs share certain commonalities when it comes to schools. Their own formal education ended early, and their own school encounters often were unsatisfactory. The beginning of a new, improved relationship between school and home is an effort to render them, as adults, more knowledgeable and to make them favorably inclined toward their children's schools. In some cases, this involves empowering parents not only by getting them into the building but also by giving them decision-making roles. Part of the move away from the culture of poverty in these settings involves encouraging people to take steps on their own behalf rather than relying on others to act in their stead.

When the Mission View Elementary School in Tucson, part of the Educational and Community Change project, wanted to get parents—mostly Spanish-speaking—more involved in their children's education, the school took measures to draw the mothers closer to the school. These were women, said school officials, who ordinarily seldom left the home. The school began by teaching them arts and crafts, including how to crochet. Soon conversation in the group became easy and flowing and the women supported each other, increasing their levels of confidence. Mission View became an important place for this small group, who felt increasingly at ease with the school staff, all of whom—except for the nurse and some cafeteria workers—spoke Spanish.

Recognizing that many parents may need help themselves in order to aid their children with their assignments, Canton Middle School instituted a homework hot line that allowed families to telephone and listen to a recorded description of the homework assigned each day in every course in the school. Parents could determine what pages their children were supposed to cover on a given night. The system also created voice mailboxes for both parents and teachers so that they could leave each other messages. The homework hot line was a natural development at a school that asked each family to agree to a contract pledging to find a quiet place for the child to do homework and to make sure that homework was completed. About 75 percent of the families signed these contracts.

But the demands of jobs, home life, and preschool children—as well as some trepidation and even lethargy—seem to limit the impact of efforts to construct a bridge to the home. Whether it is a matter of signing a homework contract or taking part in the activities of a parents' center, some parents resist getting drawn into their children's school lives. In fact, certain parents adamantly disapprove of the move by educators to involve the school in family life. These parents feel that the home is sacred territory where the family itself should determine policies affecting the children and that efforts by public schools to build partnerships represent an unwelcome infringement by governmental authority. So strong has this attitude been in some places that parents have tried to enact laws limiting the reach of government agencies on matters affecting, for instance, the health and welfare of children. Amendment 17, which voters in Colorado turned down by a narrow margin in 1996, contained language about the right of parents to direct and control the upbringing of their children.

A variation on this conflict appears in some of the enhancement programs themselves. Communities in Schools, an organization that offers programs in school districts around the country, sometimes found that its overtures were not received as well by parents as by school people. "Some of them perceive us as trying to do their jobs," Jackie Robinson of CIS said of parents. "Some don't want the program to do what they think the family ought to do. But without us some of these kids wouldn't get their basic needs attended to because no one attends to those needs in the home." Workers for the Children's Aid Society in New York City sometimes have encountered much the same attitude. "In the cases of some of these kids," said a society representative, "not only don't we get parental participation, but parents don't even acknowledge what we are doing for their kids." These are discouragements that enhancement programs try to overlook.

The path between school and home runs in two directions, and some schools use home visits to try to break down barriers and to better understand just what confronts students in their out-of-school lives. A teacher at the Expo Middle School in St. Paul, Minnesota, lauded the value of home visits. "I can approach students differently

when I see how they live," he said. "It's a real eye opener." In Los
Angeles, it was not until family liaison workers from the Vaughn
Learning Center started calling on parents that they realized that some
Mexican families actually lived in garages. Discussions of homework
took on new meaning in reference to such children.

Two Different Ways to Link
the Home to Student Assessment

In line with the conviction that parents who become more knowledgeable about schools will involve themselves more readily with the
education of their children, the Educational and Community Change
Project (ECC) in Tucson set out to enlighten parents about districtwide, nationally norm-referenced pupil testing at the schools. A goal
was to help parents decipher the meaning of test scores and to build a
receptive climate for the alternative assessments that project supporters hoped would replace the traditional examinations. The project
introduced parents to the subject of testing by encouraging them to
think about knowledge itself and what knowledge they considered it
essential for their children to learn. In other words, what should a
student study in elementary school? The question, simple enough, is
seldom asked. Yet the question ought to precede the preparation of a
test if the test is to examine what people consider important to know.

The idea of looking at testing in this manner was part of the school
restructuring that ECC promoted. The project favored alternative
assessment over traditional standardized testing. Parents were encouraged to challenge the validity of traditional tests, the very kinds of tests
that so often found their children's knowledge lacking. The notion of
a single "right" answer was called into question, and the possibility
was raised that there were numerous acceptable answers. ECC took its
battle against norm-referenced assessment into the schools in Tucson
that were affiliated with the project.

Thus in 1996 a meeting was held at Ochoa School, the lead school
of the project. Eight mothers sat in cramped fashion around a table in
a small room adjacent to the main office. The table and the chairs were
actually children's furniture, and the adults' knees bumped up against
the underside of the table. Two of the mothers had infants with them.

Viki L. Montera, the project director, led the meeting, speaking in English; the school's community worker translated her words into Spanish, then translated parents' comments back into English for Montera, who seemed to know enough Spanish to get the gist of the comments without translation.

"We're thinking about different ways of assessing what the children know," Montera said, referring to the test scores that were published annually in the local newspaper. "We're trying to bring together teachers and parents in the schools to think about what children are learning. What do you believe is valuable that your children are learning? We want you to begin a discussion about this, about what your children are learning and how you know that they are learning it."

These questions about the nature of learning prompted a discussion about a recent effort by students from the school to clean up a litter-strewn lot near the school. Montera asked the mothers what they thought the children had gleaned from the experience. One mother spoke of how her child had learned about the soil and about varieties of trees and the sort of soil that each tree needs for healthy growth. The mother appeared satisfied that the time spent cleaning the lot was a good learning experience. The parent of a first grader added that the kind of learning derived from the experience in the lot seemed to make her child more interested in school. She said that her child was already a good student who liked to read books and that she hoped other children in the class had a similar interest in books.

"What is it that you think that your children are learning?" Montera asked, apparently trying to steer the conversation toward the topic of alternative assessment. "What is it that you think is important for them to learn in school, and how do you know they are learning it?" The conversation continued, but the parents did not indicate either what they thought was important for children to learn or how they knew the children were learning it. Finally one mother said that she was concerned that the students spent too much of their time doing what appeared to be play, an apparent allusion to activities such as those they pursued at the littered lot. The mother wondered whether time used in such a manner was in concert with the purpose of school. She also voiced concern about the expectations that were put on her child in his multiage classroom, where he was supposed to take responsibility for the learning of younger children. Her son was uneasy with that burden, she said. As she talked it through, however, she decided it might be for the best. "I told him it was good to learn patience and to take responsibility. He is good about it now. He resolves the fights that other kids get into." She thought, in retrospect, that this role was important for him because he was the youngest sibling and did not ordinarily perform such a function.

Not another enhancement program followed the confrontational approach that ECC built into its efforts to educate parents about reading assessment. The idea elsewhere tended toward accepting norm-referenced tests and working within the existing system of assessment to help students do as well as they could. The talk was not about whether traditional reading examinations were good or bad but about what children could do to improve their scores. One day at Public School 5 in Manhattan, for instance, people were attending a gathering of the kinship parenting program, a group whose very existence acknowledged the fact that many students lived with grand-parents, aunts and uncles, and other relatives who were their primary caregivers. At least 5 percent of the 1,200 pupils at P.S. 5 lived with neither parent. Some of those at the meeting looked considerably older than the usual parents of elementary-age children and faced child-rearing issues that they probably had not expected to encounter at that stage of life. The kinship parenting program was trying to help them cope with their unexpected burdens.

Several dozen kinship caregivers were at the school this day for the workshop on testing. The time for the annual citywide examina-tions in reading and mathematics was fast approaching. The workshop was an attempt to tell the adults what to expect and to encourage them to take steps over the long run that would strengthen the children's reading abilities and prepare them for testing. A school representative spoke in Spanish about the tests, and the principal translated her words into English for the minority of people there who did not understand Spanish. The translation went something like this at a meeting in the cafeteria:

"If your child was in school in the Dominican Republic but not in school here in New York for 20 months, he or she doesn't take this test. Those enrolled here for at least 20 months take the test, but 20 months is not enough. If I had to go to a foreign country and take a test in 20 months, I don't know how I'd do. Yet many of the children do very well. The second part of this test, the writing portion, is given only in the fourth grade. Children are asked questions—like when you went on vacation what did you do—and then they have to answer in a story that they write on paper. They have to have a beginning, a middle, and an end to what they write. The teachers mark it. Not one teacher, but three teachers. That gives a fairer picture of what your child has written. They look to see if the English is correct and the spelling and whether the child used a beginning, a middle, and an end."

About 30 adults, all but two or three of them women, were in the room when the session began. Stragglers arrived throughout, taking seats at one or another of the tables in the sparkling clean cafeteria. "This test is untimed," the principal said, "but they say that if a child takes more than two hours you may as well take the paper away. They only have to write 175 words and they have time enough to think about it, plan it, and write it. The children have already taken a practice test so they know how to do this. Many did very nicely."

Everyone listened politely. No one asked a question. The Spanish presentation with immediate translation into English continued throughout. The principal went on: "What can we do together to help the children do well on this test? Let them read. Anything they want, just so they read. Read, read, read, everyday. They should see you reading. When you read a magazine or a newspaper, show them you're reading. Point it out so they know you are reading. It doesn't matter if you're reading in Spanish. Just so they see you're reading. So, what should you say at home to the children?"

"Read, read, read," the people at the meeting chanted responsively, as if in church.

"They can read the same story more than once. That's okay. What else can you do? You can watch TV with them and talk to them and ask questions about what they saw," the principal said. Then she referred to a leaflet that she had distributed, pointing out a list of questions that adults can ask children after watching television or reading together:

"Who are the people in the show?"
"Why do they act the way they do?"
"Use some words to describe the people."
"Where does the story take place?"
"What would happen if we changed the place?"

The list continued in this way, concluding with suggestions about what adults should ask children when they take them to a supermarket, to a park, or to a museum. The principal told them that it did not matter whether they asked the children questions in Spanish or English. "They think in two languages," she said. Then she encouraged them to get the children to think about events in sequence—what happened first, what happened next, what happened at the end. "It helps their writing to think this way," she explained. "What's it all about? Tell me the whole story. Summarize it. What's the central idea? What's the most important thing?"

Few of the people had bothered to remove their jackets and coats. Some unzipped or unbuttoned their outer garments, but they sat fully dressed for the wintery weather outside, much as high school students do at certain schools where lockers are not used. The principal continued the mock discussion that she wanted the caregiver adults to have with the children for whom they were responsible. She suggested that they ask the children to talk about the characters in a story and posed some sample questions: "Are they real or are they make-believe? When you see a dog talking, is that real?" Then she turned to the use of literary devices. "This means things such as the setting. Is it in the country or in the city? Do the people speak in the way you speak? How do the people in the story act? Why do they act that way? Are they real or are they make-believe? The questions are the same in any language." The principal spoke some more about the contents of the citywide test that the students would be taking. "The questions might well ask them to infer," she said. "Does anyone know what that means?" No response. She cited an example to illustrate an inference. Then she referred to a booklet that she distributed to help people understand more fully what would appear on the examinations from the California Testing Bureau.

The booklet explained what test questions on reading would deal with—recall of facts, sequence of events, summary of information, central theme, plot, character analysis, tone, and literary devices. It said that students would be asked to infer, analyze, interpret, predict, transfer knowledge, construct meaning, evaluate meaning, and extend meaning. The principal, with the translations from Spanish into English continuing, gave examples, saying, finally: "Now that I've given you all the information you need to start working with your children, what's the one thing to do everyday?"

In unison, they intoned once again: "Read, read, read."

EIGHTEEN

Conclusion: Looking Back, Looking Ahead

Nikki Brown, the AmeriCorps worker on assignment to the I Have A Dream program, thought that she and the 19 other college students involved in the project at Chelsea-Elliott Homes in Manhattan were making a difference even if evidence to that effect was not readily available. "There's a lot that you can't measure, like the emotional and social advances of the children," said Brown, dressed in a sweatsuit with an AmeriCorps insignia on the sleeve. "They make these gains, but maybe they are not documented. Because we started with them when they were young [the students began in the project at seven and eight years of age], you'll see real progress. But the truth is that at any age if someone comes and shows genuine caring and concern, it can make a difference. A lot of what we do is nothing more than shooting the breeze with them. I don't think they get enough chance to talk to people about their day and about life in general."

Brown, a graduate of Morgan State University in Maryland who was pursuing a master's degree in urban policy at the New School for Social Research, felt a special bond with the dreamers because they all lived in public housing, just as she had when she was growing up in the Bronx. She thought, however, that the difference between her experience and theirs was that today's youngsters were being hurried into growing up and were "missing their childhood." The impact of the drug culture, with its violence and degradation, loomed larger in their lives and they "had to put on a front and pretend to be older than they actually were." Brown believed that she had advantages over the children in the program even though she too was raised in poverty by a single mother. There were no siblings in her home, so she did not get pressed into caring for brothers and sisters as so many of the dreamers did and her mother struggled to keep her out of the public schools and send her to parochial schools. "They're living in a world that we can't completely understand," said Brown, who was only 23 years old.

An unanswerable question has to do with just how much social capital a youngster needs to overcome the circumstances of a life that surrounds him or her with obstacles at every turn. What sort of connectedness and support mechanisms can help a young person find a way through this thicket of difficulties? It is fine to say that education will make the difference, but as the vignettes in this book demonstrate, education is not pursued in a vacuum. Crime, violence, poverty, and family dysfunction threaten to undermine the efforts of the most devoted teachers. Furthermore, schooling itself—for students of all economic circumstances—poses problematic issues. Even if a child perseveres in the face of overwhelming odds and goes to class regularly, what is he or she to make of lessons that are boring and irrelevant? In other words, the struggle to change outcomes for the needy carries the added burden of absorbing the lessons of school reform. These attempts to change education face the daunting challenge of trying, at the same time, to close the achievement gap between whites and Asian Americans on the one side and blacks and Latino Americans on the other side. The progress that was made in this regard in the 1970s and 1980s appears to have come to a halt; if anything, the gap may be widening in some subjects and in some grades.[1]

And so the funders and supporters of the various enhancement programs still wrestle with questions of how to make a difference. Do test scores alone reveal the worth of such programs? What does it mean when improvement seems obvious but test scores show few or no gains? "I'm repeatedly stymied when I think about what these interventions are and how long it takes to get a changed test score," said Susan Philliber, an evaluator for several enhancement programs. "Just thinking about it makes my hair hurt." The attempt to alter the destinies of schoolchildren in need has to be more than a fad. The programs keep replicating themselves without conclusively demonstrating a statistically significant impact. As one researcher noted, if such inexactitude existed in the health field, the Food and Drug Administration would want more evidence before allowing the product to gain widespread use. On the other hand, how does someone measure over just a few years a program meant to show its effects during a lifetime?

Officials of enhancement projects initially take delight in any progress, however slight. The Educational and Community Change Project in Tucson, for instance, was pleased by the early gains, small as they may have been, of students at the Ochoa School on the Iowa Test of Basic Skills. The test, however, did not align with the school's curriculum. This is one of the problems in authenticating program impact. What teachers at Ochoa said they *did* know about the students, though, was that they were engaged in learning to a greater extent than in the past and that the type of work they did in school had greater connection to the real world. Five years after the start of the project, only 2 of the school's 17 teachers were still using reading textbooks regularly. The rest had switched over to real literature.

Canton Middle School in Baltimore welcomed the introduction of new state tests for eighth graders that encouraged thinking and were more in tune with the school's educational reforms than the former nationally-standardized, norm-referenced tests used in Maryland. Canton students' scores improved between 1991 and 1996 in reading and mathematics, generally outranking averages at the city's other middle schools. The gains continued in 1996, but, nonetheless, Canton continued to trail the state averages, attesting to the persistent achievement gap between urban and suburban schools. Satisfaction over improvement on the new examinations also was tempered by the fact that Canton's curriculum and teaching styles did not orient students toward the norm-referenced test that the city's selective high schools continued using to determine admissions. So during the month and a half leading up to the admissions test, Canton began devoting the last period of each day to preparing eighth graders for the norm-referenced test. Schools like Canton that show concern for the development of the whole child, rather than a single-minded focus on academics, are asked over and over again for evidence that such attention produces scholastic gains.

Ron Lewis of the headquarters office of Communities in Schools in Alexandria, Virginia, said that when he asked students whether a discussion in class made sense to them, their affirmative answers were reason for some gratification. An evaluation of CIS done out of the University of North Carolina, however, was less sanguine about the program's impact. The report stated: "Despite anecdotal evidence that suggests Cities in Schools [the program's old name] programs enhance the academic and social success of 'at risk' students who participate in the program, programs in the Southeast and across the country are functioning without defined and clearly operationalized outcome measures . . ."[2]

Martha Cameron at the headquarters of Children's Aid Society in New York City said: "We hope for long-term success. I accepted a long time ago that what we can do in numbers is limited. But every time we help one child, we help a whole family and all of the younger siblings. We only begin to touch the surface in filling the gaps. But we help them discover that the gaps exist and give them some of the tools so they can fill the gaps themselves. What keeps me going is when I see these kids graduate from college. I knew them when they were 13 or 14 and so I know how far they have come. I see how far they've gone beyond their peers. They are light-years ahead of peers in the neighborhood who haven't had the experiences that they have had." This did not mean that Children's Aid did not crave statistics to back up its claims. Pete Moses, Cameron's boss, said: "We take very seriously our responsibility for evaluating our efforts in a variety of ways. We know we have to demonstrate educational performance and improvement. I'm positive we're having a significant positive impact on the education of our kids. I'm anxious for the research that will back this up."

The foundations and other funders that pour millions of dollars into enhancement projects sometimes worry over a paucity of documentable success. The Danforth Foundation, based in St. Louis, was so disappointed with the progress of its efforts in working with schools for youngsters in need that it essentially scrapped the program and started over again. "If you look for hard empirical data that all of this [the enhancements] improves outcomes for children, you would be hard-pressed to come up with anything that shows it improves student learning," said program evaluator Philliber. "You even wonder if the state of research is up to the task. You're forced to measure things that aren't easy to track and people say you can't measure those things anyway."

At the I Have a Dream project at New York City's Chelsea-Elliott Houses, evidence of scholastic progress was scant, for example. But there were stories that seemed to resonate with meaning. A child who entered the program at the end of second grade able to read only her name was reading on a third-grade level by the time she finished fifth grade. Not grade level, mind you, but progress, to be sure. After testing this student originally, the school had recommended that she get special education placement, speech and language therapy, and counseling. Her mother refused to authorize any of these measures, however, and the girl continued in a regular class. The only extra attention came through the intervention of I Have a Dream, which provided her with daily tutoring. Moreover, representatives of the dreamer program worked to get the school to provide certain services that were allowable even without parental permission. The impact of such efforts by an enhancement program is not readily quantified.

The I Have a Dream organization was sensitive to questions about its effect on students. In an internal document addressing the issue of evaluation, its headquarters cautioned its projects to evaluate success based on "specific" improvement in students, not on the basis of just "any" improvement. "*Any* improvement is not necessarily *sufficient* improvement," the memorandum said. "For example, a dreamer may increase her self-esteem in real and measurable ways, but if she maintains an F average, she will not graduate from high school." The document went on to list the pros and cons of using indicators of success in seven areas: school attendance, grades, standardized test scores, graduation rates, drop out rates, rate of teen parenthood, and self-esteem.[3] Clearly, the program had some statistics that seemed to attest to a degree of success. In three dreamer projects in Chicago in which the scheduled graduation years were 1993 and 1996, for example, the cumulative graduation rate of the dreamers was 69 percent. Meanwhile, in the same high schools only 40 percent of the non-dreamers were graduating. As of 1992, 51 percent of dreamers in eight projects in New York City finished high school on time, in comparison with 32 percent of other students. Denver's first class of dreamers graduated in June 1995 with an on-time rate of 80 percent, as compared with no more than 60 percent of other students.[4]

Altogether, by the spring of 1996, about 2,500 graduates of I Have a Dream across the country were attending some 380 colleges, universities, and other postsecondary schools. About three out of four young people in the program went on to some sort of formal education after high school.[5] Early indications were that attrition rates for dreamers in college were high even though the program paid their tuition (the program does not provide for room, board, books, and transportation). The organization was considering what it could do to keep more of its students enrolled in postsecondary education.

What Makes a Difference?

The attempt continues to make scholastic outcomes for students in need more closely approximate the achievements of students from more prosperous backgrounds. Yet what is the evidence that schools affect what becomes of advantaged students from affluent families? Yes, circumstances usually turn out better for those from families of means than for the truly disadvantaged, but how much of this has to do with what happened in school itself? The amount of algebra or American history a person recalls usually has little to do with his or her ability to participate gainfully in the mainstream of American life. How many high school graduates remember how to solve equations or can discuss the role of the United States in World War I? This is not to say that substantial learning has small importance. No one associated with a project studied for this book was apt to make such a statement.

Clearly, though, social capital counts for as much as book learning, and it has much to do with the paths that open up for advantaged students. A sense of connectedness, a sense of well-being, a sense of academic initiative, and a sense of knowing that extend beyond subject matter position young people for the life, liberty, and pursuit of happiness that Jefferson had in mind for Americans when he wrote the Declaration of Independence. What this means, then, is that if schools in the United States hope to prepare all children for lives better than those they have known, instituting high academic standards will

not be sufficient in and of itself. Students from impoverished backgrounds require a support structure that will keep them from falling
off the ladder. Otherwise, chances of meeting the standards fade like a
winter sun.

A sense of connectedness ensures that school counts for something in a young person's life. Furthermore, connectedness binds the
school to the community and to the student's family in ways that
reinforce formal education. A sense of well-being helps keep the
student healthy enough to gain maximum benefit from education.
Good physical, mental, and emotional health are all at stake for a
student when it comes to getting the most out of schooling. A sense of
academic initiative builds a foundation for learning. There are very
good reasons why children are more likely to thrive in school if parents
read to them and provide them with experiences that promote their
intellectual development. Good role models set examples for a student
to emulate, and teachers who hold high expectations and know how
to engage students put other important pieces of the learning puzzle
in place.

Finally, a sense of knowing enlarges upon the social capital that
lends context to each new learning experience. Parents, teachers, and
the community itself contribute, ideally, to a child's sense of knowing.
The Japanese schools frequently cited as models of the academic rigor
that ought to be found in American schools possess other factors that
also facilitate scholastic achievement. An American researcher pointed
to the way elementary schools in Japan strive to meet the needs of the
whole child, including the sense of belonging so that students
"develop strong positive bonds to schools that meet their human
needs."[6] These human needs are what this book had in mind in its
formulation of the four senses.

The model of schooling embodied in the four senses calls for an
approach to education seldom found today, when schools still tend to
operate in isolation—cut off from families and communities and from
agencies that meet social service and health needs. The ecosystem now
understood to be integral to the natural world is still not appreciated
in the world of education. In indigent neighborhoods usually hardly
any effort is made to fortify and link the various forces that could
synergistically support children's development. Scant recognition is

paid to the fact that a student's intellectual development and receptivity to schooling depend on an array of factors beyond the classroom.

Laurence Steinberg and his colleagues, after studying more than 20,000 teenagers and their families for a decade, concluded in 1996 that "the sorry state of student achievement in America is due more to the conditions of students' lives outside of school than to what takes place within school walls."[7] Moreover, they blamed many of the shortcomings in high schools on the failure of parents to exert enough positive influence on behalf of their children's education, leaving more room for youngsters to be negatively influenced by a youth culture that holds academic achievement in disdain.[8] Schools that want children to read better in the third grade, to have a deeper understanding of mathematical concepts in the sixth grade, and to be able to cope with chemistry and physics in high school must surround students with the social capital to make this progress possible.

Collaboration is imperative. Fienberg-Fisher Elementary School in Dade County, Canton Middle School in Baltimore, and New Brunswick High School in New Jersey all addressed the health needs of their students by forming partnerships with medical providers. The Flambeau schools in rural Rusk County, Wisconsin, and El Puente Academy in urban Brooklyn reached out to embrace their communities. The Vaughn School in Los Angeles and Expo Middle School in St. Paul even made available clothing when children needed it.

One measure of the difference that some enhancements have made has to do with their effect on educational practices, if not on individual achievement. Educational and Community Change, in Tucson, dealt extensively with teaching and learning in the schools in which it was implemented. The program promoted teaching in two languages, multiage grouping, and curriculum without prescribed textbooks. Program funds also enabled the schools to hire regular substitutes so that classroom teachers could be freed for weekly dialogue sessions. For half a day each week, the teachers discussed issues with other project members, articulating theories and examining assumptions. The program at Vaughn in Los Angeles was very much connected to the effort to transform education under a charter arrangement, including the waiving of certain requirements of the teachers' union. Expo Middle School in St. Paul also had a waiver from the union, in this case allowing for hiring outside the regular channels. El Puente had nonlicensed teachers functioning in roles not unlike those of regular teachers.

Another way to gauge the impact of programs of enhancement has to do with the extent to which they inspire replication within regular school offerings, as AVID did in San Diego and elsewhere. The Foshay Learning Center, a middle school in Los Angeles, tried to model its program for seventh graders after the Neighborhood Academic Initiative in which some of its students participated in conjunction with the University of Southern California. In replication of the USC initiative, Foshay set up its own after-school and Saturday programs, also trying to involve parents, as USC did. This was clearly an example of school reform mimicking, in the best sense, an outside intervention. The presence in the school of students who participated in the Neighborhood Academic Initiative helped create a tone that educators at Foshay hoped would infect the entire school. It was not like that in the beginning, when the first Foshay students in USC's Academic Initiative were ridiculed by classmates.

It was clear, however, that teachers at Foshay held students in the Neighborhood Academic Initiative—with its full array of support services—to higher expectations than other students in the school. David Dillard, a social studies teacher who taught students who were in and out of the program, observed that sometimes those in the program got worse grades simply because he had higher standards for them. For one thing, USC required students to be at least on grade level in their reading ability in English. Many other Foshay students could not meet this standard. Furthermore, chances of a student who was certified for special education coping with the USC program were slim. Yet a considerable number of special education students were in the general student body at the school.

So, while officials of the Neighborhood Academic Initiative rejected the notion that they were "skimming off" some of the best students in the schools in which the program operated, it appeared that, in fact, this was the case. This is not to say, however, that these same students would have prospered without the program. All evidence pointed to the contrary for many participants, and it was clear that the Neighborhood Academic Initiative was a powerful force for improving outcomes and for bolstering the ability of families to reinforce their children's attainments. Stephanie Hoffman, a science teacher, surveyed her grade book and found that of the academy students, the averages were 90.3 percent for the eighth graders and 89.7 percent for the seventh graders. By comparison, among the nonacademy students, the averages were 71 percent for the eighth graders and 73.5 percent for the seventh graders.

The grounding received by the USC academy students was in evidence one day when Madeleine K. Albright, then the U.S. ambassador to the United Nations, visited Foshay. The invitation to Albright carried some clout because her sister was an administrator at the school. Earlier in the year, students in the Neighborhood Academic Initiative had spent time reading Thomas More and Machiavelli, hating having to slog through the laborious texts. They may not have been enamored of the works, but they retained some of the ideas. When Albright spoke to the students, she was surprised that some of them discussed policy with allusions to Thomas More and Machiavelli. Not bad for the inner city.

Complicating Circumstances

Schools will not have an easy time in remaking themselves in order to build social capital for children in need. Collaboration requires a rearrangement of turf. Agencies that have struggled to establish their domains may not readily overlook territorial demarcations. Furthermore, even if agencies cooperate and position themselves to deliver services effectively, is such paternalism sufficient and will it advance poor people toward the kind of self-sufficiency that social capital makes possible? Some scholars have questioned the worth of collaboration that focuses simply on delivering services while fostering dependency on outside experts. Julie A. White and Gary G. Wehlange, both of the University of Wisconsin-Madison, argued that the goal of such services should be to encourage interdependence through the development of social capital, thereby strengthening neighborhoods and communities in the process. "We contend," they wrote, "that in the long run the first priority for social policy should be to promote reforms that build social capital; i.e., to help groups of citizens develop their capacity to organize themselves to address community problems. . . . The failure of social policy, in general, and the human services in particular to address the need to build social capital has led to neglect and decline of communities, a serious issue in contemporary society."[9]

School reform itself presents issues that confound educators. One thrust of the move to improve schools, for example, calls for freeing teachers from some duties and giving them time for planning so that they can confer more readily with each other. At an elementary school in Arizona with an enhancement program, the faculty appreciated the idea of having more time to meet together, but they measured the value of any out-of-the-classroom experience in terms of whether it warranted their separation from their students. For example, one teacher fretted because her students had misbehaved when the substitute was with them. "I was sad because I trusted you," she had chided the children. The students had collaborated to write an apology that was written in both Spanish and English. They had to copy the letter in either language, and all of the letters would be presented to the substitute. It read: "We're sorry we caused trouble. We're learning how to respect teachers and follow directions. We will be nice the next time."

Teachers also may evince anxiety over the idea of schools enmeshing themselves in services that ostensibly verge away from the academic mission. While some programs, such as those at Baltimore's Canton Middle School or Brooklyn's El Puente Academy, were embedded in their schools, others such as Communities in Schools or the Children's Aid Society or the Beacons, had the aura of add-ons, seemingly exogenous to the school systems in which they operated. That these programs used personnel who were not on the payroll of the school board sometimes created a potential for conflict with the school's regular teachers. Richard Negron, who headed the Children's Aid Society's operation at I.S. 218, said: "There has always been a small group of teachers who isolated themselves from the program. They didn't think it was significant or important. We understand that it is unrealistic to expect everyone to buy into the program. But, after all these years, even those who isolated themselves are starting to see the benefits."

The citywide Beacons program in New York saw a shortcoming in its model in the limited link that the program made with instructional strategies to improve educational outcomes. A report on the program said:

> Since the initiative did not originate with schools, it is not surprising that it has involved limited dialogue with teachers and school administrators about education in the classroom. Beacons agencies have taken a support role through after-school tutoring, homework help and enrichment activities, and through provision of computers and other such tools. A few have developed direct plans with the school, for example, concentrating enrichment efforts on a particular grade level at the school's request, or working to bring a science enrichment program (through NSF funding to the school). Yet, there is far more potential that has not yet been tapped for collaboration to support educational achievement.[10]

Some classroom teachers—at Manhattan's I.S. 218 and elsewhere—were inclined to view the practice of offering health services through school as peripheral to the fundamental business of education. These teachers probably would have admitted that obstacles blocked the learning paths of poor children, but somehow they resisted the idea of the school assuming a primary role in removing the barriers. Some evaluators have observed that "school restructuring strategies may be more accessible and understandable to those who are involved in school-linked services than school-linked services strategies are to those involved in school restructuring. . . ."[11]

School-based health programs in some places simply may not have done enough to proselytize among the faculty. An English teacher at New Brunswick High School in New Jersey, for instance, said of the school-based mental health program: "I'm concerned with anything that interferes with the daily academic structure." He objected to the practice of students missing classes for counseling sessions and proposed that the sessions occur only during lunchtime. "I'm not sure," he said, "that there should be such a large program in a school if the program is not purely academic." He also criticized the recreational aspects of the school-based program, proposing instead that it offer homework help. To the clinicians in the program, however, recreation was the hook that brought students to them and helped make seeing a "shrink" acceptable. A science teacher, not acknowledging any familiarity with the concept of confidentiality accorded to the patient-practitioner relationship, felt that the mental health counselors were not sharing information with her that she ought to know about her students. "All I ever see is a note that they are supposed to leave class for counseling," she complained. "And then it becomes a problem if I refuse to let someone leave."

A social studies teacher at New Brunswick said that contact between the school-based personnel and the faculty was minimal, engendering gossip among the faculty and misunderstanding about the role of the program. "There seems to be a separation," he observed. He thought that counseling should be limited to advising students about the academic program. Also, he believed that the school-based program reached only a relative handful of students and most remained untouched by it. "I don't even know if it's for the general student population," he said. "Why do they work with certain kids and not with others who clearly need it? Anyway, it would be better to have tutoring instead of playing pool," he said.

Before growing impatient with the responses of teachers, however, the ambitious nature of the various efforts to mobilize everyone for joint action on behalf of students in need must be considered. In one report the Stuart Foundations, a San Francisco philanthropy, reminded readers that

> education practitioners at joint school restructuring and school-linked services sites are expected to undergo profound changes in the way they do business. Teachers who have traditionally enjoyed norms of privacy and autonomy are asked to share what they are doing with their students with the larger community, and actively seek the expert advice of others, even outside of their profession. At some schools, the degree to which teachers were expected to change was so great that several veteran teachers requested transfers to other sites not having either school restructuring or school-linked services. The principal, whose primary mission was to guide the instructional program for the school, now plans complex school/ health and human services programs with other agency personnel, and often supervises professionals outside of the field of education.[12]

Another personnel issue has to do with the fact that some of the most promising enhancement programs depend precariously on the work of just a handful of dedicated, hardworking individuals who extend themselves far beyond the call of duty. They cannot be expected to remain in their positions indefinitely, which prompts questions about whether the projects can thrive beyond their involvement. These exemplars were such people as a classroom teacher in one program who stayed after school two and a half hours four days a week for no extra pay. He took it on himself to be in touch with each household at least once a week. His students worshiped him, but how long this married young man with a first child on the way could keep up such a pace was questionable.

Then there is the question of the continued service of directors and program heads of various projects. Some seemed to have made the ventures work by sheer force of personality. Such charismatic individuals as Rheedlen's Geoffrey Canada, Fienberg-Fisher's Grace Nebb, Vaughn's Yvonne Chan, Nancy Updegrave at the tiny Ivydale School in Appalachia, and the Neighborhood Academic Inititative's James Fleming were larger-than-life figures without whom it would have been difficult to imagine their programs prospering. Canada, recognizing this problem, created his own leadership development program with an eye toward trying to ensure the availability of people who could keep programs operating in the future. Continuity in leadership poses problems everywhere in education. A report on the program of the Edna McConnell Clark Foundation observed that instability was ingrained in school districts and that personnel turnover, from the superintendent on down, undermined attempts to bring about change. Only one of the project's 12 schools kept a principal in place through the five-year period. The other 11 schools had a total of 27 different principals during that time.[13]

Given such problems, are schools that serve those in need in any position to help revitalize their communities? On the other hand, do they have any choice? Under the usual circumstances, it is difficult to imagine either a school or its surrounding neighborhood prospering while the other falters, locked as they are in a symbiotic relationship. It is no accident that real estate prices and the quality of local public schools are so closely linked. Viable communities provide a basis for good schools and good schools help sustain communities. The neighborhood school strengthens the neighborhood and neighborhood prosperity strengthens the school. Neighborhoods that are healthy, supportive places for children and families to reside create a climate supportive of learning. Good schools tend to have students who begin accepting civic responsibility and start contributing to the uplift of their neighborhood.

Where exceptions exist, schools and communities occupy separate worlds despite their proximity. A magnet school that attracts its enrollment from a wide geographic area, for instance, may offer solid education and, perhaps, racial integration as well but have only a tangential link to its immediate surroundings. And in such a locale as Manhattan, perfectly awful public schools may stand side by side with luxury apartment buildings inhabited by people who send their children to private schools or whose children are grown. By and large, however, in most inner-city or rural settings the fortunes of school and neighborhood ebb and flow as one, and—with struggle—each can bolster the other. Precisely because so little revitalization has occurred, time may be running out for the public schools as they are now constituted. In areas of concentrated poverty, there are all too many instances in which neither neighborhood nor school seems to be improving. Confidence ebbs as all who can find escape routes flee and living conditions deteriorate for those who remain. "People reason that, if the schools can't help individuals, they certainly can't help the larger community," said David Mathews, former Secretary of the U.S. Department of Health, Education, and Welfare.[14]

The most upbeat note on which such a story can end has to do with the individual lives that enhancements help change. This is not a tale of improving education on a massive scale. The triumphs remain limited, though the prospects for a larger victory remain tantalizing. In the meantime, the triumphs are notable, and many fewer of them would occur without the enhancements. Students in the south-central ghetto of Los Angeles found their way into the University of California because the Neighborhood Academic Initiative made it possible. Healthier students in Washington Heights could marshal more personal resources for the challenging work of the classroom. Students in

San Diego were getting more out of their courses because they acquired study skills. Black male middleschoolers in Cleveland knew that they were not alone in taking school seriously. Children in Miami Beach found a useful way to spend their after-school time. Students in rural Wisconsin saw a connection between what they learned in school and being able to earn a living in a depressed community. In Newark, students felt a closer tie to school, setting the stage for making education more important to them.

Lives change one at a time. Despite the continuing imperative to provide better educational opportunities for millions of American children in need, the altered lives of a relative few serve as testament to what is possible for the many.

Notes

Chapter 1

1. Kenneth Kitchner, "Rich Schools, Poor Schools." *The New York Times,* New Jersey Section, May 19, 1996. p. 19.
2. Francis A. J. Ianni, *The Search for Structure: A Report on American Youth Today.* New York: Free Press, 1989, p. 105.
3. James S. Coleman, "Social Capital, Human Capital, and Schools." *Independent School* (Fall 1988): 12.
4. Sharon Ramirez and Tom Dewar, *El Puente Academy for Peace and Justice: A Case Study of Building Social Capital.* Minneapolis: Rainbow Research, 1995, p. 46.
5. Robert D. Putnam, "Social Capital and the Prosperous Community." *Wingspread Journal* (Autumn 1995): 4-6.
6. Barbara Schneider, "Schools, Social Capital, and the Formation of Social Norms." Paper presented at the annual meeting of the American Educational Research Association, New York, NY, April 1996.
7. Jimy M. Sanders and Victor Nee, "Immigrant Self-Employment: The Family as Social Capital and the Value of Human Capital," *American Sociological Review* (April 1996): 231-249.
8. Sharon Waxman, "Admissions Allegations Rock California." *The Washington Post,* April 11, 1996, p. A3.
9. Philip J. Cook and Robert H. Frank, "The Economic Payoff of Attending an Ivy-League Institution." *Chronicle of Higher Education,* January 5, 1996, p. B3.
10. Bill Clinton, State of the Union Message. *The New York Times,* February 4, 1997, p. A20.
11. Margaret C. Wang, Geneva D. Haertel, and Herbert J. Walberg, "The Effectiveness of Collaborative School-Linked Services." In *School-Community Connections,* Edited by Leo C. Rigsby, Maynard C. Reynolds, and Margaret C. Wang. San Francisco: Jossey-Bass, 1995, p. 306.
12. William L. Yancey and Salvatore J. Saporito, "Ecological Embeddedness of Educational Processes and Outcomes," In *School-Community Connections.* Ed. by Rigsby et al, p. 223.
13. Rates of Homicide, Suicide, and Firearm-Related Death Among Children--26 Industrialized Countries. News release by Centers for Disease Control and Prevention, Atlanta, Georgia, February 7, 1997.

14. Annie E. Casey Foundation, *Kids Count: A Pocket Guide on America's Youth*. Baltimore: Annie E. Casey Foundation, 1996, p. 8.

15. Ibid., p. 4.

16. Susan Moore Johnson, *Teachers at Work: Achieving Success in Our Schools*. New York: Basic Books, 1990, p. 83.

17. *Urban Schools: The Challenge of Location and Poverty*. Washington, DC: U.S. Department of Education, Office of Educational Research and Improvement, NCES 96-184, 1996, pp. 3-4.

18. William Julius Wilson, *When Work Disappears: The World of the New Urban Poor*. New York: Knopf, 1996.

19. Rima Shore, "Moving the Ladder: Toward a New Community Vision." Draft report on Schooling and Families: New Demands, New Responses at the Aspen Institute, Aspen, Colorado, August 6-13, 1994.

20. Michael E. Porter, "Inner-City Newark Has Advantages; Let's Use Them." *Star-Ledger,* April 9, 1996, editorial page.

21. Kimberly Downing, "Building Communities, Developing Economies." *Connections* (December 1995): 11-13.

22. Michele Cahill, *A Documentation Report on the New York City Beacons Initiative*. New York: Fund for the City of New York, December 1993, p. 1.

23. Paul Theobald and Paul Nachigal, "Culture, Community, and the Promise of Rural Education." *Phi Delta Kappan* (October 1995): 132.

24. "What If . . . We Measured Prosperity in New Ways?" *Wingspread Journal* (Autumn 1995): 12-13.

25. Janet Maughan, "Sustainable Communities: An Idea Whose Time Has Come?" *Wingspread Journal* (Spring 1996): 4-7.

26. John W. Gardner, *Building Community*. Washington, DC: Independent Sector, 1991.

27. Annie E. Casey Foundation, *The Path of Most Resistance: Reflections on Lessons Learned from New Futures*. Baltimore: Annie E. Casey Foundation, 1995, p. 25.

28. Michelle Cahill, pp. 6-9. *Documentation Report*.

29. Ibid., pp. 6-9.

Chapter 2

1. Abraham Maslow. *Motivation and Personality*. New York: Harper & Row, 1954.

2. National Association of Secondary School Principals, *Breaking Ranks*. Reston, VA: National Association of Secondary School Principals, 1996, pp. 31-32.

3. Institute for Research on Learning, *A New Learning Agenda: Putting People First*. Palo Alto, CA: Institute for Research on Learning, 1993, p. 3.

4. Sharon Ramirez and Tom Dewar, *El Puente Academy for Peace and Justice: A Case Study of Building Social Capital.* Minneapolis: Rainbow Research, p. 22.

5. "High Schoolers Taking Longer to Graduate," *The New York Times,* April 3, 1997, p. B1.

6. Luis Rodriguez. "Our Kids Are Being Set Up." *Rethinking Schools* (Summer 1996): 3.

7. Bill Clinton, State of the Union Message. *The New York Times,* January 23, 1996, p. A13.

8. "Uniforms Nothing New to Catholic Schools." News release, National Catholic Educational Association, Washington, DC, July 11, 1996.

9. Gary G. Wehlage, *Reducing the Risk: Schools as Communities of Support.* New York: The Falmer Press, 1989, p. 113.

Chapter 3

1. Michele Cahill, *A Documentation Report on the New York City Beacons Initiative.* New York: Fund for the City of New York, December 1993, p. 19.

2. Deborah L. Cohen, "Taking Up Residence." *Education Week,* April 3, 1996, p. 30.

3. Robert Putnam, "Social Capital and the Prosperous Community." *Wingspread Journal* (Autumn 1995): 6.

4. Raymond Hernandez, "Rating of Schools Shows Skills Lag in New York City," *The New York Times,* January 3, 1997, p. 1.

5. "Unique Partnerships Supports Public School in Houston Housing Project." *School Board News,* October 15, 1996, p. 1.

6. Peter Schmidt, "Reaching Students in Public Housing." *Chronicle of Higher Education* October 4, 1996, p. A8.

Chapter 4

1. Institute for Research on Learning, *A New Learning Agenda: Putting People First.* Menlo Park, CA: Institute for Research on Learning, 1993.

2. Deborah L. Cohen, "Neighborhood Education Watch Seeks to Mobilize Communities." *Education Week,* February 28, 1996, p. 9.

3. Clifford Krauss, "U.S. Joining Local Fight on Narcotics," *The New York Times,* September 16, 1996, p. B3.

4. "Baltimore Project on Vacant Houses Gives Students Legal Insight." *The New York Times,* February 4, 1996, p. 19.

5. Ernesto J. Cortes, Jr., "Making the Public the Leaders in Education Reform." *Education Week,* November 22, 1995, commentary page.

6. Ernesto J. Cortes, Jr., "Community Organization and Social Capital." *National Civic Review* (Fall 1996): 51.

7. Kristen Cook, "Many Efforts Try to Prevent Teen Violence," *Arizona Daily Star,* January 21, 1996, p. 1.

Chapter 5

1. Norm Fruchter, *New Directions in Parent Involvement*. Washington, DC: Academy for Educational Development, 1992, pp. 33-43.
2. President's Advisory Commission on Educational Excellence for Hispanic Americans, *Our Nation on the Fault Line: Hispanic American Education*. Washington DC: President's Advisory Commission on Educational Excellence for Hispanic Americans. 1996, p. 52.
3. Philliber Research Associates, *The Family Care/Healthy Kids Collaborative*. Accord, NY: Philliber Research Associates, Fall 1994, p. 16.
4. James P. Comer, *Rallying the Whole Village*. New York: Teachers College Press, 1996, p. 48.
5. General Accounting Office, *Elementary School Children: Many Change Schools Frequently, Harming Their Education*. GAO/HEHS-94-45. Washington, DC: General Accounting Office, February 1994, pp. 7-8.
6. "Urban Student Mobility Disrupts Education and Reform Efforts." Crespar Research & Development Report, October 1996, p. 14.

Chapter 6

1. Roberta G. Doering, "School Boards Must Address Needs of the Whole Child: Health Children Are Better Learners." *School Board News*, January 23, 1996, p. 2.
2. Undated brochure from the Family Resource Center from the Connecticut Department of Education.
3. William S. White, *1993 Annual Report of the Charles Stewart Mott Foundation*. Flint, MI: Charles Stewart Mott Foundation, p. 5.
4. Annie E. Casey Foundation, *The Path of Most Resistance: Reflections on Lessons Learned from New Futures*. Baltimore: The Annie Casey Foundation, 1995, p. 2.

Chapter 7

1. U.S. Department of Education, Office of Educational Research and Improvement, *Urban Schools: The Challenge of Location and Poverty*. NCS 96-184. Washington, DC: U.S. Department of Education, Office of Educational Research and Improvement, 1996, p. 11.
2. Michelle Cahill, *A Documentation Report on the New York City Beacons Initiative*. New York: Fund for the City of New York, December 1993, p. 16.
3. James P. Comer, "New Haven's School-Community Connection," *Educational Leadership* (March 1987): 13-16.
4. Joy G. Dryfoos, *Full-Service Schools*. San Francisco: Jossey-Bass, 1994, p. xv.
5. Ibid., p. 15.

6. "Number of School Clinics Up 50 Percent Since 1994." *Education Week,* April 2, 1997, p. 13.

7. David Tyack, "Health and Social Services in Public Schools: Historical Perspectives." *The Future of Children* (Spring 1992): 21.

8. Jessica Portner, "Nurses Orders." *Education Week,* May 15, 1996, p. 23.

9. Ellen Brickman, *A Formative Evaluation of P.S. 5: A Children's Aid Society/ Board of Education Community School.* New York: The Children's Aid Society, March 1996, pp. 25-28.

Chapter 8

1. Edward G. Rozycki, "Establishing Nationally Recognized Educational Standards." *Educational Horizons* (Spring 1997): 109-111.

2. Robin Hood Foundation, *Kids Having Kids,* New York: Robin Hood Foundation, June 13, 1996.

3. Fred M. Hechinger, *Fateful Choices.* New York: Hill and Wang, 1992, p. 73.

4. Sara McLanahan and Gary Sandefur, *Growing Up With a Single Parent: What Hurts, What Helps.* Cambridge, MA: Harvard University Press, 1994, pp. 3-4.

5. Susan Philliber and Perila Namerow, "Trying to Maximize the Odds: Using What We Know to Prevent Teen Pregnancy." Paper presented at a workshop of The Teen Pregnancy Prevention Program, Division of Reproductive Health, National Center for Chronic Disease Prevention and Health Promotion, Centers for Disease Control and Prevention. Atlanta, GA, December 13-15, 1995.

6. Daniel Goleman, *Emotional Intelligence.* New York: Bantam Books, 1995.

7. Walter Turnbull, *Lift Every Voice: Expecting the Most and Getting the Best from All of God's Children.* New York: Hyperion, 1995, p. 183.

8. Peter Applebome, "For Youth, Fear of Crime Is Pervasive and Powerful." *The New York Times,* January 12, 1996, p. A12.

9. Ibid.

10. Stanley M. Elam, "Phi Delta Kappa/Gallup Poll of the Public's Attitudes Toward the Public Schools." *Phi Delta Kappan* (September 1996): 49-50.

11. Sharon Ramirez and Tom Dewar, *El Puente Academy for Peace and Justice: A Case Study of Building Social Capital.* Minneapolis: Rainbow Research, 1995, p. 21.

12. Milbrey W. McLaughlin, Merita A. Irby, and Juliet Langman, *Urban Sanctuaries.* San Francisco: Jossey-Bass, 1994.

13. Shirley Brice Heath and Milbrey W. McLaughlin, "A Child Resource Policy: Moving Beyond Dependence on School and Family." *Phi Delta Kappan* (April 1987): 579.

14. Michelle Cahill, *A Documentation Report on the New York City Beacons Initiative.* New York: Fund for the City of New York, December 1993, p. 2.

Chapter 9

1. Viki L. Montera. "Bridging the Gap: A Case Study of the Home-School-Community Relationship at Ochoa Elementary School." Doctoral diss. University of Arizona, 1996. p. 166.
2. Robert N. Bellah et al, *Habits of the Heart: Individualism and Commitment in American Life.* Berkeley: University of California Press, 1985, p. 194.
3. Robert J. Chaskin and Diana Mendley Rauner, "Research and Findings of the Program on Youth and Caring." *Phi Delta Kappan* (May 1995): 669.
4. Ibid., p. 668.
5. Eric Schaps, Catherine Lewis, and Marilyn Watson, "Schools As Caring Communities." *Resources for Restructuring.* National Center for Restructuring Education, Schools, and Teaching. (Fall 1995).
6. Daniel Solomon et al, "Creating a Caring Community: Educational Practices That Promote Children's Prosocial Development." In *Effective and Responsible Teaching: The New Synthesis.* Edited by Fritz K. Oser, Andreas Dick, and Jean-Luck Patry. San Francisco, CA: Jossey-Bass, 1992, p. 394.
7. National Association of Secondary School Principals, *Breaking Ranks.* Reston, VA: National Association of Secondary School Principals, 1996, p. 21.
8. Magnus O. Bassey, "Teachers for a Changing Society: Helping Neglected Children Cope with Schooling." *The Educational Forum,* (Fall 1996): 60.
9. *Service Opportunities for Youths.* Washington, DC: The Children's Defense Fund, 1989.
10. Sharon Ramirez and Tom Dewar, *El Puente Academy for Peace and Justice: A Case Study of Building Social Capital.* Minneapolis: Rainbow Research, 1995, pp. 25-26.
11. Karen J. Pittman and Michele Cahill, *Youth and Caring: The Role of Youth Programs in the Development of Caring.* New York: Academy for Educational Development, 1992, p. 4.
12. James Youniss, J. A. McLellan, and M. Yates, "What We Know About Engendering Civic Identity." *American Behavioral Scientist* (March/April 1997): 620-631.
13. Richard W. Paul, "Ethics Without Indoctrination." *Educational Leadership* (May 1988): 17.

Chapter 10

1. B. Bradford Brown, "School Culture, Social Politics, and the Academic Motivation of U.S. Students." Paper presented at a Conference on Student Motivation sponsored by the U.S. Department of Education, Office of Education Research and Improvement, Washington, DC November 8-9, 1990, p. 14.

2. Richard Hofstadter, *Anti-Intellectualism in American Life.* New York: Knopf, 1970.

3. Jerome Karabel, "Status-Group Struggle, Organizational Interests, and the Limits of Institutional Autonomy." *Theory and Society* (January 1984): 1-39.

4. Nat Gottlieb, "Brown: Participation Needed From Blacks." *(Newark) Star-Ledger,* February 20, 1996, p. 51.

5. Signithia Fordham and John U. Ogbu, "Black Students and the Burden of 'Acting White.'" *The Urban Review* 18, no. 3 (1986): 177.

6. Signithia Fordham, *Blacked Out: Dilemmas of Race, Identity, and Success.* Chicago: University of Chicago Press, 1996.

7. Patrick T. Terenzini, "The Transition to College: Diverse Students, Diverse Stories." *Research in Higher Education* 35, no. 1. (1994): 63.

8. Dorothy Rich, *MegaSkills.* Boston: Houghton Mifflin Company, 1992, p. 5.

9. National Center on Effective Secondary Schools News Letter. School of Education, University of Wisconsin, Madison. (Winter 1989-90): 1.

10. Jerome H. Bruns, "They Can But They Don't." *American Educator* (Winter 1992): 38.

11. Richard Sagor, "Building Resilience in Students." *Educational Leadership* (September 1996): 38.

12. Research for Better Schools, *Closing the Urban Achievement Gap: A Vision to Guide Change in Beliefs and Practice.* Philadelphia: Research for Better Schools, 1995.

13. Debra Viadero, "Beating the Odds." *Education Week,* March 29, 1995, p. 29.

14. Emily E. Werner and Ruth S. Smith, *Overcoming the Odds: High Risk Children from Birth to Adulthood.* Ithaca, NY: Cornell University Press, 1992.

15. Patricia Gandara, *Over the Ivy Walls.* Albany: State University of New York Press, 1995, p. 112.

16. 16.Peter Benson, "Random Acts of Asset Building." *Wingspread Journal* (Winter 1996): 7-9.

17. Thomas Sowell, *Migrations and Cultures: A World View.* New York: Basic Books. 1996.

18. Laurence Steinberg, B.B. Brown, and S.M. Dornbusch, "Ethnicity and Adolescent Achievement." *American Educator* (Summer 1996): 34.

19. Marylou Tousignant, "A Family Succeeds by Degrees." *The Washington Post,* May 17, 1996, p. A1.

Chapter 11

1. Mark Freedman, *The Kindness of Strangers.* San Francisco: Jossey-Bass, 1993.

2. Anthony Williams. Letter to the Editor, *The New York Times editorial page*, September 7, 1995.

3. Longitudinal Research on Middle Level AVID: Year 1 Report. Draft. Center for Research, Evaluation, and Training, 1997.

4. U.S. Department of Education, Office of Educational Research and Improvement, *High School Students Ten Years After "A Nation At Risk."* NCES 95-764. U.S. Department of Education; Office of Educational Research and Improvement, Washington, DC: May 1995, p. 9.

Chapter 12

1. Patricia A. Graham, "What America Has Expected of Its Schools over the Past Century." *American Journal of Education* (February 1993): 88.

2. Sharon P. Robinson, "Life, Literacy, and the Pursuit of Challenges." *Daedalus* (Fall 1995): 135.

3. Carnegie Foundation for the Advancement of Teaching, *An Imperiled Generation: Saving Urban Schools*. Princeton, NJ: Carnegie Foundation for the Advancement of Teaching, 1988.

4. Valerie E. Lee, "Another Look at High School Restructuring: More Evidence That It Improves Student Achievement and More Insight into Why." *Issues in Restructuring Schools* (Fall 1995).

5. Robert Rosenthal and Lenore Jacobson, *Pygmalion in the Classroom: Teacher Expectations and Pupils' Intellectual Development*. New York: Irvington Publishers, 1992.

6. Thomas L. Good, "Two Decades of Research on Teacher Expectations: Findings and Future Directions." *Journal of Teacher Education* (July-August 1987): 32-47.

7. Robert L. Hampel, "Historical Perspectives on Academic Work: The Origins of Learning." Paper presented at the Conference on Hard Work and High Expectations: Motivating Students to Learn, sponsored by the U.S. Department of Education, Office of Educational Research and Innovation, Arlington, VA, November 8–9, 1990, p. 7.

8. Gene I. Maeroff, *Don't Blame the Kids*. New York: McGraw-Hill, 1982, p. 9.

9. Antoine M. Garibaldi, "Creating Prescriptions for Success in Urban Schools." Paper presented at the conference on Hard Work and High Expectations: Motivating Students to Learn, sponsored by the U.S. Department of Education, Office of Educational Research and Innovation, Arlington, VA, November 8–9, 1990, pp. 9-10.

10. M. Kay Alderman, "Motivation for At-Risk Students." *Educational Leadership* (September 1990): 28.

11. National Association of Secondary School Principals, *Breaking Ranks*. Reston, VA: National Association of Secondary School Principals, 1996, p. 50.

12. "Motivate, Don't Isolate, Black Students." *The New York Times* editorial page, November 5, 1990.

13. Renee Smith-Maddox and Anne Wheelock, "Untracking and Students Futures: Closing the Gap Between Aspirations and Expectations." *Phi Delta Kappan* (November 1995): 222-228.

14. Chester E. Finn, Jr., "Will 'Efficacy' Help New York's Schools?" *The New York Times* op-ed page, February 6, 1996.

15. Jacques Steinberg, "U.S. Limits Law to Help Schools Chief Fight Corruption." *The New York Times*, June 25, 1996, p. B4.

16. Robert E. Slavin et al, "Whenever and Wherever We Choose: The Replication of 'Success for All.'" *Phi Delta Kappan* (April 1994): 639.

17. Educational Resources Group, *Expecting the Best from Students in Urban Middle Schools*. Princeton, NJ: Education Resources Group, 1994, pp. 51-60.

18. Ibid.

19. U.S. Department of Education, Office of Educational Research and Improvement, *Social Background Differences in High School Mathematics and Science Coursetaking and Achievement*. NCES 95-206. Washington, D.C.: Department of Education, Office of Educational Research and Improvement, August 1995.

20. Census Bureau, 1996, as reported in *The New York Times,* September 6, 1996, p. A18.

21. David Levering Lewis, *W.E.B. Du Bois: Biography of a Race*. New York: Henry Holt, 1993, pp. 34-37.

22. Ibid., p. 545.

Chapter 13

1. National Association of Secondary School Principals, *Breaking Ranks*. Reston, VA: National Association of Secondary School Principals, 1996, pp. 14-15.

2. Lillian G. Katz and Sylvia C. Chard, *Engaging Children's Minds: The Project Approach*. Norwood, NJ: Ablex Publishing, 1989, p. 3.

3. Claudia Geocaris, "Increasing Student Engagement: A Mystery Solved." *Educational Leadership* (December 1996/January 1997): 72-75.

4. Vito Perrone, "How to Engage Students in Learning." *Educational Leadership* (February 1994): 11.

5. Michael S. Knapp, "The Teaching Challenge in High-Poverty Classrooms." In *Teaching for Meaning in High Poverty Classrooms*. Edited by Michael S. Knapp and Associates. New York: Teachers College Press, 1995, pp. 1-10.

6. *Our Future Workforce, Part III. Getting and Keeping a Job,* Introduction. Curriculum at Canton Middle School. Unnumbered and undated.

Chapter 14

1. James Atlas, "Making the Grade." *The New Yorker,* April 14, 1997, p. 36.
2. James S. Coleman, "Social Capital, Human Capital, and Schools." *Independent School* (Fall 1988): 12.
3. Harold W. Watts, "Investing in Children: Closing the Real Deficit." *News and Issues* (Summer 1995): 4.
4. Rudolph F. Crew, "Building Literacy at Home and in Our Schools." *Imagine* (Fall 1996): 1.
5. Barbara Heyns, *Summer Learning and the Effects of Schooling.* New York: Academic Press, 1978.
6. Jonathan Jaffe and Karen Auerbach, "Urban Youth Complete Summer Enrichment Program." *(Newark) Star-Ledger,* August 18, 1996, sec. 1, p. 37.

Chapter 15

1. Valerie Lee and Susanna Loeb, "Where Do Head Start Attendees End Up? One Reason Why Preschool Effects Fade Out." *Educational Evaluation Policy Analysis* (Spring 1995): 62-82.
2. Gene I. Maeroff, "Withered Hopes, Stillborn Dreams: The Dismal Panorama of Urban Schools." *Phi Delta Kappan* (May 1988): 635.

Chapter 16

1. Hugh Mehan, Irene Villanueva, Lea Hubbard, and Angela Lintz, *Constructing School Success.* New York: Cambridge University Press, 1996, pp. 79-80.
2. Sharon P. Robinson, *The Conditions Necessary in Urban Schools for Supporting the Academic and Intellectual Growth of Poor Minority Students.* Washington, DC: U.S. Department of Education, Office of Educational Research and Improvement, 1997.
3. Wayne Flynt, "Rural Poverty in America." *Phi Kappa Phi* Journal (Summer 1996): 32.
4. Robert Fulghum, *All I Really Need to Know I Learned in Kindergarten.* New York: Villard Books, 1988, pp. 6-7.
5. Bob Morris, "Is it Hip to Be Cool? Not in This Charm School." *The New York Times,* January 28, 1996, p. 33.
6. John Lahr, "Speaking Across the Divide." *The New Yorker,* January 27, 1997, pp. 35-42.
7. Ricardo D. Stanton-Salazar, "A Social Capital Framework for Understanding the Socialization of Racial Minority Children and Youths." *Harvard Educational Review* 67, no. 1 (Spring 1997): 1-40.
8. Amherst H. Wilder Foundation, "Key Strategy Recommendations for Promoting the Productive Capacity of Individuals." Report. St. Paul, MN: March 10, 1993, p. 4.

9. Ann Bradley, "Teachers Make Style Statement by Dressing Up." *Education Week,* September 11, 1996, p. 1.

10. Neil Postman, "Of Luddites, Learning, and Life." *Technos* (Winter 1993): 25.

11. Mike Allen, "Separatism Is In, Except for White Men." *The New York Times,* June 30, 1996, p. 5, Week in Review Section.

12. Samuel D. Proctor, "To the Rescue: A National Youth Academy." *The New York Times,* September 16, 1989, p. 27.

13. Neil MacFarquhar, "When the Way Out of the City Is the Fairway." *The New York Times,* May 20, 1996, p. B1.

Chapter 17

1. William Raspberry, "Firing Smith Won't Fix D.C.'s Schools." *The Washington Post* op-ed page, August 30, 1996.

2. Kathleen V. Hoover-Dempsey and Howard M. Sandler, "Parental Involvement in Children's Education: Why Does It Make a Difference?" *Teachers College Record* (Winter 1995): 319-322.

3. Ibid., pp. 321-326.

4. *The Urban Learner Framework: An Overview.* Philadelphia: Urban Education Project, Research for Better Schools, 1994, p. 2.

5. Viki L. Montera, "Bridging the Gap: A Case Study of the Home-School-Community Relationship at Ochoa Elementary School." Doctoral diss., University of Arizona, 1996, p. 20.

6. Educational Testing Service, *America's Smallest School: The Family.* Princeton, NJ: Educational Testing Service, 1992.

7. Betty Hart and Todd R. Risley, *Meaningful Differences in the Everyday Experiences of Young American Children.* Baltimore: Paul H. Brookes Publishing Co., 1995, p. 132.

8. David W. Grissmer, *Student Achievement and the Changing American Family: An Executive Summary.* Santa Monica, CA: RAND, 1994, p. 10.

9. William H. Honan, "Income Found to Predict Education Level." *The New York Times,* June 17, 1996, p. A11.

10. A.M. Garibaldi, "Creating Prescriptions for Success in Urban Schools." Paper presented at the Conference on Hard Work and High Expectations: Motivating Students to Learn, sponsored by the U.S. Department of Education, Office of Educational Research and Evaluation, Arlington, VA, 1990, p.12.

11. Michele Cahill, *A Documentation Report on the New York City Beacons Initiative.* New York: Fund for the City of New York, December 1993, pp. 9-10.

12. *Raising Our Future: Families, Schools, and Communities Joining Together.* Cambridge, MA: Harvard Family Research Project, 1995, pp. 4-5.

Chapter 18

1. *Education Watch: The 1996 Education Trust State and National Data Book.* Washington, DC: The Education Trust, 1996.
2. Gary L. Bowen et al, "Toward an Understanding of School Success: An Ecological Perspective." A report, University of North Carolina School of Social Work, January 1993. p. 3.
3. John Gargani. A Very Brief Guide to Evaluating IHAD Projects. New York: I Have a Dream Foundation, March 7, 1996.
4. I Have a Dream Foundation, "How Successful Is 'I Have a Dream' Program?" New York: I Have a Dream Foundation, March 1, 1996.
5. Report on dreamers in college. New York: I Have a Dream Foundation, March 1996.
6. Catherine C. Lewis, "The Roots of Japanese Educational Achievement: Helping Children Develop Bonds to School." *Educational Policy* 9, no. 2 (June 1995): 129-151.
7. Laurence Steinberg, "Failure Outside the Classroom." *The Wall Street Journal* Editorial page, July 11, 1996.
8. Laurence Steinberg, *Beyond the Classroom: Why School Reform Has Failed and What Parents Need to Do.* New York: Simon & Schuster, 1996.
9. Gary G. Wehlange and Julie A. White, "Citizens, Clients, and Consumers: Building Social Capital." Paper prepared by the Center on Organization and Restructuring Schools, University of Wisconsin-Madison. Supported by the U.S. Department of Education, Office of Educational Research and Improvement, May 30, 1995.
10. Michele Cahill, *A Documentation Report on the New York City Beacons Initiative.* New York: Fund for the City of New York, December 1993.
11. Margaret Gaston and Sally Brown, *School Restructuring and School-Linked Services: Working Together for Students and Families.* A paper written for the Stuart Foundations, 1994, p. 12.
12. Ibid., pp. 18-19.
13. Anne C. Lewis, *Believing in Ourselves: Progress and Struggle in Urban Middle School Reform 1989-1995.* New York: Edna McConnell Clark Foundation, 1995, p. 72.
14. David Mathews, *Is There a Public for Public Schools?* Dayton, OH: Kettering Foundation Press, 1996, p. 4.

Bibliography

Alderman, M. K. "Motivation for At-Risk Students." *Educational Leadership* (September 1990): p. 28.

Annie E. Casey Foundation. *Kids Count: A Pocket Guide on America's Youth.* Baltimore: Annie E. Casey Foundation, 1996.

Annie E. Casey Foundation. *The Path of Most Resistance: Reflections on Lessons Learned from New Futures.* Baltimore: Annie E. Casey Foundation, 1995.

Atlas, J. "Making the Grade." *The New Yorker,* April 14, 1997.

Bassey, M. O. "Teachers for a Changing Society: Helping Neglected Children Cope with Schooling." *The Educational Forum* (Fall 1996): 60.

Bellah, R. N., et al. *Habits of the Heart: Individualism and Commitment in American Life.* Berkeley: University of California Press, 1985.

Brickman, E. *A Formative Evaluation of P.S. 5: A Children's Aid Society/Board of Education Community School.* New York: The Children's Aid Society, March 1996.

Brown, B. B. "School Culture, Social Politics, and the Academic Motivation of U.S. Students." Paper presented at a Conference on Student Motivation sponsored by the U.S. Department of Education, Office of Educational Research and Improvement, Washington, DC, November 8-9, 1990.

Bruns, J. H. "They Can But They Don't." *American Educator* (Winter 1992): 38.

Cahill, M. *A Documentation Report on the New York City Beacons Initiative.* New York: Fund for the City of New York, December 1993.

Carnegie Foundation for the Advancement of Teaching. *An Imperiled Generation: Saving Urban School.* Princeton, NJ: Carnegie Foundation for the Advancement of Teaching, 1988.

Chaskin, R. J. and D. M. Rauner. "Youth and Caring: An Introduction." *Phi Delta Kappan* (May 1995): 669.

Coleman, J. S. "Social Capital, Human Capital, and Schools." *Independent School* (Fall 1988): 12.

Comer, J. P. "New Haven's School-Community Connection." *Educational Leadership* (March 1987): 13-16.

Comer, J. P. *Rallying the Whole Village.* New York: Teachers College Press, 1996.

Cortes, Jr., E. J. "Community Organization and Social Capital." *National Civic Review* (Fall 1996): 51.

Downing, K. "Building Communities, Developing Economies." *Connections* (December 1995): 11-13.

Dryfoos, J. G. *Full-Service Schools*. San Francisco: Jossey-Bass, 1994.

The Education Trust. *Education Watch: The 1996 Education Trust State and National Data Book*. Washington DC: The Education Trust, 1996.

Education Resources Group. *Expecting the Best from Students in Urban Middle Schools*. Princeton, NJ: Education Resources Group, 1994.

Educational Testing Service. *America's Smallest School: The Family*. Princeton, NJ: Educational Testing Service, 1992.

Elam, S. M. "Phi Delta Kappa/Gallup Poll of the Public's Attitudes Toward the Public Schools." *Phi Delta Kappan* (September 1996): 32.

Flynt, W. "Rural Poverty in America." *Phi Kappa Phi Journal*, (Summer 1996): 32

Fordham, S. *Blacked Out: Dilemmas of Race, Identity, and Success*. Chicago: University of Chicago Press, 1996.

Fordham, S., and J. U. Ogbu. "Black Students and the Burden of 'Acting White.'" *The Urban Review*, 18, no. 3 (1986): 177.

Freedman, M. *The Kindness of Strangers*. San Francisco: Jossey-Bass, 1993.

Fruchter, N. *New Directions in Parent Involvement*. Washington, DC: Academy for Educational Development, 1992.

Fulghum, R. *All I Really Need to Know I Learned in Kindergarten*. New York: Villard Books, 1988.

Gandara, P. *Over the Ivy Walls*. Albany: State University of New York Press, 1995.

Garibaldi, A. M. "Creating Prescriptions for Success in Urban Schools." Paper presented at the Conference on Hard Work and High Expectations: Motivating Students to Learn, sponsored by U.S. Department of Education, Office of Educational Research and Innovation, Arlington, VA, 1990.

Gaston, M., and S. Brown. *School Restructuring and School-Linked Services: Working Together for Students and Families*. A paper written for the Stuart Foundations, 1994.

General Accounting Office. *Elementary School Children: Many Change Schools Frequently, Harming Their Education*. GAO/HEH S-94-45. Washington DC: General Accounting Office, February 1994.

Geocaris, C. "Increasing Student Engagement: A Mystery Solved." *Educational Leadership* (December 1996/January 1997): 72-75.

Goleman, D. *Emotional Intelligence*. New York: Bantam Books, 1995.

Good, T. L. "Two Decades of Research on Teacher Expectations: Findings and Future Directions." *Journal of Teacher Education* (July/August 1987): 32-47.

Graham, P. A. "What America Has Expected of Its Schools over the Past Century." *American Journal of Education* (February 1993): 88.

Grissmer, D. W. *Student Achievement and the Changing American Family: An Executive Summary*. Santa Monica, CA: RAND, 1994.

Hampel, R. L. "Historical Perspectives on Academic Work: The Origins of Learning." Paper presented at the Conference on Hard Work and High Expectations: Motivating Students to Learn, sponsored by U.S. Department of Education, Office of Educational Research and Innovation, Arlington, VA, 1990.

Hart, B., and T. R. Risley. *Meaningful Differences in the Everyday Experience of Young Children*. Baltimore: Paul H. Brookes Publishing, 1995.

Harvard Family Research Project. *Raising Our Future: Families, Schools, and Communities Joining Together*. Cambridge, MA: Harvard Family Research Project, 1995.

Heath, S. B., and M. W. McLaughlin. "A Child Resource Policy: Moving Beyond Dependence on School and Family." *Phi Delta Kappan* (April 1987): 576-580.

Hechinger, F. M. *Fateful Choices*. New York: Hill and Wang, 1992.

Heyns, B. *Summer Learning and the Effects of Schooling*. New York: Academic Press, 1978.

Hofstadter, R. *Anti-Intellectualism in American Life*. New York: Knopf, 1970.

Hoover-Dempsey, K. V., and H. M. Sandler. "Parental Involvement in Children's Education." *Teachers College Record* (Winter 1995): 319-322.

Ianni, F. A. J. *The Search for Structure: A Report on American Youth Today*. New York: Free Press, 1989.

Institute for Research on Learning. *A New Learning Agenda: Putting People First*. Menlo Park, CA: Institute for Research on Learning, 1993.

Johnson, S. M. *Teachers at Work: Achieving Success in Our Schools*. New York: Basic Books, 1990.

Karabel, J. "Status-Group Struggle, Organizational Interests, and the Limits of Institutional Autonomy." *Theory and Society* (January 1984): 1-39.

Katz, L. G., and S. C. Chard. *Engaging Children's Minds: The Project Approach*. Norwood, NJ: Ablex Publishing, 1989.

Knapp, M. "The Teaching Challenge in High-Poverty Classrooms." In *Teaching for Meaning in High Poverty Classrooms*. New York: Teachers College Press, 1995, pp. 1-10.

Lahr, J. "Speaking Across the Divide." *The New Yorker*, January 27, 1997.

Lee, V. E., J. B. Smith, and R. G. Croninger. "Another Look at High School Restructuring: More Evidence That It Improves Student Achievement and More Insight into Why." *Issues in Restructuring Schools* (Fall 1995): 1-10.

Lewis, A. C. *Believing in Ourselves: Progress and Struggle in Urban Middle School Reform 1989-1995*. New York: Edna McConnell Clark Foundation, 1995.

Lewis, C. C. "The Roots of Japanese Educational Achievement: Helping Children Develop Bonds to School." *Educational Policy* (June 1995): 129-151.

Lewis, D. L. *W.E.B. DuBois: Biography of a Race*. New York: Henry Holt, 1993.

McLanahan, S., and G. Sandefur. *Growing Up With a Single Parent: What Hurts, What Helps.* Cambridge, MA: Harvard University Press, 1994.

McLaughlin, M. W., M. A. Irby, and J. Langman. *Urban Sanctuaries.* San Francisco: Jossey-Bass, 1994.

Maeroff, G. I. *Don't Blame the Kids: The Trouble with America's Public Schools.* New York: McGraw-Hill, 1982.

Maeroff, G. I. "Withered Hopes, Stillborn Dreams: The Dismal Panorama of Urban Schools." *Phi Delta Kappan* (May 1988): 635.

Maslow, A. *Motivation and Personality.* New York: Harper & Row, 1954.

Mathews, D. *Is There a Public for Public Schools?* Dayton, OH: Kettering Foundation Press, 1996.

Maughan, J. "Sustainable Communities: An Idea Whose Time Has Come?" *Wingspread Journal* (Spring 1996): 4-7.

Mehan, H. *Constructing School Success.* New York: Cambridge University Press, 1996.

Montera, V. L. "Bridging the Gap: A Case Study of the Home-School-Community Relationship at Ochoa Elementary School." Doctoral diss., University of Arizona, 1996.

National Association of Secondary School Principals. *Breaking Ranks.* Reston, VA: National Association of Secondary School Principals, 1996.

Paul, R. W. "Ethics Without Indoctrination." *Educational Leadership* (May 1988): 17.

Perrone. V. "How to Engage Students in Learning." *Educational Leadership* (February 1994): 11.

Philliber Research Associates. *The Family Care/Healthy Kids Collaborative.* Accord, NY: Philliber Research Associates, Fall 1994.

Philliber, S., and P. Namerow. "Trying to Maximize the Odds: Using What We Know to Prevent Teen Pregnancy." Paper presented at a workshop of The Teen Pregnancy Prevention Program, Division of Reproductive Health, National Center for Chronic Disease Prevention and Health Promotion, Centers for Disease Control, Atlanta, GA, December 13-15, 1995.

Pittman, K. J., and M. Cahill. "Youth and Caring: The Role of Youth Programs in the Development of Caring." Paper presented at Youth and Caring Conference, Miami, FL, February 26-27, 1992.

Postman, N. "Of Luddites, Learning, and Life." *Technos* (Winter 1993): 25.

President's Advisory Commission on Educational Excellence for Hispanic Americans. *Our Nation on the Fault Line: Hispanic American Education.* Washington DC: President's Advisory Commission on Educational Excellence for Hispanic Americans, 1996.

Putnam, R. D. "Social Capital and the Prosperous Community." *Wingspread Journal* (Autumn 1995): 46.

Ramirez, S., and T. Dewar. *El Puente Academy for Peace and Justice: A Case Study of Building Social Capital.* Minneapolis: Rainbow Research, 1995.

Research for Better Schools. *Closing the Urban Achievement Gap: A Vision to Guide Change in Beliefs and Practice.* Philadelphia: Research for Better Schools, 1995.

Rich, D. *MegaSkills.* Boston: Houghton-Mifflin Company, 1992.

Rigsby, L. C., M.C. Reynolds, and M.C. Wang. *School-Community Connections.* San Francisco: Jossey-Bass, 1995.

Robin Hood Foundation. *Kids Having Kids.* New York: Robin Hood Foundation, 1997.

Robinson, S. P. "Life, Literacy, and the Pursuit of Challenges." *Daedalus* (Fall 1995): 135.

Robinson, S. P. *The Conditions Necessary for Urban Students to Achieve at High Levels.* Washington DC: U.S. Department of Education, Office of Educational Research and Improvement, 1996.

Rodriguez, L. "Our Kids Are Being Set Up." *Rethinking Schools* (Summer 1996): 3.

Rosenthal, R., and L. Jacobson. *Pygmalion in the Classroom: Teacher Expectations and Pupils' Intellectual Development.* New York: Irvington Publishers, 1992.

Rozycki, E. G. "Establishing Nationally Recognized Educational Standards." *Educational Horizons* (Spring 1997): 109-111.

Sagor, R. "Building Resilience in Students." *Educational Leadership* (September 1996): 38.

Sanders, J. M., and V. Nee. "Immigrant Self-Employment: The Family as Social Capital and the Value of Human Capital." *American Sociological Review* (April 1996): 231-249.

Schaps, E., C. Lewis, and M. Watson. "Schools As Caring Communities." *Resources for Restructuring* (Fall 1995): 1-6.

Schneider, B. "Schools, Social Capital, and the Formation of Social Norms." Paper presented at the annual meeting of the American Educational Research Association, New York, NY, April 1995.

Shore, R. "Moving the Ladder: Toward a New Community Vision." Draft report based on meeting at Aspen Institute, Colorado, August 6-13, 1994.

Slavin, R. E. et al. "Whenever and Wherever We Choose: The Replication of 'Success for All.'" *Phi Delta Kappan* (April 1994): 639.

Smith-Maddox, R., and A. Wheelock. "Untracking and Students' Futures: Closing the Gap Between Aspirations and Expectation." *Phi Delta Kappan* (November 1995): 222-228.

Sowell, T. *Migrations and Cultures: A World View.* New York: Basic Books, 1996.

Stanton-Salzar, R. D. "A Social Capital Framework for Understanding the Socialization of Racial Minority Children and Youths." *Harvard Educational Review* (Spring 1997): 1-40.

Steinberg, L. Beyond the Classroom: *Why School Reform Has Failed and What Parents Need to Do.* New York: Simon & Schuster, 1996.

Steinberg, L., B. B. Brown, and S. M. Dornbusch. "Ethnicity and Adolescent Achievement." *American Educator* (Summer 1996): 28-48.

Terenzini, P. T. "The Transition to College: Diverse Students, Diverse Stories." *Research in Higher Education* 35, no. 1, (1994): 63.

Theobald, P., and P. Nachtigal. "Culture, Community, and the Promise of Rural Education." *Phi Delta Kappan* (October 1995): 132.

Turnbull, W. *Lift Every Voice: Expecting the Most and Getting the Best from All of God's Children.* New York: Hyperion, 1995.

Tyack, D. "Health and Social Services in Public Schools: Historical Perspectives." *The Future of Children* (Spring 1992): 21.

U.S. Department of Education, Office of Educational Research and Improvement. *High School Students Ten Years After "A Nation at Risk."* NCES 95-764. Washington DC: U.S. Department of Education, Office of Educational Research, May 1995.

U.S. Department of Education, Office of Educational Research and Improvement. *Social Background Differences in High School Mathematics and Science Coursetaking and Achievement.* Washington DC: U.S. Department of Education, Office of Educational Research and Improvement, August 1995.

U.S. Department of Education, Office of Educational Research and Improvement. *Urban Schools: The Challenge of Location and Poverty.* NCS 96-184. Washington DC: U.S. Department of Education, Office of Educational Research and Improvement, 1996.

Wang, M. C., G. D. Haertel, and H. J. Walberg. "The Effectiveness of Collaborative School-Linked Services." In *School-Community Connections,* ed. L.C. Rigsby, M. C. Reynolds, and M. C. Wang. San Francisco: Jossey-Bass, 1995, pp. 283-309.

Wang, M. C., and H. J. Walberg, Eds. *Strategies for Improving Education in Urban Communities.* Philadelphia: Temple University Center for Research in Human Development and Education, 1996.

Watts, H. W. "Investing in Children: Closing the Real Deficit." *News and Issues* (Summer 1995): 4.

Wehlage, G. G. *Reducing the Risk: Schools as Communities of Support.* New York: The Falmer Press, 1989.

"What If . . . We Measured Prosperity in New Ways?" *Wingspread Journal* (Autumn 1995): 12-13.

Wilson, W. J. *When Work Disappears: The World of the New Urban Poor.* New York: Knopf, 1996.

Yancey, W. L. and S. J. Saporito. "Ecological Embeddedness of Educational Processes and Outcomes." In *School-Community Connections,* ed. L. C. Rigsby, M. C. Reynolds, and M. C. Wang. San Francisco: Jossey-Bass, 1995, p. 223.

Youniss, J., J. A. McLellan, and M. Yates. "What We Know About Engendering Civic Identity." *American Behavioral Scientist* (March/April 1997): 620-631.

Index